'RESEARCHING THE VISUAL,

Images, Objects, Contexts and Interactions in Social and Cultural Inquiry

Michael Emmison and Philip Smith

LIBRARY ST. MARY'S COLLEGE

SAGE Publications
London · Thousand Oaks · New Delhi

First published 2000

 SAGE Publications Ltd
6 Bonhill Street
London EC2A 4PU

SAGE Publications Inc
2455 Teller Road
Thousand Oaks, California 91320

SAGE Publications India Pvt Ltd
32, M-Block Market
Greater Kailash - I
New Delhi 110 048

British Library Cataloguing in Publication data

A catalogue record for this book is
available from the British Library

ISBN 0 7619 5845 2
ISBN 0 7619 5846 0 (pbk)

Library of Congress catalog card number available

Typeset by Type Study, Scarborough, North Yorkshire
Printed in Great Britain by The Cromwell Press Ltd,
Trowbridge, Wiltshire

Contents

List of Exercises and Projects

Preface

It is now commonplace to observe that we live in a massively visual society. The famous art historian Ernst Gombrich is just one of many to point to this self-evident visuality. He writes:

> We are living in a visual age. We are bombarded by pictures from morning to night. Opening our newspaper at breakfast we see photographs of men and women in the news, and raising our eyes from the paper, we encounter the picture on the cereal package. . . . (Gombrich, 1996: 41)

Gombrich goes on to document an imaginary day in which we open glossy junk mail, drive past billboards, encounter maps, graphs and blueprints at work, watch television, and collect coffee table books and photographs in our homes. The overall picture is of a world in which the total volume of visual material is increasing and our exposure to it is incessant. The argument is one that few could disagree with. Yet it is also curiously short sighted – the social world may be visual in far more ways than Gombrich suspects. To our reading, Gombrich may be correct to assert that we 'are entering a historical epoch in which the image will take over from the written word' (ibid.: 41). But like so many other scholars, he common-sensically equates the study of the visual with the study of images and representations of a kind we shall refer to as two-dimensional visual data. Moving beyond this position is a key task of this text. Let us begin this process by reconstructing Gombrich's imaginary day along different lines:

> Putting the bread in the toaster we notice its quaint retro styling. After eating we visit the bathroom, which is hidden in a part of the house that is away from public view. Driving to work in our 4WD car whose bulk symbolizes our status and whose styling pays homage to the frontier ideologies of our country we read the play of traffic in the road in order to ensure a safe passage. We arrive at the security gate to our office building and pass by the panopticon-like security cameras. As we walk in from the car park we notice how the design of the office building gives off an impression of power and wealth. Standing in the elevator full of strangers, we are pressed close to other people. We make only minimal eye contact and try to appear normal by standing stiffly and looking straight ahead. We are reassured when we see that the other people in the lift are dressed

conservatively, suggesting that they are not a threat. Entering our office we water the plants which give it a homely feel and pin up some new postcards. During our first appointment with a subordinate we slouch back in our chair whilst our visitor sits straight and still. Visiting the park at lunchtime we take care to select an attractive and safe spot where there is no graffiti or other signs of disorder. We take out a newspaper and start to read so as to discourage interaction with others who are also sitting on the benches. . . .

The day could continue, but we feel we have enough material here to make our point. Social life is visual in diverse and counterintuitive ways. Consequently there are many more forms of visual data than the photograph, the advertisement and the television programme. Objects and buildings carry meanings through visual means just like images. Clothing and body language are significant signs which we use to establish identity and negotiate public situations. Eye contact plays a role in regulating social life among strangers. Tensions between surveillance, visibility and privacy regulate our lives and our uses of space. In all of these areas there are, we suggest, rich supplies of material for the visual researcher.

Much of this book is about this overlooked domain of visual inquiry. In giving up the idea that visual research is only the study of photographs, advertisements, etc., then, a far broader range of data becomes available for investigation. From our vantage point, visual inquiry is no longer just the study of the image, but rather the study of the seen and observable. It includes issues of visibility, mutual interaction and semiotics as they relate to objects, buildings and people as well as to the study of images. Rethinking visual research in this way will better allow it to be connected to mainstream social scientific traditions as opposed to its field-specific knowledge base. At the time of writing, visual sociology, to take one subdiscipline as an example, is perceived as an isolated, self-sufficient and somewhat eccentric specialism. There have been notable problems in connecting up visual sociology as a subfield to the central theoretical traditions and debates of social science. A symptom of these conceptual shortcomings is the widespread tendency to use visual materials (photographs) in a purely illustrative, archival or documentary way rather than giving them a more analytic treatment. One result is that most other sociological researchers simply aren't interested in what visual sociologists have to say. By reconstructing the concept of visual research in the way we are suggesting, possibilities arise for fruitful interchange between such isolated fields and the bigger pictures of social science and cultural theory. Ideas about display, status and interaction allow us to tap into the rich vein of Goffmanian interactionism. Ideas about surveillance, visibility and privacy bring to mind Elias and Foucault. Readings of objects, buildings and places allow reference to Lévi-Strauss on nature/culture or to postmodern theory on architecture and so on.

Once this reconstruction is accomplished we can position visual research as a central theme of investigations into society and culture. It allows us to demonstrate that scholars in a diverse range of areas (not just those looking at photographs) have been 'doing the visual'. In Molière's play, *Le Bourgeois Gentilhomme*, the character of M. Jourdain is informed that there are two kinds of language – poetry and prose. On being told this fact he declares triumphantly that he has always been speaking prose, only without knowing it. In a similar way, we suggest, many investigators have been exploring visual data and using visual methodologies but have not been aware that they were undertaking a visual inquiry (see also Banks and Morphy, 1997). Under a diverse collection of methodological and theoretical banners they have explored issues which, in as far as they amount to an exploration of the seen and seeing, can be called visual research. Understanding and using visual data, then, is a central skill for those interested in social and cultural processes. Becoming more reflexive about this activity and tradition, and becoming more methodologically skilled within it, should enhance the quality of our research.

The argument that visual research should be taken seriously can be supported by pointing to change in society itself as well as to continuity with core traditions in social theory. Many commentators have suggested that we have entered a new historical era, one in which the visual has become more important as a pivotal aspect of social life. Accounts of the rise of civilization and modernity have long pointed to the ties between written language and the formation of complex societies. Weber and his followers like Ernest Gellner suggest that writing is central to the organization of modern, bureaucratic industrial societies. Such accounts have rightly been criticized for ignoring the continuing role of visual information other than writing in this social formation (Kress and van Leeuwen, 1996). But the point is well taken that writing has played a key part in making possible the emergence of complex modes of social organization. Yet if writing or the 'textual' is said to be fundamental to modernity, what can be said about postmodernity? Some theoretical work suggests that the organizing principle of such a social formation might be the visual rather than the written.

In his seminal discussion of the postmodern, the French philosopher Jean-François Lyotard (1984) speaks of the 'decline of grand narratives'. Lyotard suggests we have lost faith in the big stories of our time: progress, reason, science, emancipation. Such narratives are implicated in the core of modernity, whether in social theory or in social policy or in popular culture. Several critics assert that this movement away from grand narratives has been accompanied by a shift from a textual, diachronic culture – a culture of discourse – towards a synchronic culture characterized by images and unmediated, forceful visual impacts. According to Scott Lash (1988) the cultural logic of postmodernity has seen a visual sensibility replace a literary one. We live in a world, he says, where images have replaced texts as the dominant cultural form. Citing Stallone and

Schwarzenegger films as well as authorities like Susan Sontag (1977), Lash claims that such an image-based culture is founded on spectacle and the immediate representational impact of a visual which defies a depth hermeneutic. These themes mirror Fredric Jameson's (1991) arguments that the postmodern era is one which lacks a sense of history and narrative. It is one where visual and spatial forces are coming to organize our social life in ways which defy easy comprehension. One might also point to Baudrillard's (1988, 1990) arguments about the triumph of the 'simulacrum', with the 'real' world becoming hopelessly infiltrated by models, events and trends which mimic and feed off the spectral images of popular culture.

Whilst such arguments by postmodernists appear plausible enough, it is equally possible to argue that humans have always lived in strongly visual cultures. A selection of evidence for this proposition might include the following. From popular maxims to metaphysics, the sense of sight seems to be the one that is most valued. As Anthony Synnott (1993) points out, (in the West at least) sight is equated in complex ways that are both literal and metaphorical with wisdom, truth, God, understanding, masculinity and power. Anthropological reports on non-modern societies indicate the centrality of visual communication in ritual, symbolism, totemism and everyday life to 'primitive' social organization (Banks and Morphy, 1997). Richard Sennett (1977) tells us that through clothing, make-up and insignia, the public life of early modern Europe was dominated by visible markers of identity, status and belief (we return to this theme in the last chapter of the book). In a sensitive and revealing memoir of the experience of being blind in contemporary Australia, John Hull (1990) speaks of difficulties as diverse as navigating public spaces, avoiding public stigma, and producing appropriate facial expressions during interaction. The experiences of exclusion and routine problems that confront blind people in all societies are a powerful reminder of the centrality of visual information to the ways that humans organize their social life. Those who doubt we live in such a society should trying living for just a day without the use of sight.

Whichever theoretical position one chooses to endorse about the existence, timing and nature of epochal historical transformations, we can all agree that studying the visual is important because we live in a world where the 'visual' is of tremendous significance. Yet just how to conduct research in such an important and staggeringly diverse field is far from clear. The purpose of this book is to map some of the various routes for investigating this realm. We will suggest that methods from photography to ethnography to semiotics to observation can all be applied to visual materials. We will also suggest that visual data can be located in sources as diverse as wedding albums and pornography, living rooms and waiting rooms, living bodies and stony statues, august museums and playful shopping malls. Coming to terms with this wealth and diversity is the major purpose of this book.

About this book: claims and disclaimers

Like all texts, this one has defined aims and objectives. Making these clear at the outset of the book is a useful task.

What this book does do

- We provide an overview of the various forms of visual data that are available for social research by bringing together in one accessible text a variety of approaches and perspectives which have previously been unconnected.
- We broaden out the concerns of visual research to include issues of visibility, invisibility, surveillance and presentation of the self, in addition to established understandings which centre on the study of the image.
- We offer an approach which is grounded in both social science and cultural inquiry. We anticipate that this book will be of most relevance to researchers in disciplines such as sociology, anthropology, cultural and media studies, geography and urban studies. There are also scattered themes and ideas that will be of interest to those in history, economics, environmental science, criminology, psychology and art and design.
- We suggest numerous small-scale, low-budget exercises and projects that students can undertake. Some involve pure interpretation, others involve testing a hypothesis. *Exercises* are generally activities which can be completed in an hour or so by an individual student. They are intended to be thought-provoking as opposed to formal explorations of an issue. Exercises can often form the basis of a tutorial, with material collected or reflected upon during these activities being used to generate group discussion on methods and findings. *Projects*, on the other hand, will need a longer time to complete and are often best accomplished by a group of students. A project requires collecting data using systematic sampling and recording techniques and often involves testing a hypothesis or resolving a puzzle derived from the literature. For these reasons, many projects could be expanded in scope and sophistication to form the basis of a thesis or a published article.
- Where possible we point to links joining the kinds of data we discuss with social and cultural theory. This will demonstrate the rich theoretical heritage available to visual inquiry and enable researchers to conduct projects which have a strong analytic purpose. We are particularly concerned to show how visual data can be used as an indicator with which to explore abstract theoretical ideas.

What this book doesn't do

- Whilst we devote some space to the analysis of photographs and images, much of this book will be given over to other visual resources and data forms, such as objects, places and people. We certainly do not claim to offer an exhaustive treatment on what to do with photographs. Other texts are available which provide these skills (Collier and Collier, 1986; Wagner, 1979).

- We do not claim to provide specialist knowledge about how to take photographs or produce a video. Nor do we provide lengthy classifications of types of image and the ways in which visual language works. We are also unable to address important debates about the philosophy, psychology and physiology of perception which consider how the brain processes visual information.

- The analysis of moving images requires a detailed exposition of techniques which is beyond the scope of this text. Consequently, we will pass over the analysis of film and television material. Studies of kinesics likewise generally make use of videotapes of human movements and gestures. We provide only a brief discussion of this field and suggest some simple projects which do not require this technology.

- We will not go through basic methodological issues like sampling techniques, coding sheets, displaying and writing up results, remaining unobtrusive, staying out of danger and being ethical. Again these are covered in numerous other methods texts (e.g. Neuman, 1994).

- The book is intended for the most part as a student text. We do not claim to be constructing a profound new theory of the visual or a path-breaking method for studying visual materials. We do claim, however, some originality for our argument that visual research should expand in scope and theoretical orientation beyond the study of photographs. We also see the organization of this book as a modest innovation. In so far as we show there is extreme and unexpected diversity in visual research and data, imposing some kind of order on the field is of great importance. The conceptual categories informing the division of material between the last four chapters provide a noteworthy initial step in accomplishing this task.

Acknowledgements

This book could not have happened without the generous donation of ideas, skills and time by various friends, students and colleagues. Some of the material presented in Chapter 3 derives from teaching strategies developed in conjunction with Jim McKay. We thank him for sharing his expertise with us. David Silverman was an instigator of the book and provided a valuable commentary on the entire manuscript. Monique Hudson and Laura Emmison are responsible for much of the graphic design and artwork in the book. Keitha Brown offered technical advice with word processing. Ian Woodward, Lisa Kennedy, Stephanie McGrane, Brad West, Andrew Peake, Monique Hudson, Rosemary Aird, John Western, Kirstyn Shaw, Emma Ogilvie, Lindy Creighton, Renae Mahboop and others who wished to remain anonymous, agreed to appear as models in the Safe-Campus posters or otherwise allowed themselves to be photographed for the book. We thank the student groups 'Lanark' and 'Mass Media Monopoly' from our 'Media, Culture and Society' course for the 'Do-it-Yourself' advertising posters which they produced as part of their assessment for the course. Funds from the University of Queensland supported some of the costs involved in our research.

The editorial and technical staff at Sage assisted in all stages of the book. We thank in particular Simon Ross and Beth Crockett for guidance in shaping the direction of the text and to Claire Cohen for her assistance with production.

Grateful acknowledgement is made to various bodies for kind permission to reproduce the following copyright material.

Figure 2.1 appears courtesy of the New York Academy of Sciences.
Figure 2.2 appears courtesy of the Keystone Agency.
Figure 2.3 appears courtesy of Robert Doisneau/Network/Rapho.
Figures 3.5 and 3.6 are courtesy of J. Walter Thompson Pty Limited.
Figure 3.9 appears courtesy of Alan Moir.
Figure 3.10 appears courtesy of Mark Lynch.

Every effort has been made to trace copyright holders. The authors and publishers would be happy to hear from those we were not able to locate.

1

Introduction: Putting Visual Data into Focus

This chapter will:

- highlight some current confusions about the meaning of 'visual data'
- argue that visual research must go beyond the use of photographic images
- suggest that visual researchers must also embrace issues of spatiality and visibility
- account for the marginalization of visual data in many fields of social science
- summarize the content of the remaining chapters.

Assessing the place of visual data within the social sciences is made diffi-cult by the fact that there is no obvious unanimity about either what this term should embrace or – perhaps more significantly – how such data are to be incorporated into these disciplines' analytical concerns. Drawings, maps, sketches, diagrams, advertisements, directional signs, but above all, photographs, are the most commonly occurring items to be found in the existing discussions of 'visual research'. But despite the superficial simi-larity which these items appear to enjoy – a similarity which is aided by the fact that in many cases it is only *as* photographs that the various forms of visual data become available for analysis and discussion[1] – there is no general theoretical agreement about their status or utility or how to approach this analysis.

For example, advertisements have typically been viewed as 'texts' and subject to semiotic or similar forms of cultural interpretation; sketches, diagrams, maps and signs have, in various ways, been investigated as sites for the display of common-sense or practical reasoning by those who work in the ethnomethodological tradition; documentary photographs have generally been regarded as 'raw materials' – the visual accompaniments for more traditional forms of anthropological ethnography. There are those who maintain that visual data are inherently qualitative: a domain of genres, narratives and codes. For others, visual information can be readily quantified through content analysis procedures. Cross cutting each of these distinctions is, perhaps, the most basic issue of all: should visual researchers generate the images which they seek to analyse or is visual research primarily concerned with analyses of the numerous images already produced within the institutions of the culture?

Despite this initial air of confusion which confronts the neophyte visual researcher, two observations can, however, be quickly established on the basis of even a cursory inspection of the available literature. The first is tantamount to a complaint that visual information has been marginalized from the core concerns of the social sciences. Even though our social world confronts us above all as a visual experience, the social sciences have, with one or two notable exceptions, remained largely indifferent to questions of visual depiction. In the case of sociology, where this tendency is probably the most pronounced, visual researchers consequently have been ghettoized and reduced to communicating with each other about a narrow range of specialist issues. The second observation, to which we alluded above, is that where social and cultural researchers have considered 'the visual'; this has been almost entirely focused on the use of photographic images as the prevailing currency. We want to suggest that these two observations are far from coincidental; that is, it has been the inability to see beyond the use of photography which has been the major impediment to the development of a vibrant tradition in visual research. Whilst we are in broad agreement with the view that the systematic use of visual data does not appear to figure prominently in the tool boxes of most empirically oriented social researchers, we hope to persuade students that a wealth of visual information awaits those who are prepared to look afresh at what this might entail. The title of our introductory chapter is designed to capture this alternative vision.

Our primary aim in writing this book is to propose analytical frameworks for the investigation of visual data, which rest on conceptual foundations that are both theoretically informed and empirically productive. In contrast to the claims that visual information has been neglected or marginalized, we hope to show that 'the visual' is a pervasive feature not only of social life but of many aspects of social inquiry as well. In order to do this we must first break with the common-sense view which has led to photographs – or images more generally – having so much prominence in discussions about the visual. Stated in its bluntest form our reservations about an image-based visual social science rest on the view that photographs have been misunderstood as constituting forms of data in their own right when in fact they should be considered in the first instance as means of preserving, storing, or representing information. In this sense photographs should be seen as analogous to code-sheets, the responses to interview schedules, ethnographic field notes, tape recordings of verbal interaction or any one of the numerous ways in which the social researchers seek to capture data for subsequent analysis and investigation. Mainstream social researchers capture their data with surveys, questionnaires and interviews amongst other methods; visual researchers have traditionally captured images. But unlike the former, who can readily appreciate the difference between the reality they investigate and their means of apprehending this reality, amongst the latter this distinction has become confounded.

Consider, by way of example, photographic images of the following items: newspaper cartoons, statues or other civic monuments, the interiors of shopping malls, and people standing in queues or negotiating their way along busy sidewalks or pavements. It is entirely conceivable that each of these disparate objects could occur in a collection of 'visual social research' whose only apparent unifying theme was the reliance on photography as a means of recording or displaying information. The list has, in fact, not been randomly compiled: they are all phenomena which we will be examining in more detail in later chapters. The point we wish to make, however, is that the apparent unity these phenomena have as a consequence of being thus collected is entirely spurious. Their utility as data does not stem from their character as photographs but lies elsewhere. To appreciate what their utility might be we have to focus on the characteristics of these phenomena as objects in their own right.

Of course, there are many complex philosophical issues concerning photographic representation which our discussion can only allude to here. The data which are captured by photographs appear to be qualitatively different from those recorded through other kinds of research methods. Perhaps the obsession with photographs in visual research lies in these perceptions about their ontological specificity and privilege. Unlike other forms of storing information, photographs are signs which bear an iconic resemblance to the reality they represent (we deal with this matter more fully in Chapter 3 on pages 66 to 69 – the reader is asked to consult the relevant section there if they are unfamiliar with this terminology). Yet this should not negate their fundamental similarities with completed surveys, notebooks and so on as storage devices. Confusions about the ontological status of the photograph as 'data' are compounded by everyday language and common-sense reasoning. On the face of it what could be more self-evident than a visual researcher referring to a collection of photographs as 'my data'? But to pursue the analogy of storage even further: what if these photographs had been taken by a digital camera and the images collected on a CD-ROM? Would the material CD-ROM be seen as a form of 'visual data'? Would the bits and bytes of computer code which encode the image be seen as visual data? Probably not. In both cases the data would only be thought of as 'visual' once it was reproduced on a monitor or printer. Or, working in the other direction, it would be possible to take photographs of quantitative computer-generated statistical output such as a SAS or SPSS listing file, but the result surely would not be generally regarded as 'visual data'. Such confusions and paradoxes point to the fact that the concept of 'visual data' has never really been thoroughly explicated.

Distinctions between the various analytical levels in photographs have often been made in the context of arguments about realism and photography. For example, Ball and Smith (1992) speak of a differentiation

> between (1) what is given in the photograph – its *content*; (2) whatever the photograph is of – its *referent*; and (3) the presentation of the photograph once made – the *context* in which it appears and the use made of it. (Ball and Smith, 1992: 19–20, emphasis in original)

It is the coexistence of these analytical levels which has contributed to the widely held view that photographs are not simply reflections of reality or 'windows on the world'. Despite Barthes' philosophical commitment to photographic realism – his insistence that the photographic image was 'a message without a code' (Barthes, 1977a: 17), the prevailing view amongst academic analysts, and, we suspect, amongst an increasingly sophisticated and media-literate lay public, is that photographs are, or at least have the potential to be, social constructions, consciously or unconsciously manipulated images which can serve ideological ends. But it is not this specifically 'political' sense of the photograph which concerns us here. Our point is rather that the uncritical reliance on 'the photograph' as a form of data in its own right has prevented visual researchers from discovering a more fundamental level of analysis. What needs to be considered, we suggest, is the way in which the visible features of the social world which are readily available to the naked eye – not their representation in photographic images – constitute data for investigation. Stated in its simplest form, we are proposing that visual data should be thought of not in terms of what the camera can record but of what the eye can see. Photographs may be helpful sometimes in recording the seen dimensions of social life. Usually they are not necessary.

We understand visual data to potentially encompass any object, person, place, event or happening which is observable to the human eye. Couched in these terms the list of possibilities is enormous, perhaps endless. Newspaper headlines, cartoons, magazine advertisements, billboards, traffic signs, war memorials, flags, cemeteries, graffiti, museum exhibits, domestic dwellings, gardens, parks, shopping malls, parades, fast-food outlets, bus terminals, hotel lobbies, sports arenas, beaches, waiting rooms, lifts, public toilets, seating arrangements, glances, hair styles, clothing accessories, body decorations and much more all qualify for inclusion in this understanding of the visual. The crucial word, then, is 'potentially'. The objects, persons, events or happenings which provide the raw materials for visual investigation must be also be viewed, understood, or placed in some analytical framework before they can be regarded as data. Our understanding of visual data, then, is both data-driven and theory dependent. It is data-driven in the sense that we aim to capture the phenomenal features of whatever visual materials we use in our investigations and make these the object of our analysis. It is theory dependent in the sense that it is only through a conceptual framework that a given 'object' can become 'data' for investigation. As a means of encompassing both of these dimensions we make the point that visual is also spatial. That is, we propose to utilize spatial considerations in determining the various categories or types of visual data that are available for analysis, and spatial considerations also enter into the ways we think about the meaning, or the relevance of these items as data. The objects, people and events which constitute the raw materials for visual analysis, are not encountered in isolation but rather in specific contexts. For the most part we observe the myriad features of our environment as also having a spatial existence, and it is this spatial existence which serves as the means whereby much of their sociocultural significance is imparted. Visual data, in short, must be understood as having more than just the two-dimensional component which its representation in the photographic image suggests.

If we move away from the common-sense equation of visual data with images and embrace the claims being advanced here, it is possible to regard many aspects of twentieth-century social science, and many of the major figures in these disciplines, as contributing to the development of visual research. Amongst classical social theorists, Simmel is the most obvious candidate for inclusion when one considers his detailed observations of the changing character of human conduct under the changed conditions of modernity or urbanism. Indeed Simmel explicitly addressed the issue of the observability of social interaction in a famous essay first published in 1908. We shall consider Simmel's account of the visible features of social life in Chapter 6.

Less obviously, but no less significantly, there are many other figures in the history of social and cultural inquiry who, it can be argued, have been thinking about the visual or using visual methodologies in their work although not necessarily as explicitly or self-consciously as Simmel. In addition, and as a consequence, we would argue that a surprising number of forms of social science data can be readily recoded or reworked as instances of visualization/spatialization. For example, to the extent that it has been concerned with reading the urban landscape, much of the tradition of urban research from the Chicago ecologists to writers such as Lyn Lofland (1973), as well as the more recent postmodern accounts of Soja (1996) and Harvey (1989), is, in our terms, engaged in a form of visual research. But the social organization of space has also received attention from elsewhere. As Prior has demonstrated, a case can be made for 'a sociology of space rather than a sociological geography' (1988: 87) through focusing not so much on the spatial relationships which exist between buildings, settlement patterns and the like characteristic of urban landscapes, but on the internal features of buildings – upon their architectural configurations. Prior's own work on the changing architecture of hospitals, which we consider in Chapter 5, draws extensively upon Foucault in developing a discursive conception of spatial organization, knowledge and control. Foucault's example of the panopticon and gaze similarly can be very easily seen as a major contribution to theorizing the role of the visual in social life, more particularly their links to power and social control.

Although he published only one book which contained pictorial illustrations, Goffman, Simmel's intellectual heir, must also be regarded as a significant contributor to our understanding of visual aspects of social life. Many of Goffman's most important concepts, particularly those he considers in *Behaviour in Public Places* (1963) and *Relations in Public* (1971) are specifically designed to illustrate observable aspects of social conduct. Indeed it is something of a puzzle why Goffman relied on purely verbal accounts of the interactions he so painstakingly documented. From Goffman it is but a short step to the field of proxemics and the work of Edward Hall (1966), who did employ photographic illustrations and diagrams to visualize his work. A longer and possibly more contentious route also connects Goffman to the conversation analysis tradition where the video recording of naturally occurring talk is emerging as an increasingly required empirical component, particularly in the emerging corpus of studies which have begun to document workplace activities and environments involving forms of computer-mediated interaction (e.g. Heath, 1997; Heath and Luff, 1997). Taken as a whole this literature suggests that we can reread much of the history of social thought as a tradition of visual inquiry. It is a tradition where the camera has been marginal rather than central, and where theoretical imagination and spatial considerations have played more important roles. Before we consider the contribution that photography has played in the social sciences in more detail, it is useful to illustrate the ability of social research to consider these themes without recourse to the camera.

The visibility of space and place as social science data

We are not, of course, the first to call for spatial considerations to be given more prominence in discussions of research methodology, although we are not aware of any contemporary practitioners of visual social research making this connection. In a recent article Stimson (1986) has noted that questions of place and space have been virtually ignored in most recent qualitative research, to such an extent that any talk of participant *observation* is misleading: most ethnography is about listening rather than looking. Stimson develops his call for a visual ethnography by describing in detail the room in which the General Medical Council in the UK holds its disciplinary hearings. Most of us will never have occasion to attend the regulatory activities of professional groups like the GMC but we can readily appreciate from Stimson's description how the room can be viewed, not simply as a place where the hearings are conducted, but a constituent element of the hearing itself. All aspects of the room – the oak panelling, leather chairs, high ceilings, the glass-fronted bookcases, the spatial arrangements of the tables, the presence of a uniformed commissionaire – he argues, convey the formality and solemnity of the occasion:

This is a room in which serious matters are discussed: the room has a presence that is forced upon our consciousness. This is a room that, even when unoccupied, impresses on the visitor a solemn demeanour and subdued speech. When occupied, it retains its solemnity, and speech is now formal, carefully spoken, and a matter for the public record. (Stimson, 1986: 643)

The visible features of the room all contribute, Stimson suggests, to invoke a further dimension which is equally crucial to the functional ends of the disciplinary tribunal: a sense of history, tradition and permanence. There are crests commemorating each of the past presidents of the council as well as spaces where future incumbents of the office will one day be on display. Other individuals who have contributed to the organization are portrayed in oil paintings or marble busts. Photographs would be inappropriate in such a setting, he suggests. The quality of the physical materials out of which the room is constructed and furnished enhance this sense of tradition and continuity. Once again, it is the effect of these historical particulars on the ensuing speech which is most relevant:

Words spoken in this room, evidence, deliberations, and disposals, become part of this history. This is not a place for trivial speech and fickle judgements: this institution was here prior to the present incumbents, and will continue after them. Their decisions are bound by precedent, and will become, in turn, precedent for those who follow. (Stimson, 1986: 645)

In short there appears to be a necessary connection between the spatial arrangements of the room and its participants, and the discourse which transpires there: an organic connection between the demand for formality in speech and formality in setting. We should be cautious, therefore, in thinking that such deliberations could successfully occur in settings which are radically 'informal'. Atkinson (1982) makes a similar point about the functional ends of formal activities by reference to the ill-fated attempt of Pope John Paul I to appear more 'informal' through his refusal to be carried aloft in the papal chair. This was a strategy which was supposed to endow the Pope with more humility in his contact with the crowds in St Peter's Square. However, an unanticipated effect of the abandonment of the chair was a decrease in the Pope's visibility for the assembled crowds. Atkinson reports that the Vatican was 'inundated with thousands of letters from frustrated pilgrims' who each expressed the same complaint: that they were no longer able to see Pope John on his newly instituted 'walkabouts'. It appears that the tradition of carrying the Pope, although appearing as 'ostentatious' or 'formal', may well have been devised to meet the practical purpose of enhancing papal visibility, and in abandoning this practice the Vatican had failed to take this matter into account. The papal chair was, in fact, reinstituted shortly before the Pope's death.

Stimson concludes his discussion of the disciplinary tribunal by rhetorically posing the question of how successful the hearings would be if they were conducted in a radically different architectural space such as a

McDonald's restaurant. In contrast to the tradition and permanence of the disciplinary setting, everything about the fast-food restaurant signifies transience and informality. Furnishings and equipment are plastic, vinyl and polystyrene; lengthy stays are discouraged through uncomfortable seating, noise and proximity to the kitchen areas. 'Conversation here, for customers, is informal. For staff it is rehearsed and repetitive. . . . Speech here will not make history. It would be difficult to conduct a disciplinary hearing in this setting' (ibid.: 650).

On the appropriate use of photographs as research data

By any account, Stimson is making a contribution to the 'sociology of the seen' in his discussion of the spatial organization of the Medical Council's hearing room. His work, however, is unlikely to be claimed by contemporary visual social researchers because he does not include visual material in his article. But this raises the question, then, of just how essential photographs are. Visual researchers, we suggest, have become fixated on the collection of images to the detriment of the wider concerns of a sociology of visual information. We can illustrate this point most clearly by contrasting two studies which share a number of assumptions about visual aspects of social life and how 'the visual' can be employed as a resource for making claims about aspects of social structure. The two articles are Harper's (1997) recent analysis of the social structure of a dairy farm community in the United States and Enninger's (1984) study of grooming and dress codes in an Old Order Amish community. Note, first, the analytical similarity to the titles of the respective articles:

- Harper: *'Visualizing Structure: Reading Surfaces of Social Life'*
- Enninger: *'Inferencing Social Structure and Social Processes from Nonverbal Behaviour'*

Harper's research involved the use of aerial photographs of dairy farms in St Lawrence County, New York, in an attempt to discover whether the two types of farms he had identified in an earlier phase of his inquiry – 'craft' and 'industrial' – looked different from the air and to what extent the photographs could add to the further clarification of these concepts. Historically all farms in the region had once been of the craft variety but some had undergone development to the 'industrial' form. The difference between these types is partly one of size but it also refers to a difference in the organization of the whole milk production process, which in turn is reflected in the spatial layout of the farm buildings. Harper's argument, however, is that at ground level these differences are not at all apparent:

From the road, most farms in my study appear to be quite similar. Most have a farmhouse and outbuildings made from either wood or metal. It is difficult from the eye-level view to see how many outbuildings there are, or their relationship to each other or to the living quarters. It is difficult for the eye-level observer to note differences in divisions of labour which these buildings encapsulate. (Harper, 1997: 63–64)

Hence the point of his article: do the two types of farms have spatial organizations reflecting their contrasting industrial organization which are visible from above? Harper's research suggested that they do. The craft farms can be conceptualized as complex spaces in which the individual farmer retains overall responsibility for the entire production process, using his own locally developed arrangements of tools and equipment. From the air the craft farms appear to embody this craft 'mode of production', that is the craft farms have retained most of their former layout since they still retain many of these earlier aspects of production:

> The spatial logic suggests craft work: working areas with enough space and separatedness for an uncluttered work routine; organized so that a single worker may move easily between tasks. (ibid.: 64)

In a similar fashion the technological changes which characterize the development of industrial farms, manifested in the spatial differentiation of the various milking, feeding, and manure treatment processes, are all visible from the air in a way unavailable to the earthbound observer. Harper also argues that the photographs reveal more subtle features of the craft/industrial dichotomy as well as information about other social processes occurring in the community: for example rural gentrification involving the development of non-working farms. Harper includes 12 photographs in his article which are designed to illustrate these points. Our argument is that, although these are helpful additions to his written text, they are not essential for the completion of his research. Harper could just as easily have observed the differences in the farm spatial layouts as he flew over them, noting pertinent features on a code-sheet and so on. The data which are essential for his research are the observed arrangements in the farm buildings, not the representation of these arrangements in a photographic image. The photographs are cosmetic: they assist in the dissemination of his research findings but they are not responsible for generating those findings in the first place.

Enninger's research, although concerned with a quite different topic, employs essentially the same analytical strategy as Harper, how can the observable features of a phenomenon be used to tell us something else or something more informative about the phenomenon? In Enninger's case the issue is what sociostructural information can be learnt from observations of male grooming and dress codes within Old Order Amish culture? Amish culture has specific institutional norms regarding male hair length and beard growth as well as a complex code which governs clothing arrangements above the waist. All Amish males are supposed to have their hair cut in the same 'crock-pot' style and, once baptised, must begin the growth of a beard in a specified manner. Upon marriage, further norms regarding beard growth operate. Enninger argues that these male grooming patterns 'leak' specific information about membership categories which are significant within the culture: for example visible signs of marital status which are used to differentiate males over a certain age. Moreover, because some of the appearance norms operate on the basis of the norm having a minimum requirement to be fulfilled, then it is possible to observe the extent to which groups within the culture seek to exert a 'personal' rather than a 'social' identity from their degree of conformity to the norm. For example the younger Amish males tend to display hair styles which fulfil minimum requirements, whereas higher-status groups may 'show a distinct tendency to overfill appearance norms' (Enninger, 1984: 85).

With regard to dress the Amish have a complex system of permitted combinations governing the three layers – shirt, waistcoat and jacket – of above-waist clothing. Enninger shows how these clothing arrangements can be used to infer specific information about the wearer's 'bio-social status' [sic] – for example age, baptised/non-baptised, minister/non-minister – and the social event for which the clothing corresponds – everyday use, travel or shopping, visiting, church, etc. Indeed his point is that the clothing arrangements are, in part, a means of constituting the nature of a social occasion. In this way he suggests that the Amish can dispense with preparatory or opening verbal moves and begin the 'business phase of the interaction immediately' (ibid.). In contrast to Harper's research on the spatial arrangements of the dairy farms, however, photographs play no part in Enninger's study. Had he included them to illustrate the grooming and clothing codes then his article may have gained in appearance, but photographs would not have added in any way to the *substance* of his analysis.[2]

Our argument is that visual social research is better modelled on Enninger's study of the Amish community than on Harper's photographic investigation of the aerial layout of dairy farms. Simply availing oneself of information which is readily available to the eye is, we suggest, the logical starting point for a methodologically robust visual social science rather than the prevailing assumption that this must be founded on the technology of the camera. But this does not mean that photographic images play no part in our agenda. To the extent that such images are a conspicuous part of the seen world, then, they constitute data for investigation in exactly the same way as all other visible phenomena. To repeat: our argument is directed against the view that the features of the social world must be photographed before they become available as data for investigation.

The marginalization of the visual in the social sciences

Having argued that the use of photography is not an essential research device, it may seem curious at this juncture to address the question of the underutilization of visual information within the social sciences. But 'visualization' is a more complex matter than the decision whether or not to photograph, and it is worth examining the issues at stake in more detail. We noted earlier that the 'marginalization' of visual depiction has been a recurring theme in virtually all the recent overviews of the image-based discussions of visual research (Ball and Smith, 1992; Chaplin, 1994; Fyfe and Law, 1988; Wagner, 1979). Social scientists, the charge goes, have been largely indifferent not only to the use of visual depiction as a means of disseminating their research findings but also to the ways technologies of visualization are used in the topics they study. The marginalization of the visual dimension is therefore debated primarily as an issue of representation and communication. It is not, it should be stressed, posed as a failure to observe or to take note of the visual world.

Gordon Fyfe and John Law have provided the most comprehensive account of the marginalization of the visual, although we shall suggest that in their effort to deal with the neglect of visual evidence primarily as a theoretical matter they may have overlooked some more obvious reasons. A superficially appealing reason for the absence of visual depiction – but one that they have no qualms in rejecting – is based on economic considerations. Publishers of social science books and editors of journals, it is suggested, baulk at the inclusion of visual material, citing the costs involved with reproduction, copyright, paper quality, etc. But such arguments conveniently overlook the fact that for many forms of publication, from newspapers and magazines to books on cooking and art history as well as many branches of natural science, 'the visual' is an integral component:

> the pages of a scientific journal such as *Nature* depend upon depictions: tables, graphs, scattergrams, maps, sketches and photographs – all of these and more are to be found in the articles it publishes. The science that it reproduces would be impossible without visualisation: depictions are *constitutive* of scientific production. (Fyfe and Law, 1988: 3, emphasis in original)

Fyfe and Law advance three more substantial reasons for the neglect of visual depiction in the manner of the natural sciences. Most fields of scientific inquiry, they maintain, have legitimate 'technologies of summarization'. The objects which serve as the discursive currency for such fields are, for the most part, uncontroversial and readily subject to quantification and simplification using 'the normal technologies of statistical manipulation': graphs, charts, tables, etc. But quantification, they suggest, has a more ambivalent status in the social sciences:

> Sociology does not have and has never possessed a generally agreed set of methods for identifying, discriminating and counting what it takes to be significant objects of study, and it may be that the meaning and lack of significance assigned to the visual reflect paradigmatic struggle within the discipline. (Fyfe and Law, 1988: 4)

Although this could conceivably be advanced as a reason for the relative absence of visual forms of summary data it does not, in their view, account for the absence of the visual in relation to individual empirical elements. Again, the natural sciences provide evidence of the ubiquity of photographs, sketches, diagrams and maps with the inference that in all these cases 'seeing is believing'. Why are the social sciences different? In relation to sociology part of the answer lies with its hermeneutical character – the fact that sociology attempts to understand or interpret social action and must therefore place far more premium on words. Elizabeth Chaplin makes a similar point when discussing the relative neglect of photography as a tool in the process of data collection. She points out that social science has developed in such a way as to privilege verbal forms of communication:

> Our conventions about what counts as social science relate overwhelmingly to verbal discourse. In social science, therefore, a photograph depends on caption and textualisation to give it authentic and precise social scientific meaning. In this way it loses its autonomy as a photograph, and thus any claim to make a contribution 'in its own right'. In social science, as in most other discipline areas, images need words, while words do not necessarily need images. (Chaplin, 1994: 207)

However, Fyfe and Law see this as only part of the reason for the absence of visual elements. Instead they suggest, second, that it the 'theoretical fragmentation' of the social sciences rather than their hermeneutical character which serves as a more likely reason for the absence of visual depiction:

> In the natural sciences disputes about visualization tend to be rather specific and do not undermine the general legitimacy of virtual witnessing. However in sociology the general position is quite different. The centre of gravity of sociology, lying close, as it does, to the expression and articulation of general philosophical differences, neither lends itself well, nor allocates much priority to differences that might be resolved by recourse to visual depictions of its subject matter. (Fyfe and Law, 1988: 5–6)

Their third reason derives from the arguments advanced by writers such as Turner about the removal of the body as an analytical category from mainstream social theory (see Turner, 1984). Although they do not hold Durkheim directly responsible for this excision, the disappearance of bodies was one obvious effect of Durkheim's call for sociological explanations *sui generis*, with its explicit opposition to the role of biological or psychological processes in human conduct. Indeed they argue,

> it is only in the last ten or fifteen years, with the writing of Foucault, that an interest in the body has been reintegrated with the concerns of broader social theory. . . . However Turner's argument also helps explain the marginalization of the visual. Thus when the body was deleted from social theory, so, too, was

the eye. The analysis of perception and representation disappeared into psychology, biology, art history or, indeed, anthropology – which with its different intellectual struggles was never led to deny the physical and the biological. (Fyfe and Law, 1988: 6)

Fyfe and Law raise some intriguing epistemological questions about the status of visual information and visual depiction within the social sciences but, although we do not wish to discount these, their discussion has arguably overlooked some more basic considerations. We want to suggest that an additional reason for the absence of visual representations – in this case we are referring specifically to photographic images – from the mainstream social science publications lies in the political nature of the 'relations of viewing' which is felt, in some quarters, to attach to the generation and consumption of images. In part this entails revisiting the arguments advanced by Foucauldian writers such as Tagg (1988) who have historically linked the development of photography to a broader concern for the surveillance, regulation and control of populations. To the extent that disciplines such as sociology, social work and social administration invariably 'study down' then the inclusion of photographic images in research accounts of subjects such as 'the underclass', welfare recipients, street kids, factory labourers and so on may be construed as a continuation of this regulatory regime.

But the issue extends beyond a concern for the surveillance of the poor or marginalized. There is evidence to indicate that certain other forms of photographic representation have been deemed insulting, invasive, or degrading in some quarters of these disciplines. On the face of it this may seem strange amongst a scholarly community committed to the open dissemination of information, but the issue does appear to be contentious. For example, in their paper comparing images of parenthood in the United Kingdom and Japan, Dingwall, Tanaka and Minamikata (1991) report that the then editorial board of *Sociology* refused them permission to include a fifth image in their article 'on the grounds that some readers might consider that pictures of this kind portrayed women at a private and vulnerable moment in an objectifying and offensive manner' (Dingwall et al., 1991: 443). The image in concern was that of a birth scene which had already been published in a well-known UK pregnancy advice book.[3] The authors felt that this particular image dramatically highlighted the main finding of their research that, in comparison with their UK counterparts, Japanese birthing manuals marginalize women and present birth as a matter for medical authority in that although such scenes 'occur in all the newer UK texts . . . it is quite impossible to find any Japanese equivalent' (ibid.: 438).

However, it is not just editors who censor the appearance of certain images: authors also exercise a form of – albeit unconscious – self-censorship on some occasions. A recent issue of the journal *Women's Studies International Forum* contains an article by Cindy Jenefsky and Helen Miller

(1998) titled 'Phallic intrusion: girl–girl sex in *Penthouse*'. The article seeks to demonstrate that these apparent depictions of lesbian sexual activity in the magazine are, in fact, represented in ways which serve the gratification of the (male) viewers or spectators. Rather than faithful phenomenological portrayals of an alternate form of sexuality, the *Penthouse* images 'colonize' lesbian sex and 'effectively reinscribe and renaturalize heterosexuality'(Jenefsky and Miller, 1998: 375). The point we seek to make here is that the authors do not include any photographs of the images in their article, one consequence being that much of their article is taken up with descriptive details of the sexual activity under consideration. Had the images been included then arguably the empirical basis of their analysis would have been strengthened in that readers 'could see for themselves' the accuracy of their observations. But, of course, against this, the argument could – and should – be made that their inclusion would have reflexively embodied the very point about scopophilic pleasures the authors were seeking to make. By contrast it is instructive to compare Jenefsky and Miller's article with Morgan's (1989) investigation of dominatrix pornography which does include illustrative material. The difference here would appear to be that, unlike the former where the images are degrading to women, in the latter, although manifestly pornographic, they present an image of the female as empowered.[4] What seems to be happening here, we suggest, is that images are selected for incorporation according to non-cognitive criteria. Where images are considered to be degrading or morally offensive, authors and editors feel uncomfortable about reproducing them. When they are considered to be progressive, liberating, or neutral then there is a greater likelihood of their being included in an article. What is ironic, we suggest, is that whilst photographs are often deemed to be unacceptable by authors and editors, textually explicit descriptions of morally suspect materials are considered less so. Such a 'double standard' tells us quite a lot about the relationship of our society to the image as opposed to the text. Whilst texts are associated with reason and higher mental faculties, images are seen as subversive, dangerous and visceral. As the French writer Louis Aragon put it, for 'each man there awaits . . . a particular image capable of annihilating the entire universe' (quoted in Hamilton, 1997: 108). The aesthete Walter Benjamin also pointed to the unique powers of the photographic image. He suggested that '. . . the most precise technology can give its products a magical value' and implied that in the photograph 'a space informed by human consciousness gives way to a space informed by the unconscious' (1985: 243). He traces this back to the realist qualities of the medium and its uncanny, almost mystical ability to capture and fix forever the Here and Now of particular locations and subjectivities.

The matter of whether or not to include visual examples of the phenomenon under discussion appears, paradoxically, to be most acute in precisely those areas of social and cultural inquiry – gender relations, sexuality, the media – where illustrations are most likely to be found in abundance. However, there appears to be no consensus on the question of their appropriateness. Matacin and Burger (1987) display a similar atti-tude to visual material as Jenefsky and Miller in their article dealing with sexual themes in *Playboy* cartoons, which is based on purely verbal accounts of the cartoon content. However, Margaret Duncan (1990) includes several images in her article examining representations of women in sports photography. Indeed many of her photographs illustrate – as she intends – the points about the objectification of women and voyeuristic pleasures which flow to viewers which concerned Jenefsky and Miller. We would argue that Duncan's article is enhanced by these photographs and that, *ceteris paribus*, the analytical purposes served by the inclusion of visual materials should outweigh other considerations.

Whilst sociology has vacillated on issues of visual propriety, anthro-pology (until quite recently) has taken a more affirmative position on the need for visual materials to be incorporated into its texts, even those which might be considered highly offensive. Bateson and Mead's (1942) *Balinese Character*, for example, which we consider in the following chapter, con-tains depictions of ritual self-wounding (plate 55), the disinterring of corpses for ceremonial purposes (plate 90) and a dog consuming the faeces emerging from a crawling infant (plate 33). We suggest there are several reasons for this liberal attitude towards the photograph. First, anthropo-logical monographs typically report on cultures with which their readers have little familiarity. Photographs of huts, canoes, costumes (or lack thereof), daily activities and so on can obviate the need for lengthy descriptions and provide readers with a shortcut to getting a 'feel' for the kind of society they are dealing with. Second, colonial discourses and power relations provided a context in which photographs of possibly sen-sitive matters could be taken and reproduced with little fear of censure by those observed. Third, and relatedly, the quality of the 'primitive' as 'Other' allowed photographs to be taken without fear of moral contagion. Distance in terms of geography, culture and race allowed the ethnographic photograph to be positioned as a neutral and scientific document rather than as pornographic or voyeuristic, exploitative or as potentially cor-rupting. Evans-Pritchard's (1940) *The Nuer*, to pick a well-known text at random, contains close-up pictures of completely naked (black) men and women with visible genitalia. Some of these people are obviously in their early teens. It is an interesting thought-experiment to consider what would happen if equivalent images were to appear in a sociology text dealing with western, white subjects.

Somewhat more prosaically, decisions whether to include illustrative material may also be influenced by purely legalistic considerations of intellectual property and the rights of photographic subjects to own their images. Looking at recent French legal cases, Bernard Edelman and Edgar Roskis (1998) argue we are living in an era where the concept of a public domain in freely reproducible images is being attacked by market forces (see also Frow, 1998). In the late nineteenth century the engineer Gustave

Eiffel attempted to claim copyright on images and reproductions of his famous tower. It took a court ruling in 1893 before the tower could be reproduced by anyone in a photograph, with the court deciding that the public had a 'right to procure itself an image . . .' (Edelman and Roskis, 1998: 15). More recently, efforts have been made to restrict these sorts of rights. Edelman and Roskis provide some examples which are worth repeating here to give a flavour of the issues at stake. The architects of France's Grande Arche de la Defense, a more recent major Parisian landmark, stipulated in their contract that they had copyright over images of the structure and successfully sued a postcard vendor. The owner of a picturesque cottage used in a Brittany tourism campaign won $1600 damages for unauthorized use of an image of the property. The artist Christo, who specializes in wrapping large structures, did not allow photographs to be taken of the Pont-Neuf after he had packaged it, claiming that, although the bridge was public property, he had executed an 'original work'. These kinds of issues can pertain to people as well as their things. In French law, as in many other legal systems, individuals whose image appears in a reproduction without permission can sue. Complex legal debates often take place over whether the photograph was simply a reproduction of the person's 'effigy' (in which case the rights belong to them) or if it involved some kind of artistic and creative activity (in which case they belong to the photographer). Because the photograph is an iconic form of representation, it is much harder to claim it is a creative work than, say, a painting. Thanks to several high-profile cases in which ordinary people (as opposed to models) claim their image has been reproduced and commodified without their permission, the humanist photography of everyday life has moved from the streets of Paris and London to the streets of Calcutta and Rio. According to Edelman and Roskis: 'No photographer can operate any longer without having to sign stacks of forms in order to get the assent of every private person who happens to cross his path. And even then he can still be sued, since the signatory can change his mind at the time of broadcast or publication. . . . How can you blame the photographer for travelling further and further, under more clement legal skies, to seek out subjects less inclined to sue?' (1998: 15). In conclusion, then, undertaking visual research can result in an inadvertent trip through legal minefields.

In the course of writing this book we had our own experience of these problems. We wished to incorporate into one of the following chapters (see pp. 67–73) a discussion of a campus safety campaign as an illustration of the various ways in which photographs and their accompanying texts can be read. After spending some time working on the images and talking to students about what they meant to them we approached the relevant body. Permission was denied. We can only speculate on the reasons for this, but we suspect that two factors are at work. Firstly, the models (probably unpaid volunteers) would have had their images reproduced in a book with international circulation. Yet they had agreed only to be part of a local poster campaign. Secondly, the organizers of the campaign were probably concerned that their efforts, and those of the models, would be subject to ridicule or exposed as incompetent.

Because our book is largely concerned with what can be seen, rather than what has been photographed, we have, however, effectively side-stepped the issues of visual propriety, copyright and surveillance. Unlike the overwhelming majority of methodological discussions on visual research, our text is not dependent on images to make its point. For the most part the examples of research using visual information that we consider in the following chapters do not depend on the reader actually having to inspect an image of the phenomenon under consideration. A number of images have been included – we toyed briefly with the idea of producing a book on visual data which contained none at all but decided that this might be too iconoclastic – but overwhelmingly we rely on descriptions of what can be seen for our inspiration.

One of the most important consequences of the conceptual reconfiguration we are proposing here is that there may well be instances of researchers using forms of visual data which commentators have conflated and which demand quite different forms of analysis. Perhaps the most obvious example concerns two studies which, on the surface, both use the world of advertising as their empirical domain: Goffman's *Gender Advertisements* (1979) and Judith Williamson's *Decoding Advertisements* (1978). Our argument is that only one of these books – Williamson's *Decoding Advertisements* – is actually about advertising as a phenomenon. Williamson is concerned to provide an analysis of the ideological work that advertisements do – how they create desire, how they manufacture 'subject positions' from which their intended messages are designed to be read and understood. Williamson's conceptual framework primarily draws upon the work of structuralist and Marxist writers such as Barthes, Lacan, Althusser and Lévi-Strauss.

In contrast, Goffman's book, we argue, is not 'about' advertising at all despite the fact that, almost without exception, it *has* been treated as a contribution to the literature on advertising. Goffman is concerned with exploring the characteristic ways in which gender is ritually invoked in interpersonal or face-to-face conduct, and he uses as his primary empirical materials several hundred images of men, women and occasionally children, culled from published advertisements. A small number of news photographs, which illustrate his analytical themes, are also included. Goffman's book, like all his others, is really a contribution to the study of the interaction order: indeed his essay was first published in the journal *Studies in the Anthropology of Visual Communication*. Goffman could conceivably have used photographs of 'naturally occurring' gendered interaction for his illustrations. That he did not says something about the ease of availability of such posed 'fictional' advertisements and perhaps, more critically, something of the cavalier attitude he displayed towards methodological issues such as replicability, validity, etc.[5] Williamson, on the other hand could not have used photographs of natural interaction in her analysis despite the fact that many of the images which advertisers create are purportedly drawn from or seek to represent 'real life'. In terms of the framework developed in our book, then, advertising images such as those which Williamson examines are two-dimensional and will be considered in Chapter 3 along with other examples of media texts. In contrast the issues which Goffman addresses with his corpus of images are those of gesture, gaze, touch, display and other forms of micro-interactional behaviour, and we consider this in a separate chapter (Chapter 6) which has the body as a site of living visual data as its focus. In part these analytical conflations are simply another expression of the failure of visually oriented researchers to distinguish between the information they examine – the seen – and the methodological means they have established for capturing this information – the photographic image.

The remainder of the book is organized into five chapters. In Chapter 2 we present an overview of the principal trends in 'visual research'. We identify four major areas before focusing in detail on the use of photographs in visual inquiry. The chapter takes the form of a critical review in which we highlight ambiguities about the meanings of 'visual data' and point to some limitations as well as potential uses of photography. As is the case in all the chapters, the text will include detailed analysis of particular representative studies and follow-up exercises which students can undertake. Chapter 3, 'Two-dimensional visual data: images, signs and representations', moves beyond the uses of photography to consider other forms of two-dimensional data. Most of the examples we consider are drawn from the media, and the theoretical frameworks which we utilize in this investigation tend primarily to be those which are current in media research. In this chapter we give some consideration to the ways in which visual data from the media have been subject to both quantitative and qualitative techniques of analysis. Visual data is generally assumed to be qualitative, but some of the most interesting uses to which visual information has been put have come from researchers employing quantitative methods. Our major focus in the chapter, however, lies with the analysis of two-dimensional images such as cartoons, advertisements and signs. We draw upon critical semiotics and ethnomethodology to point to the ways in which these operate in everyday social life.

In Chapter 4, 'Three-dimensional visual data: settings, objects and traces', we look at objects of material culture which operate as signifiers in social life. We have in mind here the range of objects from those of everyday life in the home which carry personal meanings to those in public spaces, such as statues, which represent official public discourses. Our argument is that such objects provide a rich vein of visual information which can be read for clues about selves and societies. We will argue that although such forms of data can be analysed in traditional semiotic terms, they are also implicated in human actions. Exploring how agents react towards, use and modify these items is therefore an important research issue which pushes us towards the analysis of people and space. Hence this chapter points towards the next by arguing the need to combine semi-otic and observational forms of analysis given certain research questions. The chapter will also discuss graffiti, 'hot rod' cars, and other forms of marginalized material culture. Finally it highlights the study of traces, rubbish and unintended visual clues as a resource for finding out about social life. In many cases we will find that 3D data, unlike 2D data, must often be interpreted in terms of its spatial context. It exists not as an abstraction in splendid isolation on the page, but rather as part of a field of lived objects and spaces. These provide a context through which its meanings are shaped and in terms of which it can be read.

Chapter 5 on 'Lived visual data: the built environment and its uses', brings these spatial issues to the foreground in considering some of the various locales of modern societies – the shopping mall, the museum, the beach, the suburban home and garden – as 'lived texts' where both actions and sign systems can be read to unpack their cultural significance. We offer a dual focus both on the place or locale itself and on the ways that action is patterned in response to such locales. We show that issues of visi-bility, spatiality and semiotics combine in complex ways in such places, making them a fascinating resource for sociological inquiry. Finally Chapter 6, 'Living forms of visual data: bodies, identities and interaction', moves the discussion from inert texts, objects and places towards a focus on the human body and human interaction. Whilst the previous chapter placed an emphasis on how people read and use places, here we are more concerned with how people respond to each other. One organizing theme for the chapter is the claim that interactions in contemporary cities are regulated by norms about display, dress, eye contact and body language behaviour. Visual signals therefore play a central role in regulating social life in public settings. We explore how these operate not only on the body itself, but also in physical contexts as diverse as waiting rooms, queues, offices, trains and public parks. We suggest that the body, unlike the 'soul' or the 'self', is inherently and ineluctably visual and as such constitutes a rich source of data for anchoring various research projects. Whilst we touch upon iconic representations of the body as found in two- and three-dimensional visual data, our primary concern here is with the ways that the body is used as a living signifier in social life and the ways that it codes into issues of self- and collective-identity.

We recognize that by enlarging the scope of visual data in the manner we have suggested, we lay ourselves open to the charge that our concep-tion of 'the visual' is so extensive that it embraces the subject matter of the social sciences almost in their entirety. To an extent we would accept that this is the case. Our defence – to echo our earlier remark – would be that the social sciences have not recognized this ubiquitous visuality as self-evident. We do not think that the frequently made claims that the visual has been ignored or marginalized are an accurate assessment of the real state of affairs. Rather it has been the inability to recognize the pervasive-ness of the visual beyond the image which provides the major impediment to visual research taking its rightful place in the methodological canons. In the following chapter we look in more detail at this issue and at the kinds of activities that currently pass for visual research in social and cultural inquiry.

Notes

1   We return to this central ambiguity as regards the status of photographs as visual data in the next chapter.
2   The issue of photographic representation of his data does have a number of additional aspects. Enninger admits that, even if he had wished to obtain photographs the use of such recording technology in the Amish community would have been impossible because of cultural prohibitions. However, his argument is that this was not necessary. Although audiovisual technology is essential for research into many aspects of paralinguistic and nonverbal behaviour because of its fleeting and transient character – and a reason why field studies of these issues are not as common as those made under laboratory conditions – studies of nonverbal behaviour which focus on dress and grooming are not subject to the same constraints. Dress behaviour is generally constant across long periods of time and so the researcher is not faced with the same need to 'capture' the information for later extended analysis. The same argument can, of course, be made in relation to the spatial arrangement of buildings or locales such as Harper's dairy farms, which are even less likely to undergo change.
3   The picture is included on page 47 of M. Stoppard (1985) *Pregnancy and Birth Book*.
4   We discuss Morgan's research in more detail in Chapter 6.
5   This point has frequently been mentioned by commentators, even those who are otherwise generally sympathetic to Goffman. See for example Schegloff (1988), McGregor (1995).

2

Current Trends in Visual Research: a Conceptual Review

This chapter will:

- identify and discuss the prevailing trends which characterize visual research in social and cultural inquiry
- review the history of photography as a research tool and discuss earlier summaries and typologies of the field
- discuss some exemplary uses of photographically based research
- highlight some of the epistemological concerns which accompany the study of the image.

Notwithstanding the title of this book, it is a matter of some conjecture whether a subfield of 'visual research' actually exists as a coherent entity. The term itself is not in doubt – books, journals and professional associations can all be found claiming to embody the practice – but on closer inspection there is very little that is common to them. What the various branches of visual research do share, however, is a concern with images. As we have seen in the previous chapter, terms such as visual depiction, visualization, visual anthropology and visual sociology have become the code words for a field which is concerned with generating, using and analysing images. We argue that four quite different approaches to the use and interpretation of visual materials have emerged, each with its own distinctive theoretical and methodological underpinnings. Our verdict on this work is mixed: some branches have used visual information to make important theoretical arguments which are only available through image-based methodologies, but a good deal of visual data is used in ways which are simply illustrative. In this chapter we propose to offer an overview of these traditions before turning to our alternative, more inclusive, conceptual framework for the analysis of visual data which we employ in the rest of the book.

The four existing approaches to the use of visual materials which we examine are as follows:

- The generation and use of photographic still images primarily by ethnographically oriented researchers as an additional means of documenting social and cultural processes. Anthropologists and qualitative sociologists tend to be the main users of this method.
- The analysis of existing, commercially produced images such as advertising and other media content primarily by semioticians as a way of uncovering ideologies and cultural codes. Advocates of cultural studies approaches are most associated with this technique.
- The analysis of 'practices of visualization', primarily the use of diagrams, sketches and figures in scientific research and communication. Such research has generally been conducted by ethnomethodologists and constructivists who conduct social studies of science.
- The use of video-recordings of naturally occurring social interaction, particularly studies of work-based, technologically mediated communication. This branch of visual research has developed within the conversation analysis tradition, but its roots can be found in the pioneering proxemic and kinesic studies into spatial organization, gesture and body language originally conducted in the 1960s.

These four approaches do not enjoy an equivalent amount of research attention among 'visually' oriented researchers. By far the most effort has been devoted to the first two of these, and in some quarters the taking of photographs or their interpretation is seen as the *sine qua non* of visual research. Our discussion reflects these priorities in that we will look in most detail at the existing literature on the uses of photography and the cultural analysis of images, whilst only outlining the principal developments in the other two.

Photography and the social sciences

One of the most frequently made observations by commentators on the social scientific uses of visual data is that sociology and photography share the same approximate birth date – 1839. In that year Comte published his *Cours de Philosophie Positive* and Daguerre's technique for fixing an image on a metal plate was publicly announced at an open meeting of the French Academy of Sciences. But it was not as a proto-social scientific technique that photography was first recognized or discussed. Rather it was the opposition between its scientific or realist and its artistic manifestations – a tension whose legacy is arguably still apparent today – which initially captured public imagination. For Daguerre the verisimilitude of the photographic image was his pre-eminent achievement; Daguerre spoke of his invention as having 'given nature the power to reproduce herself'. But for the painter Paul Delaroche, photography meant something else. 'From this day painting is dead', Delaroche is reported to have said on encountering his first photographic image (quoted in Trachtenberg, 1980). For much of its history, photography has been engaged in a struggle against a '... fetishistic and fundamentally anti-technical concept of art' (Benjamin, 1985: 241), sometimes touting its realist credentials, at others its potentialities as an interpretative medium. Throughout the twentieth century, although the realist conception of photography has been dominant, it has refused to forego its expressive function, lingering ambivalently at the recognized borders of the art world.[1] This tension is manifested in treatments of the photograph within the social sciences. As we shall see, for some it is best thought of as a document or tool for faithfully capturing what 'really' goes on. For others it is a text – an artefact, best thought of as an expression of culture which has to be read or interpreted much like a painting.

The social documentary uses of photography emerged sometime later in the work of Jacob Riis and Lewis Hine. Riis, a reporter, used photography as a means of drawing attention to the slum conditions in New York in the 1890s, whilst Hine, who had some training as a sociologist, is famous for his images of newly arrived immigrant labourers and the conditions of child labour in mines and factories. Their work is seen, in part, as contributing to the passage of new labour legislation. At the turn of the century, then, sociology and photography were historically linked as practices which shared a common interest in exploring and documenting society. Nevertheless it was not an enduring marriage, as contemporary visual researchers continue to remind us.

The flirtation of American sociology with photography deserves to be looked at in more detail. As several commentators have noted, visual data in the form of still photographs was a conspicuous feature of American sociology in the early decades of this century. However, photographs disappeared almost without trace in 1916, and it was not until the late 1960s that they made their next tentative re-emergence and the first professional networks for visual sociology were established. Stasz (1979) and Henry (1986) have provided useful accounts of this early period of visual sociology. Between 1896 and 1916 the *American Journal of Sociology* published 31 articles which contained 244 photographic illustrations. The majority of these were, as Henry suggests, used simply as support for the articles dealing with social reform and he suggests that today we look at them 'with some nostalgia and some scepticism' (Henry, 1986: 1).

The latter sentiment would appear to reflect the 'official' institutional position of the journal for, as Stasz notes, an article dealing with the first 50 years of the journal (Shanas, 1945) made no reference whatsoever to them. In her analysis of the photographs, Stasz found that publication had not been evenly distributed over this period. The majority of illustrated articles (20) had appeared between 1896 and 1904; there were none between 1905 and 1909 and then a further 11 between 1910 and 1916. She suggests that the editorial policy that eventually led to the abandonment of illustrations after 1916 may have occurred as early as 1905. It may only have been the institutional affiliation between the journal and the sponsors of the Chicago

Housing Project (the Russell Sage Foundation) – the subject dealt with in the later articles – which persuaded the editor of the journal, Albion Small, to run the Housing Project pictures at all. Stasz's argument is that the disappearance of photographs from the *AJS* after 1916 (and by implication the whole of mainstream American sociology) was a direct outcome of Small's concern to establish American sociology on a more scientific basis. For Small it was the association of the discipline with reform and social amelioration, the subjects which the illustrated articles addressed, which had to be countered in successfully moving sociology 'out of amateurishness, not to say quackery, and advance toward responsible scientific procedure' (Small, 1905: 637, quoted in Stasz, 1979: 132).

With the possible exception of some of the Housing Project illustrations, Stasz found that many of the images were contrived or of questionable technical quality and that, rather than supplying additional 'evidence', their inclusion was transparently linked to the reforming zeal of the contributors. She concludes that

> Overall, two-thirds of the articles employed photographs in a way that contemporary visual sociologists would question. Crassly manipulated prints, iconographic poses, inconsistent before-and-after pictures, portraits out of context, and images based on clumsy techniques are among the styles of shooting and presentation considered today to be inappropriate in careful research reporting. They would be good illustrations for that as yet unwritten book every social science student would be required to read before graduation, *How to Lie with Photographs*. (Stasz, 1979: 128)

The United States remains, however, the country in which the social sciences have been most sympathetic to photography as a research tool. After lying dormant for several decades, an interest in photography re-emerged in the 1960s and the first professional associations for visual research were established. To all intents and purposes photographic 'visual research' today is an offshoot of North American social science.[2] Photography, here, is understood in quite different ways from the prevailing European traditions of visual inquiry where photographs are images for interpretation and decoding. For American visual social scientists, photographs are invariably images which are taken by the researcher, generally as part of a wider ethnographic project. Photographs are forms of data which the researcher has obtained with their camera as opposed to administering a survey, or conducting an interview. As a consequence, the use of photographs, and visual data more broadly, appears to be largely debated as an issue of methodological adequacy.

To a significant extent the boundary between contemporary visual inquiry in anthropology and sociology is permeable, with researchers from both of these disciplines publishing in each others' journals, citing each others' work and attending the same conferences and symposia. Accordingly, in the following discussion, we shall concentrate on the theme of the 'sociologist as photographer', which serves as the defining motif in accounts of visual research methodology. But photographs also feature in discussions of the use of documentary materials and finally as an example of an unobtrusive method of data collection. We shall look briefly at each of these in turn, although it should be realized that there is frequently some overlap between these different modes.

Sociologist as photographer

To the extent that it can be considered to have a founding father, the name of Howard Becker is invariably linked with the establishment of visual social science as this field has come to be understood in the United States. First published in the journal *Studies in the Anthropology of Visual Communication* there appears to be general agreement among practising visual researchers that Becker's (1974) article 'Photography and Sociology' stands as a seminal contribution to their field.[3] However, Becker's discussion turns out to be not so much a set of guidelines for doing visual sociology as a commentary on the occupational ideologies of photographers and sociologists and what the two groups might learn from each other. Becker's focus is primarily on the social documentary tradition in photography and specifically with the way in which sociology and photography share a common ground in the study of organizations, institutions and communities. For Becker, though, this turns out to mean little more than sociologists being prepared to use visual materials in their research, but in a way which takes advantage of their more extensive knowledge of social organization. In effect this means being more sophisticated in the appropriation of their photographic evidence so as to improve on the deficiencies of the documentary photographers. In Becker's view the primary fault with documentary photographers is that that their work is theoretically undeveloped:

> Close study of the work of social documentary photography provokes a double reaction. At first, you find that they call attention to a wealth of detail from which an interested sociologist could develop useful ideas about whose meaning he could spin interesting speculation. . . . Greater familiarity leads to a scaling down of admiration. While the photographs do have these virtues, they also tend to restrict themselves to a few reiterated simple statements. Rhetorically important as a strategy of proof, the repetition leads to work that is intellectually and analytically thin. (Becker, 1974: 11)

For Becker the most important way in which the photographic explorations of social life can be made more sophisticated (sociologically) is for the researcher to avoid the accumulation of isolated images and seek instead to photograph 'sequences of action' which try to capture something of the dynamic aspects of social organization or the patterns of cause and effect. This means that the sociologist-photographer must learn to record their images in a manner analogous to the process of data collection in fieldwork. The essence of fieldwork for Becker is that it involves a continual 'grounded-theory' style of testing tentative hypotheses in the context of a series of repeated observations. The researcher enters the field without any rigid or preconceived conceptual ideas. Initial hunches are confirmed, refined, or rejected as further observations are made. Data collection and data analysis are not separate phases of the research process: 'analysis is continuous and contemporaneous with data-gathering' (ibid.: 13).

Photographers must carry out the same process. This means that they must be prepared to spend much longer in the recording of their images than they normally would expect. Initially they may try to photograph as much as possible of the group or community they are studying, but on subsequent visits their choice of images must be more theoretically informed. They can also anticipate having a closer relationship with the people whose activities they are recording and may well seek their advice and reactions as the research develops. Photographic fieldwork and sociological fieldwork become almost identical for Becker:

> As the work progresses the photographer will be alert for the visual embodiments of his ideas, for images that contain and communicate the understandings he is developing. . . . His theories will help him to photograph what he might have otherwise ignored. Simultaneously he will let what he finds in his photographs direct his theory-building, the pictures and ideas becoming closer and closer approximations of one another. (Becker, 1974: 14)

Becker's overall aim is thus to establish the similarities between photography and sociology. Both 'vocations' – the choice of this term conveys a good deal about how he himself sees their commonalities – are faced with issues such as the reliability of the evidence they collect, and the extent to which generalizations can be made on the basis of a limited amount of data. For example, elsewhere in his preface to the edited collection, *Images of Information: Still Photography in the Social Sciences* (Wagner, 1979), in which Stasz's article is to be found, Becker demonstrates that he is clearly cognisant of the charges of methodological distortion which he feels mainstream sociology is only too ready to level against the use of photography. Becker speaks of the 'manifold difficulties' faced by anyone who attempts to use photographs in their research, 'the very difficulties which lead other social scientists to be sceptical of the results'. He adds:

> but, in every case, it is easy to see that the difficulty is not unique to photographic work. On the contrary, visual materials simply make obvious the difficulties we have with every variety of data. Do we worry because the photographic frame, putting a line around much that is of interest to us, excludes everything else? We should, just as we should worry that a questionnaire finds out something about what it asks about, and tells us nothing about the rest. Do we worry about the way the relation between the photographer and the people being photographed affects the material we get? We should, just as we should try to understand the effect of the relationship between the investigator and the people investigated in participant observation or experiments. (Becker, 1979: 7–8)

Photography and sociology thus must both deal with issues of gaining access to relevant information and to the problem of reactivity in data gathering. Where they differ according to Becker is in the manner in which they move between concepts and the indicators or images which reflect these. Sociologists generally begin with more abstract concepts and then work towards specific empirical indicators of these. Photographers, in contrast, work the other way round. They capture an image and then seek to discover what idea the image is expressing. Sociologists can learn something from this. When sociological concepts invoke clear and explicit images, they can be more readily criticized, revised and their relationships with other concepts are facilitated. If a sociological concept cannot be easily visualized, he suggests, 'we might take this as a warning that the concept is not explicitly related to its underlying imagery. Looking for an appropriate visual image might help clarify that relationship' (ibid.: 20).

Uses of photography: conventional distinctions

Since Becker first sought to establish the relevance of photography for the social sciences, there have been a number of attempts to provide overviews of visual inquiry. Although it was still restricted to the use of photography, Jon Wagner's (1979) edited collection which appeared five years later did include a much wider variety of uses than Becker's rather limited focus on social documentary photography. According to Wagner there are five distinct modes of research involving the use of photographs currently in use by visual social scientists.

First, there is the use of *photographs as interview stimuli*. Wagner cites an eclectic range of studies that have used photographic triggers in this way, but the method hardly rates as the analysis of visual data at all. As a practice it seems to have much in common with certain forms of commercial market research where participants are asked, for example, to match types of holiday setting with demographic categories on the basis of idealized visual representations of settings and people.

Second, there is the use of photography in what is referred to as *systematic recording*. Wagner traces the antecedents of this mode in the use of the camera to record animal and birdlife and refers to studies of facial expressions, seating arrangements and pedestrian traffic flows as (then) current examples of the kind of systematic recording of human behaviour made possible by the camera. Significantly, he suggests that this mode can involve both 'still and motion picture cameras'.

Third, Wagner refers to the *content analysis of naïve photographs*. These are not photographs generated by the researcher; however, it is not clear from his discussion whether the images he has in mind are the everyday cultural records of ordinary members of society or alternatively those generated by official or commercial organizations: advertisements, tourism promotion brochures, police records, corporate presentations, press photographs and so on. His point, however, is that 'all photographs contain data in addition to that "intended" by the photographer' (1979: 17) and that such information is of potential use to social researchers. The examples he offers – the use of photographs in a study of regional differences in 'smiling', or representation of male and female imagery in the work of famous photographers – appear to embrace both lay and professional depictions.

Wagner's fourth mode is that of *native image-making*, essentially the process of providing an indigenous group with the means of filming or photography and examining the outcomes. The idea is to discover something about the cultural worldviews of the group in question. As a technique this has been largely confined to anthropologists (e.g. Worth and Adair, 1972). Finally Wagner identifies the tradition of *documentary photography*, which had been Becker's principal concern. He refers to this use of photography as *narrative visual theory*, which involves in his terms 'exploring with a camera the visual coefficients of social organization'. The majority of researchers who use this mode are ethnographers, and there are several examples to be found in his collection. The distinctive feature of this mode is the 'commitment to the narrative organization of photographs in which implicit elements of social theory are clearly acknowledged' (Wagner, 1979: 18). Although it is not made explicit, this appears to be the mode which he regards as most central as a social scientific tool.

Douglas Harper has claims to being the most vocal advocate of contemporary visual research (see e.g. Harper, 1988, 1994, 1997). In his appraisal of the field a decade after Wagner's, he offered a different classification but still retained the use of photographs 'to portray, describe or analyse social phenomena' as the defining feature of visual sociology. Harper identified two major areas of investigation by researchers in this field:

> The first involves using photographs in the conventional sense of data gathering. . . . Visual sociologists also study photographs produced by the culture for example in advertising, newspapers or family photo albums. Put simply the distinction between these approaches is that some sociologists *take* photographs to study the visual world, whereas others *analyse* photographs others have taken in institutionalized occupational settings or their family lives. (Harper, 1988: 55, emphasis in original)

Harper admits that the boundaries between these two approaches are fluid and that visual sociologists often work in both fields. However, he suggests that the former activity is more central to the practice of visual sociology. Somewhat confusingly, when it comes to describing the various uses of photography, he expands these practices to include the use of film and video. For Harper there are four major methodological frameworks for the use of photography: 'the scientific', 'the narrative', 'the reflexive' and 'the phenomenological'. This typology has a number of questionable assumptions built into it and serves as a useful example of the kind of difficulties to which we have suggested discussions of photographs as 'visual data' are prone.

The *scientific* mode is the most commonly occurring use of photographic data. This mode rests on the assumption that 'many sociological categories are based on observable phenomena and ... these can be understood better if frozen in a photographic image' (ibid.: 61). The scientific mode, in other words, is essentially another name for the use of photography as a storage device, which we discussed in the previous chapter, where the photograph is primarily a means for preserving an item of data for subsequent investigation. Harper regards the standard uses of photography in ethnographic research as belonging to the 'scientific mode'. What the various examples of the scientific mode appear to have in common is the use of photography to capture information 'too fleeting or complicated to remember or describe in writing'. In addition, this use of photography, he suggests, is ideal for studying social change in communities. If archival records exist then the same community can be re-photographed at a later time.

The underlying assumption of the *narrative* mode, for Harper, is the use of images to study the *process* of social life as it naturally unfolds. The narrative mode is more commonly found in ethnographic films, but he believes that it can become a component of still photography as well. Harper cites one of his own research papers (Harper, 1987) – a photographic study of tramps which demonstrates the cyclical nature of their life as they 'get drunk on skid row, dry-out on a cross country freight ride, and take up work again, a typical "cultural story"' (ibid.: 64) – as an example. He also argues that the study of small-group processes through video-recording in laboratories is a form of narrative research, citing the work of the social psychologist Carl Couch (1987) as representative. Harper adds that researchers in the ethnomethodological tradition 'could use photographic or film recording to add rigour to their observations'. As we have noted, this has indeed been the case, although it is more than debatable whether those working in this tradition who have begun to employ video would regard their work as involving 'the narrative mode' of photography. The essential feature of this work, as with all the work emanating from within the conversation analysis tradition, is the rigorous description of naturally occurring social interaction. If this work belongs anywhere in Harper's typology then it would surely be the 'scientific mode'.

The scientific and narrative modes have in common that 'the authority of definition lies with the sociologist'. In contrast Harper sees the *reflexive* mode as a use of photography in which 'the subject shares in the definition of meaning'. In the reflexive mode the sociologist actively involves the research subjects in the interpretation of the images. The most common form is a process referred to as 'photo-elicitation'. In this the researcher begins by taking photographs as part of a wider ethnographic study but then uses these as a prompt during subsequent in-depth interviews. In this mode the content of the photographs, the settings or images which they capture are of secondary importance. The photograph is essentially a device for generating the (more important) verbal information from the interview.

Harper's final category is the *phenomenological* mode. This appears to be inspired by Roland Barthes' (1981) distinction in *Camera Lucida* between two separate aspects to photographs: the *studium* and the *punctum*. Barthes argued that some photographs – he suggests the majority – provoke only a general or 'polite' interest. This quality to create a rational or disinterested response he refers to as *studium*. However, other photographs – or perhaps aspects of the same photograph – can rupture or break this complacency and inspire a more emotionally charged response, and this Barthes refers to as *punctum*. Louis Aragon's epithet about the disturbing power of photographic images, which we noted in the previous chapter, captures this distinction perfectly. For Harper the phenomenological mode opens

> the question of how our data may play two roles. Photographs may literally describe but leave us unmoved; other images may inspire our emotions but not be useful (or even lie) sociologically. Some photographs may, however, do the opposite: that is communicate sociological insights in an artistically stimulating manner. (1987: 66)

Harper suggests that the phenomenological mode thus involves eliciting one's own knowledge through photographs which have a personal meaning – something which seems rather like the sociologist making herself both researcher and subject in the reflexive mode. He adds that this is the most 'experimental' area of visual sociology and one where sociology and art merge.

Harper's typology – like that of Wagner's before him – has a number of problems which are typical of the difficulties which practising visual social scientists confront when they attempt to systematize their discipline in this fashion. For example, it is not clear why these uses of photography are to be seen as mutually exclusive modes rather than different aspects of the same practice. As we have suggested, those researchers whom Harper deems to be engaged in the narrative mode would no doubt wish to be considered scientific as well. Documenting the processes of social life, it might be argued, is precisely what provides this work with its rigorous, scientific character. Much the same argument could be advanced by those engaged in reflexive uses of photography who practice 'photo-elicitation', a technique which is frequently linked to quantitative methods of analysis as we shall see shortly. Rather than examining further classifications of the field, it might be more instructive at this point to look in detail at some influential studies which have been based on photographic methods and attempt to learn directly from these. To do this we must journey back in time, for it is now well over 50 years since one of the most important books was published.

Seminal studies

Bateson and Mead: Balinese Character: a Photographic Analysis   When the achievements of visually oriented social sciences are discussed, one study is invariably cited as an exemplar of the use of photography as a research tool. We refer here to Gregory Bateson and Margaret Mead's photographic inquiry into Balinese culture, which was carried out between 1936 and 1939. Visual researchers rightly take inspiration from it, although it is not always clear that its full significance has been appreciated. Becker (1981: 13) eulogizes over the images, remarking on the 'visual vitality and complexity we associate with the work of fine art photographers'. Harper cites it as a model of the scientific mode of photographic use, a designation which further serves to highlight the problems with his categorization given their concern to capture the processes of Balinese cultural life. Ball and Smith (1992) remark more accurately that the significance of Bateson and Mead's study lay in the ways in which the authors had moved beyond the standard ethnographic uses of photographic materials, where these remain largely underanalysed devices.

> Photographs usually only serve illustrative functions for anthropological work or at best stand as constituents of slide-show travelogues. What makes Bateson and Mead's work exemplary and ground breaking is its use of photographs as topics of investigation. (Ball and Smith, 1992: 14)

In their introduction, Bateson and Mead refer to the form of presentation of their research materials as 'an experimental innovation' (Bateson and Mead, 1942: xi) in which they tried to communicate the intangible aspects of culture which previous, purely verbal renditions had failed to capture. Photographs, they argued, were ideally suited to identify 'similar emotional threads' which run through otherwise disparate forms of behaviour:

> By the use of photographs, the wholeness of each piece of behaviour can be preserved, while the special cross-referencing desired can be obtained by placing the series of photographs on the same page. It is possible to avoid the artificial construction of a scene at which a man, watching a dance, also looks up at an aeroplane and has a dream; it is also possible to avoid diagramming the single elements in those scenes which we wish to stress – the importance of levels in Balinese inter-personal relationships – in such a way that the reality of the scenes themselves is destroyed. (Bateson and Mead, 1942: xii)

Balinese Character, then, is not a book about the customs of the Balinese but rather an attempt to show how the Balinese 'as living persons, moving, standing, eating, sleeping, dancing, and going into trance embody that abstraction which . . . we technically call culture' (ibid.). To achieve this goal the book is organized into two complementary parts: first, an introductory essay written by Mead, structured as an ethnographic commentary on the topics covered in the photographic material; the second part of the book presents the photographs which Bateson had taken, arranged into 100 plates each containing between 4 and 11 photographs, although the majority feature 6–8 images. In all there are 759 photographs which he reports had been whittled down from about 25,000 originally taken. The 100 plates are organized into 10 major groups which reflected the authors' primary interest in socialization and its constitutive part in shaping Balinese cultural ethos: 'spatial orientation and levels', 'learning', 'integration and disintegration of the body', 'orifices of the body', 'autocosmic play', 'parents and children', 'siblings', 'stages of child development' and *'rites de passage'*.

Each full-page plate is accompanied on its opposing page by an explanation of the context for the photographs and then captions, many detailed, for each of the individual images. It is clear that both images and written texts are equally essential, but – and this is where the uniqueness of their monograph lies – there is nevertheless a degree of autonomy to the pictures. Whilst the texts would be meaningless without the corresponding images, the reverse is not the case. The contextual details and captions, of course, assist in the overall interpretation we reach of the images, but the photographs alone frequently let us *observe* the manner in which the particular cultural item they are focusing on at that juncture is enacted.

One of the primary ways in which this is achieved is through the close proximity of images which were recorded in relatively short duration. For example, plate 47 'Stimulation and Frustration', which we reproduce as Figure 2.1, contains nine images of a mother and child which were recorded in a period of only two minutes of interaction. As we move through the images on the page, we can almost observe the sequences of behaviour as they were produced in 'real time' and the ways in which each interactant's gestures are responded to by the other party. It is this level of behavioural detail which stamps their use of photographic imagery with its uniqueness. No other ethnographers have attempted to use visual data in this way. A case could be made for suggesting that Bateson was actually engaged in a form of sequential or interactional analysis *avant la lettre*. There is a delightful historical irony in the realization that in the year that Harvey Sacks – the late founder of conversation analysis – was born, Bateson was already busy in the field engaged in his own brand of visual documentation of turn-taking.

Goffman: Gender Advertisements   Closely following *Balinese Character* in visual social sciences' Hall of Fame is Goffman's *Gender Advertisements* (1979). On the face of it they would appear to have little in common, but closer inspection suggests that this is not the case. Although both the substance and provenance of the images analysed are different, the two studies share a number of methodological similarities. We have already noted that Goffman's research was originally published in an anthropological journal, which gives us some clues. Goffman does refer to *Balinese Character* in his own book but only once in a rather pointed aside, somewhat inconspicuously located in a footnote. The context is his adoption of

Bateson and Mead's idea of 'kinaesthetic learning', the term they use for a form of instruction in Balinese society in which children are physically taken through the steps or movements of a behavioural sequence, such as a dance or ceremony, by an adult. In the commercial advertisements which are his focus, Goffman reports that 'men seem to be pictured instructing women this way more than the reverse'. His footnote to *Balinese Character* runs as follows:

> This book brilliantly pioneered in the use of pictures for study of what can be neatly pictured. The work stimulated a whole generation of anthropologists to take pictures. However, very little analysis was – and perhaps could be – made of what these students collected. Somehow a confusion occurred between human interest and the analytical kind. Dandy movies and stills were brought home of wonderful people and fascinating events, but to little avail. Much respect and affection was shown the natives and little of either for the analytical use that can be made of pictures. (Goffman, 1979: 34, note 10)

There is more than a suggestion here that Goffman believed his own work should be anointed as the rightful analytical descendant in the tradition of visual analysis. Is this justified? There are certainly similarities between the two studies. Perhaps the most surprising given that they share a provenance in anthropology is that they both rely initially on sheer quantitative incidence to make their respective points. Goffman includes 508 images, somewhat less than Bateson but from a potential pool conceivably equalling – if not surpassing – the 25,000 the latter had available. Both studies, therefore, seek to prioritize the use of visual depiction by the simple technique of presenting their photographic images *en masse* with a minimum of accompanying text. Goffman's comment regarding the advantages of using photographic materials in this way could apply equally to Bateson's work. He suggests that a researcher

> can exploit the vast social competency of the eye and the impressive consensus sustained by viewers. Behavioural configurations which he has insufficient literary skill to summon up through words alone, he can unambiguously introduce into consideration. His verbal glosses can serve as a means to direct the eye to what is to be seen, instead of having to serve as a full rendition of what is at issue. (Goffman 1979: 25)

Consequently the two books look similar. As is the case with *Balinese Character*, the visual material in *Gender Advertisements* is prefaced by a purely verbal discussion of the subject. In Goffman's case this serves to introduce the reader to his core theoretical concern with the micro-rituals of gender display and, secondly, an intriguing account of the epistemological issues which attend the taking of photographs and what is thereby represented. In part, Goffman returns to themes which he had already rehearsed in his earlier, more philosophically inflected, work *Frame Analysis* (1974). Finally both studies use similar devices to present their visual material with the close juxtaposition of thematically related images on the

Plate 47

STIMULATION AND FRUSTRATION

We have already noted (Pl. 38) that the child's responsiveness is played upon by the mother. In practice, this means that the give-and-take of stimulus and response between mother and child lacks the sort of climax structure which is characteristic of love and hate in our own culture. The Balinese mother stimulates her child, but when he responds, she is unresponsive and never allows the flirtation to end in any sort of affectionate climax.

1 to 9. About two minutes of inter-personal behavior between mother and child. Extracts from M. M.'s verbal record:

"12:20 P.M. Men Goenoeng (the mother) calls I Raoeh (her son) over to her. He goes to her, and holds her breast; holds his penis; holds his knee, and begins to fret.

"Men Goenoeng bumps her head against him (figs. 1 and 2).

"Men Goenoeng settles I Raoeh astride her lap and I Raoeh plays with both nipples (fig. 3).

"I Raoeh sucks (fig. 4) and holds the other breast (figs. 5 and 6).

"Men Goenoeng pats his back rhythmically, and I Raoeh screws the right breast way over to the center of the body.

"Men Goenoeng traces a pattern on the side of her foot with her own hand (figs. 7 and 8).

"I Raoeh holds the other breast in a tight grip.

"12:22 P.M. I Raoeh looks around; hand still on breast" (fig. 9).

In this sequence, the mother's gesture in figs. 1 and 2 was in response to the child's fretting, but when he responds with affection her attention is away. Immediately after her advance, her face goes completely blank (fig. 3) and later she laughs at some unrecorded outside stimulus (fig. 4). It is probable that the "rhythmic patting of his back" recorded in the notes was performed without paying any attention to the child. In fig. 7, the camera records her with her hand in a caressing gesture on the child's head, while she looks up, laughing at something else (cf. Pl. 44 for the connection between spectatorship and sensuous skin contacts).

At the end of the sequence, both mother and child appear bored (fig. 9).

Men Goenoeng and her son I Raoeh, aged 580 days.

Bajoeng Gede, Aug. 19, 1937. 14 G 22, 23, 27, 28, 29, 30, 31, 33, last.

148

FIGURE 2.1   *'Stimulus and Frustration', Plate 47 from Bateson and Mead, Balinese Character (1942), New York: New York Academy of Sciences*

same page. Goffman arranges his visual material into five categories: 'relative size', 'the feminine touch', 'function ranking', 'the family', 'the ritualization of subordination' and finally 'licensed withdrawal' which accounts

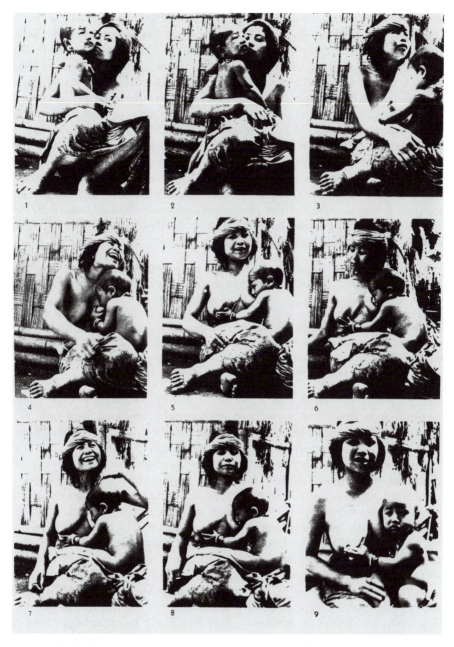

for nearly half of all the images presented. In Goffman's case the images span both pages and his accompanying verbal text has a decidedly more theoretical flavour than the largely ethnographic commentary which Bateson provides. But the major distinction between the two studies, of course, is that Bateson procured his own visual material whereas Goffman chose to analyse already-generated commercial photographs.

Related projects   *Balinese Character* and *Gender Advertisements* have set standards which have yet to be matched by other researchers. It is a telling indicator of the state of photographic visual social science that it continues to take its bearings and inspiration from two studies published so long ago. A useful way to try to highlight the analytical strengths of these studies would be to conduct your own modest photographic project based on the suggestions given in Box 2.1. We hope your experiences with this project draw attention to the difficulties inherent in capturing social life photographically and in making use of the results. There are, however, a number of other ways in which photography can be utilized for research purposes which are not as exacting as the documentary approach. Involving the subjects of the research in the task of interpreting your photographs, the basic idea in the photo-elicitation method is one of these. Schwartz, who employed the method in her study of a rural farming community, explains the benefits as follows:

> Because photo-elicitation generates extensive verbal commentary, use of this interview technique yields several benefits. Informants responded to photographs of their community, neighbours and family without hesitation. By providing informants with a task similar to a naturally occurring family event (i.e. viewing the family photo album), the strangeness of the interview situation was averted. Interviewees often responded directly to the photographs, paying less heed to my presence and the perceived demands of the task than in more traditional formal interview settings. (Schwartz, 1989: 151–2)

The project described in Box 2.2 outlines a simple form of photo-elicitation research. Involving subjects in photographic research, however, can also be found in other branches of social science besides these more traditional ethnographic approaches. Within social psychology a method known as 'autophotography' has been employed for a number of years in quantitative studies of the self. Autophotography differs from photo-elicitation in that it is the research *subject* who is responsible for taking the photographs, with the analytical task of interpreting the photograph remaining with the researcher. Pioneers in the use of autophotography such as Robert Ziller (e.g. Ziller, 1990), see the use of self-generated photographs as a natural extension to the traditional verbal inquiries into the self concept. Indeed, there are aspects of the self which can arguably be more reliably gauged with such photographs. For example Ziller and Rorer (1985) have investigated shyness using this technique. They found that first-year university students were less likely to include pictures of people when asked to portray their environment photographically than those in later years who were presumably more settled into their college life. Overall, 'shy' people were less likely to include other people in their photographic depictions of self.

Clancy and Dollinger (1993) have used the autophotography technique in an investigation of sex role differences. An initial hypothesis concerning gender differences in social connectedness was borne out in their

BOX 2.1 DOCUMENTARY PHOTOGRAPHY VERSUS THE ANALYSIS OF EXISTING IMAGES PROJECT

As we have suggested in this chapter, one of the major distinctions in conventional visual social science is between the researcher who takes photographs (e.g. Bateson) and the researcher who uses existing images (e.g. Goffman). This project requires you to undertake both strategies in order to familiarize yourself with different ways of working with photographs, and to learn about their comparative merits and problems. As there is quite a lot of work involved, you may wish to complete this with other people.

1. First, select a group or subculture in which you have an interest. This might be participants in a sport (e.g. a basketball club), people who share the same hobby (e.g. stamp collectors), or fans of a particular musical subculture (e.g. punks).
2. Next take a series of documentary photographs which aim to faithfully record the activities of this group. Try to take an anthropological or sociological approach, with an interest in the 'way of life' within the activity, the values of its members and their forms of sociability.
3. The third step is to collect existing images of people involved in the same activity as the group you study. You should be able to find these in commercial magazines devoted to the particular interest of the participants (e.g. basketball, stamp collecting, music magazines).
4. Compile two brief (750 word) photo essays (text with accompanying photographs or vice-versa) which provide a simple overview of the activity you have chosen.
5. Now compare and evaluate the two methods in terms of the following criteria: (a) the account of the activity each offers (e.g. glamorous, mundane, gendered, formal, informal); (b) the 'objectivity' of each approach as a true record of what 'really goes on' in a particular activity (e.g. what got into the photographic record and what didn't); (c) the flexibility of the approach (e.g. limitations on topics that can be covered in the photo essay using each method); (d) the resources used for each project (time, money, equipment, etc.). What seem to be the strengths and weaknesses of each approach? What have you learnt about the role of photographs in assisting social research?

research. For example, they found that men were significantly more likely than women to provide photographs featuring themselves alone. Women, alternatively, provided photographs which revealed them to be more interpersonally connected: their photographs contained more depictions

BOX 2.2   PHOTO-ELICITATION PROJECT

Return to the group or subculture you investigated in the previous project, armed with your two sets of photographs. Divide the participants into three samples. With one sample work with your own photographs and with another use the media photographs. Show each of the photographs in turn and ask the participants to talk about what the pictures mean to them. With the third group just have an unstructured discussion about the group's activities without using any photographs. Tape record and transcribe each session. When you have finished, write a report evaluating the various methodologies. Compare the following things: (a) group dynamics (e.g. which discussions seemed more natural, honest, open, unforced?); (b) the kinds of things that were talked about (e.g. range of topics, levels of abstract/concreteness in discussions). What do you conclude about the photo-elicitation technique? What are its strengths and weaknesses compared with the traditional unstructured focus group? What seemed to be the advantages/disadvantages of each kind of picture (your photographs of the group vs magazine pictures) as a photo-elicitation resource?

of people touching, smiling, groups of people and family-oriented pictures. By contrast, men's photographs more frequently included activities such as sport and other leisure activities, as well as picture of prize possessions – cars and motorcycles.

The technique can also be used to investigate cross-cultural differences in perception. Ziller (1990: 107–21) reports a study in which students from four different nationalities (the USA, Japan, Taiwan and Venezuela), but who were all resident in the United States, were asked to take photographs which depicted what the USA meant to them. When comparing the American students' photographs with those of the other national groups, six categories of photographs, out of a much larger corpus, were found to be significantly different. American students were more likely to take pictures which depicted 'freedom' or 'patriotism' (e.g. photographs of flags, political posters, churches) whereas the foreign students were more likely to photograph images of 'sport' and 'food' (e.g. images of McDonald's restaurants, Coca-Cola dispensing machines).

Photographs as historical documents: problems and issues

Although ethnographic forms of inquiry in which the researcher is also the photographer are most commonly found in discussions of visual inquiry, this does not exhaust photography's research potential. The use

BOX 2.3   AUTOPHOTOGRAPHY AND GENERATIONAL CHANGE PROJECT

Ziller's cross-national research could be easily modified by employing age as the key independent variable. An autophotographic project with this design would be an excellent way to explore a topic such as generational difference in conceptions of national identity. For this assignment you would require representatives of three generational cohorts, for example young adults (18–24), the generation in early middle age (45–50) and finally an older cohort aged, say, between 70 and 80. Members of each of the cohorts would be required to take a series of photographs – ten would be sufficient – which they feel best express their country's national identity – the images which they feel best capture what their country means to them.

To ensure some comparability in the images obtained you should attempt to control for region or location and ask your participants in the project to restrict their photographing to their residential location. This will avoid the problems of having to compare images generated by inner city residents (e.g. the Sydney Opera House or the Melbourne Cricket Ground, to use Australian examples) with those which people who are resident in rural areas could obtain. As with Ziller's research you should be able to develop a number of coding categories for these images which should give you some insight into the ways in which conceptions of national identity vary according to age.

An additional dimension to the project could be to ask the members of the two older cohorts if they have photographs in their possession which capture images of national identity which have now disappeared and see whether they feel these older images are more authentic expressions of their country.

of photographs is also found in discussions of documentary research where the focus tends to be historical and interpretive and where the researcher plays no role in generating the actual images they investigate. John Scott (1991), for example, includes photographs as part of his discussion of the use of 'personal documents' – such things as letters, diaries and autobiographies – in social research. He argues that photographs should be regarded in the same light as handwritten or printed documents; that is they should be considered as 'texts whose meaning must be disclosed like any other' (Scott, 1991: 185). For Scott all documentary source material must be assessed with four key criteria in mind: *authenticity*, *credibility*, *representativeness* and *meaning*. However, these criteria raise rather different questions in the case of photographs than they do in the case of the majority of documentary source material. The question of authenticity, for example, does not really arise in the case of photographs despite the fact that it may be an important issue in the case of visual material such as paintings. Originality and authenticity have historically been central to the assessment of paintings as 'works of art'. But, as Scott notes, the idea of an 'original' photograph makes no sense, as the very nature of photographs are that they are reproducible images.[4]

However, the credibility of photographs as documentary evidence is more of an issue. Scott has in mind here the question of the technical control which the photographer can exert over the final production of the photograph. Although this may not involve the use of props or forms of 'dark-room trickery' the fact that the photographer plays an active role in producing the final image must mean that a photograph should be considered to be a selective account of reality. A researcher must always be alert to these possibilities in interpreting any photographic image:

> At the level of literal understanding, for example, a photograph of a Victorian family may appear to give us evidence about dress styles, affluence, and demeanour, and also about attitudes, intimacy and formality in family relations. Similarly the background may provide evidence on street activity and forms of transport, and on occupational and residential segregation. But can these perceptions be relied upon? Were the family dressed in 'Sunday best' and adopting a pose and what part did the photographer play in constructing the scene? (Scott, 1991: 191)

Stuart Hall (1991) raises a different, but equally important, set of considerations in his discussion of the problems of interpretation attending the photographic record of the history of black settlement in Britain during the 1950s. Hall's argument is that many of the photographs which could serve as documentary evidence of post-war migration have already 'made a public appearance in the field of representation' and as a consequence will have already acquired meanings and inflections through their earlier positioning within the discourses of the news-photo agency, the photographic studio, or magazine colour supplement. For Hall this means that

> It is difficult, if not by now impossible, to recapture the earlier meanings of these photographs. In any event, the search for their 'essential Truth' – an original founding moment of meaning – is an illusion. The photographs are essentially multiaccentual in meaning. No such previously natural moment of true meaning, untouched by the codes and social relations of production and reading, and transcending historical time, exists. . . . Black historians, especially, handling these explosive little 'documents', will have to steer their way through the increasingly narrow passage which separates the old Scylla of 'documentary realism as Truth' from the new Charybdis of a too-simplistic 'avant-gardism'. (Hall, 1991: 152–3)

Whereas Scott approaches the question of photographic credibility rather more as a positivist might canvass the issue of reliability, Stuart Hall appears to undercut the positivist assumption that, with sufficient care and a large enough sample to inspect, an accurate assessment of the photographic record can be gauged. For Hall the idea that the original meaning of an image can somehow be grasped is futile, a position which would seem to cast some doubt on their documentary value as anything other than texts for hermeneutic analysis.

In relation to the interpretation of a photograph – the meaning which can be reasonably assigned to it – Scott suggests that the issue which underpins this is a knowledge of its genre: specifically whether it was produced professionally in a studio or, alternatively, a 'home-mode' variety. This is relevant in that commercial photographers would have exerted far more control over the photographic subjects and the context in which they were taken. The use of various props, backgrounds and poses were subject to changing fashions; moreover 'the subjects of studio photographs have in general acquiesced in the aesthetic contexts chosen for the pictures' (1991: 193). Scott argues that studio portraiture would have drawn significantly upon historically accepted family and gender roles:

> Photographer and subject connived to present a stylized presentation: who is seated and who standing symbolize authority relations, and whether the subjects are smiling or serious can convey an image of respectability or conviviality. . . . Nevertheless, a close examination of studio photographs can often disclose discrepancies between the image and the reality: a middle-class drawing room setting for people in ill-fitting and shabby clothes can signal social aspirations rather than established social standing. (ibid.)

Home-mode photography, although generally less concerned with the technical or aesthetic issues of the studio variety, nevertheless can reveal a good deal about the assumptions governing family life provided that the researcher is 'attuned to the conventions' which are drawn upon in the generation of such images. Finally he stresses that documentary researchers should not assume that the photographs which can be found in archives or private collections are necessarily representative of all those which were taken. For example, photographs which are technically deficient or, possibly more importantly, which did not seem to fit the desired family self-image may be discarded.

Scott's injunction for documentary researchers to pay close attention to the representativeness of photographic source material is clearly illustrated in Dowdall and Golden's (1989) historical study of a US mental hospital. In their analysis of the photographs pertaining to the institution, Dowdall and Golden observed that images of patients engaged in some form of occupational activity were overwhelmingly those of men. Indeed, in their collection as a whole, they found that 58 per cent of the photographs showed only male patients or a preponderance of males, compared with 41 per cent which showed women, or a preponderance of women. However data from the Hospital Annual Reports indicated that both of these observations were misleading. The institution actually housed more women than men, and women were also more actively engaged in the various institutional labour activities. Dowdall and Golden emphasize the need for photographic data to be continually assessed at each stage of inquiry in the light of what is known about the research topic from other, predominantly written, sources. Their own strategy of inquiry is an exemplary illustration of this point.

Dowdall and Golden utilize what they refer to as 'a layered analysis' which involves subjecting their photographic data to increasingly detailed forms of investigation and to being attentive to the connections between the various levels of analysis. The first level, which they refer to as 'appraisal', involves viewing the images in a historical context and paying close attention to any incongruities between the visual and the written record. At this level they were able to establish that the hospital was invariably photographed in such a way as to represent it as having a rural setting when in fact it was situated in an industrial area of the city. This point, together with the misleading gender composition of the hospital inmate population referred to earlier, may be part of the attempt by the hospital authorities to present a generally more favourable image of the institution. As they suggest:

> In a culture in which men are expected to be employed, the photographs may have reflected the normative expectations of the photographers and/or the intended audience. To show patients at work is to suggest they are regaining health and may be able to resume their expected roles. (Dowdall and Golden, 1989: 190)

The second level – 'inquiry' – is concerned to discover themes which can be observed in the collection as a whole. Where possible a precondition for inquiry is to view the photographic evidence in chronological sequence. In this way the major changes which have occurred in the institution are highlighted. In their data one of the most vivid images concerned the way in which a previously spacious and well-furnished corridor had become transformed in the space of a few decades into a rather shabby overcrowded day room for elderly male patients. Other photographs provide similar insights into the working and living conditions of the hospital staff, including several scenes of ' "remotivation classes," a not-so-subtle hint that the hospital needed a conscious on-going effort to boost morale and skills' (ibid.: 194). Dowdall and Golden comment that these images help contextualize the references to high labour turnover to which the hospital Annual Reports make reference.

The final level of analysis they refer to as 'interpretation' involves examining specific photographs in detail as a way of 'comprehending the texture and nuances of institutional life' (ibid.: 197). Two aspects of the organization of the mental hospital become apparent on the basis of this close examination of images: 'compelled activity' and 'enforced idleness'. A number of the pictures show the hospital patients doing nothing but sitting. The images, however, are not those of individuals 'at rest' but rather regimented rows of patients subject to a bureaucratically dictated idleness. Other pictures show posed images of the patients engaged in craft or handiwork activities: threading beads on strings, weaving cane. Some of the patients are slumped over the work benches and tables, physically present but not actively engaged. The photographs, in themselves, cannot resolve the question of whether these behaviours are a consequence of the patients' mental and physical conditions, or rather a regime imposed by the hospital or perhaps some combination of both of these. But it is through such photographic images, they suggest, that:

> the narrow range of institutional behaviour from idle to active become apparent. Much sociological literature on mental hospitals stresses the interactions of patients and staff. The present photographs suggest that these interactions were perhaps more episodic and infrequent than presumed. Seeking to observe and explain social activity, sociologists may have unwittingly exaggerated its significance and ignored the long periods of institutional torpor and individual lethargy that the photographs reveal. (Dowdall and Golden, 1989: 205)

Photographs as unobtrusive or non-reactive measures

The final example of social scientific utilization of photographs we consider is closely related to the documentary use but, rather than being reliant on a historical corpus of images, perhaps of questionable provenance, in this mode the researcher has some control over the images that are collected. However, this third technique also differs from the ethnographic approach in that it generally involves the utilization of photographic images not of people but rather of objects and places. Photographs, in other words, can be employed as the basis of an unobtrusive or non-reactive technique for studying social phenomena. Unobtrusive methods of data collection are, of course, much broader than this. They comprise a range of techniques which have in common the fact that they do not require the active cooperation of the research subject in the data collection process. The vast majority of methods employed by social researchers, whether quantitative (surveys, questionnaires) or qualitative (in-depth interviewing, participant observation, case studies, life histories, etc.) – or for that matter ethnographic or social documentary photography – are what researchers term reactive. That is, as Schwartz and Jacobs have pithily observed

> They have the investigator going into some arena of social life (and/or diverse social occasions) and 'making a mess', so to speak. The investigator becomes a part of the social process he is investigating. His presence and activities constitute events in this process, with their own consequences and effects. (Schwartz and Jacobs, 1979: 75)

The classic statement concerning the possibilities of non-reactive research remains Webb, Campbell, Schwartz and Sechrest's (1966) *Unobtrusive Measures: Nonreactive Research in the Social Sciences*. In their preface they refer, somewhat cryptically, to a working title for the book – *The Bullfighter's Beard* – an allusion to an observation that on the day of a fight the bull-fighter's beard growth is noticeably longer. Implicitly, the length of facial hair could be seen as an indicator of the fighter's emotional state although '[n]o one seems to know if the torero's beard really grows faster that day because of anxiety or if he simply stands further away from the blade, shaking razor in hand' (Webb et al., 1966: v). Webb and his colleagues discuss three broad categories of non-reactive measures: physical traces, archival records and simple observation. We shall be considering various aspects of unobtrusive measurement in the context of our own discussion of visual data in later chapters and so we will not expand on these categories here. The use of photographs is considered briefly by them as part of a discussion of mass media content but mainly as an issue of investigating media bias.

Schwartz and Jacobs provide a more informative treatment of photography as a non-reactive technique. As we have observed, many of the examples of photography discussed earlier are clearly reactive in that they involve the cooperation of subjects. Schwartz and Jacobs bypass this problem by photographing not people but signs which are designed to be noticed and acted upon by people. The theme of their photo essay is 'signs of prohibition'[5] – that is, signs which are predominantly located in public places and which regulate such everyday matters as parking, eating and drinking, smoking, the categories of people who can enter certain buildings and at what times, playing games, doing business and 'many other social transactions too numerous to list here'. Such signs, they maintain, are of obvious sociological interest:

> Signs of all kinds constitute unobtrusive measures, *par excellence*. The kinds that are found, where they are placed, how prevalent they are, and who is subject to them are all valuable indicators of group life. (Schwartz and Jacobs, 1979: 90)

However, they also suggest that the prevalence of such signs has theoretical significance as well. Here they draw upon Durkheim's conception of a transition from the mechanical to organic form of solidarity, in particular the changes in the workings of legal institutions which he believed accompanied this transition. The earlier forms of society characterized by mechanical cohesion had more restrictive or repressive legal arrangements – 'thou shalt nots' – whereas the organic form of society rested on a solidarity of differentiation, a heightened awareness of moral dependency and a diminution of the role of collective constraint. However, Schwartz and Jacobs suggest that there seem to be 'many counterindicators' to this. Their photo essay – a collection of approximately 30 'signs of prohibition' – is just one example of this. They add that it is ironic that so many such signs can be witnessed 'in a permissive society currently populated by the "Spock generation" ', an irony compounded by the realization that the signs were all observed in one of the most liberal parts of the USA, the San Franciso Bay Area. Schwartz and Jacobs conclude that the prevalence of such signs is an indication

> that the number of 'thou shalt nots' is not decreasing but increasing. Not only have the duly constituted authorities formulated and displayed a series of prohibitions on the populace, but private citizens have joined in this undertaking in earnest. [We] take this to be an indicator of a perverse lack of trust on the part of the citizenry, which in turn is taken to indicate not a sense of growing morality, but a lessening of it. (ibid.: 91)

Much more can be said about signs as sources of visual information, and we shall briefly consider some of the other theoretical considerations which have been raised in relation to signs, in addition to their status as unobtrusive measures, in the following chapter. Despite the fact that *Unobtrusive Measures* had reportedly sold 125,000 copies up to 1979 (Kellehear, 1993: 4), interest in the use of these techniques is not widespread amongst social scientists. Kellehear offers a number of reasons why this might be the case. Amongst these is the rather cavalier attitude to ethical issues which accompanies some of the techniques, such as experimental manipulation, which many researchers find questionable. Kellehear argues that a lack of awareness by subjects that they were being researched 'may indeed be unobtrusive for the purpose of validity but it is nevertheless intrusive for those people because those activities have been disturbed by the researcher's activities' (ibid.: 4). Methods which utilize experimental manipulation, such as staging shoplifting to assess shopper reporting behaviour, are therefore '*socially* as well as *ethically* intrusive' (emphasis in original). It was perhaps recognition of the concern with social intrusion which led to a change in title when the book appeared in a second edition in 1981. In the later edition the term 'Unobtrusive Measures' was dropped and replaced by 'Non-reactive Measures'.

Despite the change in title, Kellehear suggests that many aspects of the book were also 'outdated'. He refers here to new technological developments as well as theoretical movements such as post-structuralism which have had implications for the research process. In addition, the rise of cultural studies and related forms of textual methodologies has opened up an entirely new vista in the analysis of much media, documentary and even archival material. Television, cinema, popular music as well as the print media are now all more likely to be studied within their own specialized cultural studies frameworks than as domains of non-reactive measurement or investigation. However, the investigation of material culture and its traces remains a viable arena in which unobtrusive methods can be turned to advantage by visual researchers and we explore this issue in more detail in Chapter 4. In the remainder of the chapter, we turn to consider the other branches of visual inquiry we identified, touching only on their principal themes and developments.

The analysis of existing images

The examples of photographically based research discussed in the previous section are predominantly those found in North America. In contrast, within European countries the use of photographs as visual data generally does not entail the first-hand collection of subject material by the researcher/photographer but rather a reliance on already produced images. In the influential continental traditions of structuralism and semiotics photographs are thus 'texts' for analysis and interpretation. Roland Barthes' work (e.g. Barthes, 1977a, 1977b, 1981) on the photograph as a sign provides the primary exemplar here, but there has also been some important work on photography from a broadly Foucauldian perspective which links the taking of photographs by institutions such as the police, welfare and social reform bodies, hospitals and educational institutions to an interest in the surveillance and control of populations (McHoul, 1991; Tagg, 1988).

For Barthes, and others who work in the semiotic tradition, the primary issue is the interpretation of the photograph and its place in a system of cultural representation. Barthes' work, nevertheless, entails something of a paradox in relation to the use of photographs as visual data to the extent that he was forced to rely on non-visual elements to account for their meaning. In his famous essay 'Rhetoric of the Image' Barthes (1977b) came to argue that the meaning of images is always related to and dependent upon an accompanying verbal text. All images were seen by him as 'polysemous' – signifiers which generated 'a "floating chain" of signifieds'. Hence Barthes argued 'in every society various techniques are developed intended to fix the floating chain of signifieds in such a way as to counter the terror of uncertain signs; the linguistic message is one of these techniques' (1977b: 39). In taking this step Barthes was reiterating a point that had been made by Walter Benjamin some years earlier. According to Benjamin (1985: 256), despite the realism of the photographic medium, meanings could only be 'arrested in the approximate'. He argued that the duty of the photographer (and especially the progressive photographer) was to provide some kind of closure and asked: 'Will not the caption become the most important part of the photograph?' (ibid.). We shall explore the core ideas in the semiotic tradition in Chapter 3 in the context of examples of research which illustrate Barthes' key terms of anchorage and relay as well as Benjamin's key terms, insistence on the importance of the caption.

Stuart Hall (1973) has provided one of the seminal arguments that photographs should be studied as indicators of underlying cultural forces. Drawing on the work of Roland Barthes, Hall argues we should decode images in terms of connotation and denotation. Denotation is 'precise, literal, unambiguous' (ibid.: 226) whilst codes of connotation 'are more open-ended' (ibid.). Hall argues that the 'expressive codes' determining gesture and facial expression can often play a major role in shaping these connotations. By comparing photographs from various papers issued on the same day, he shows how a head and shoulders photograph of a politician who quit office denotes the politician, but can take on varying connotations depending on the expressive codes at work. The politician can be shown to be 'angry', 'defiant', 'tragic', or 'resigned'. Hall suggests that in determining which connotation is valid we have to draw upon our stock of common-sense knowledge in order to make a reading of the image in terms of its expressive content. This can involve knowledge about our society, the meanings of its symbols and the codes that govern face, body and posture. Hall argues that, in the context of news photography, expressive codes and connotations often combine to give an ideological value to the photographic sign, by positioning newsworthy events within a 'moral-political discourse' (ibid.: 231).

Hall demonstrates this thesis with reference to a photograph of a demonstrator kicking a police officer (Figure 2.2). According to Hall the denotated message 'a man in crowded scene is kicking a policeman' is ideologically read as 'anti-war demonstrators are violent people who threaten the state and assault policemen unfairly'. For Hall the extraordinary power of the news photograph lies in its ability to obscure its

THE KICK-PHOTO
Photo: Keystone Agency

FIGURE 2.2   *Newspaper photograph of a policeman being kicked from Stuart Hall 'The determinations of news photographs' in S. Cohen and J. Young (eds) (1973)* The Manufacture of News: deviance, social problems and the mass media. *London: Constable. Photo: Keystone Agency*

own ideological dimensions by appearing as a 'literal visual-transcription of the real world' (ibid.: 241). Selection and framing decisions made by photographers and editors are ignored (the newspaper might have printed, for example, a picture of a demonstrator being hit by the police) and so we tend to read such photographs as a truthful document of what really happened, ignoring the possibility of other interpretations of the event.

Hall's own take in his exploration of British news photos of the 1970s is to read the hidden forces behind them as those of authoritarian capitalism. According to Hall the media played a key role in maintaining public support for harsh policing. This ideology also projected the blame for social problems like mugging onto minority groups. As a result the systematic inequalities arising from capitalism were excluded from public analysis. It is worth remembering, however, that the press has often been attacked by the right as a liberal enclave. In the United States, for example, the press was accused of hounding Republican President Richard Nixon out of the White House but of supporting Bill Clinton during his impeachment. It is quite probable, then, that the ideological values embodied in news photographs might vary from place to place and time to time. They may also be expected to vary according to the constituency, ownership and editorial control of each paper.

Most work on the ideological force of photographs has centred on a neo-Gramscian decoding of news photographs and more recently news footage. Investigation of the deeper resonances of photographs need not be restricted to the news arena. Nor do they have to be grounded in critical theory. One of the best examples of an alternative approach is Peter Hamilton's (1997) work on French humanist photography from the end of the Second World War until the late 1950s. This is the photography of public life associated with great names like Robert Doisneau, Willy Ronis

BOX 2.4   NEWS PHOTOGRAPHS EXERCISE

Look at your own newspapers for pictures relating to an industrial dispute or public demonstration. Decode them in terms of denotation and connotation. What kinds of ideologies and values do you find hidden in the photographs? Now look at the accompanying text in the newspaper or perhaps at the editorial section. Are there any clues here to suggest your reading of the photographs was correct?

Note: It may be instructive to compare photographs and coverage in two newspapers with different political outlooks (e.g. *Socialist Worker* and *The Times*). In this way issues of ideological framing in news photographs can be dramatically foregrounded.

and Henri Cartier-Bresson. Hamilton argues that the 'dominant representational paradigm' of these photographs was one which attempted to capture a quintessential 'Frenchness'. Whilst the photographs were intended and promoted as 'documentary' photo journalism about everyday life by magazines such as *Paris Match* and *Life*, the selection of images from the infinite universe of potential images inevitably involved subjective and cultural elements. According to Hamilton, images of the French humanists promoted themes of community, happiness and solidarity. They celebrated everyday life through pictures of street life, cafés, children, lovers and homes. These themes can be illustrated with reference to Doisneau's famous picture of a young couple kissing outside the Hôtel de Ville (Figure 2.3). Hamilton notes that the couple are dressed as 'ordinary' people and that we view the scene from an 'ordinary' café table. Other persons in the picture are also members of the *classe populaire* (note the humble beret) and they are going about their ordinary business. The picture depicts the universal human emotion of love and situates it as a slice of everyday life in the streets. The overall effect allows the viewer to feel empathy and a sense of commonality with the persons in the photograph and to appreciate the joy of human sociability.

Hamilton's interpretation of the paradigm is almost Durkheimian. He sees the French humanists as responding to a crisis in French identity.

Le Baiser de l'Hotel deVille, 1950

FIGURE 2.3 *Photograph by Robert Doisneau: 'Kiss outside the town hall, 1950'. Copyright Robert Doisneau/Network/Rapho.*

German occupation and French collaboration during the Second World War had threatened and dishonoured French national identity. Humanist photography operated as an integrating force by offering inclusive and attractive definitions of Frenchness. It spoke of the importance of solidarity and human association amongst ordinary people. Hamilton's work, then, suggests that we should look at genres of photographs as a whole and try to identify key themes. These can then be related to the decoding of individual images, on the one hand, and to underlying social processes, forces and values on the other. Whilst these may be 'political' in orientation, they might also refer to less contested cultural needs such as issues of identity and the search for the good society. The following chapter provides more details concerning the analysis of existing images, including advertisements, posters and cartoons as well as the news and documentary photographs we have just considered. We now turn briefly to the two remaining traditions in visual analysis identified at the start of the chapter.

The analysis of practices of visualization

Researchers interested in visual information not only take photographs and analyse existing commercial images but have also looked at the issue of visual depiction or representation, particularly as this relates to the practices of scientific communication. This third area involving the use of visual data is almost totally ignored in the North American literature on 'visual social science' although it features prominently in two of the (UK) overviews of the place of visual data in sociology which have been published in the last ten years. For example, Fyfe and Law's (1988) edited collection *Picturing Power: Visual Depiction and Social Relations* devotes eight out of its ten chapters to studies of visual depiction, and Elizabeth Chaplin (1994) also considers this topic in some detail in her book *Sociology and Visual Representation*. It is nevertheless a specialist domain in an already marginalized area of sociology and as a field of inquiry it is characterized by many apparently idiosyncratic studies. As Chaplin notes

> any attempt to generalize from the findings of sociological analyses of scientific depictions is fraught with complexities . . . scientists represent nature in many different ways, and depiction is only one of them. We cannot, therefore, talk of a 'sociology of scientific depictions' nor draw firm conclusions from close comparisons between sociological studies of scientific depictions. (Chaplin, 1994: 183–4)

Research into these practices of visualization has been largely undertaken by ethnomethodologically influenced scholars as part of what has become known as the 'strong programme' (e.g. Barnes, 1974; Bloor, 1976) in the sociology of science. Although this embraces a number of disparate elements, it is, nevertheless, possible to detect some common themes in these studies. Perhaps the most basic is the insistence that sociological explanations can be developed to explain scientific knowledge and beliefs, regardless of whatever accuracy is deemed to be associated with these beliefs. Proponents of the strong programme argue that the development of scientific knowledge in the abstract as well as the day-to-day conduct of scientific research must be viewed as the outcome of complex social practices. Science as an organized domain of activity is thus characterized by competing interests, rivalries, negotiation of credit for discoveries and the like, all of which are amenable to sociological investigations. More mundanely but equally importantly, the 'technical contents' of scientific knowledge, it is argued, must be understood as 'inscriptions': that is they are something more than simply representations of the natural world. In their introduction to *Representation in Scientific Practice* Lynch and Woolgar make this point as follows:

> Manifestly what scientists laboriously piece together, pick up in their hands, measure, show to one another, argue about, and circulate to others in their communities are not 'natural objects' independent of cultural processes and literary forms. They are extracts, 'tissue cultures', and residues impressed within graphic matrices; ordered, shaped and filtered samples; carefully aligned photographic traces and chart recordings; and verbal accounts. (Lynch and Woolgar, 1990: 5)

Studies of visualization in science have been largely confined to the physical and life sciences such as astronomy, biochemistry and molecular biology. Although this is to simplify a complex issue, the research interest for those undertaking these inquiries turns on the fact that the objects which comprise the focus of the day-to-day laboratory practices of scientists in these fields are theoretically derived rather than empirically 'given'. Attention is thus focused on how these 'invisible' objects are made 'visible' for the purposes of scientific communication. The early – and still influential – ethnomethodological studies of scientific practice, however, paid rather less attention to the issue of visual representation and more to the analysis of the everyday discourse of laboratory practice which constituted the work of scientific discovery. For example, Garfinkel, Lynch and Livingstone's (1981) examination of the discovery of an optical pulsar at the Steward Observatory in Arizona is largely indebted to data they obtained in the form of recordings of the conversations between the scientists after the tape recorder they used to document their discovery was left running. Garfinkel et al.'s interest in examining the conversations is exactly *how* the scientists worked so that the object which appeared on their oscilloscope display came to be seen by them as an optical pulsar.

A word of warning: although this is an important and pioneering study into scientific visualization it is written in a style which has become the hallmark of certain branches of ethnomethodology. The task which Garfinkel and his colleagues set themselves is to produce an account which faithfully captures the 'real time' or 'first time through' process of discovery and for this they develop a particular form of analytical language which is not easy to grasp. Essentially the problem facing the astronomers was that they had no prior 'visual' conception of what the pulsar was. Garfinkel et al. liken the astronomers to bricoleurs who work with whatever materials are at hand to achieve their goal. They also employ the imaginative metaphor of 'the potter's object' as a means to capture this process. In the same way that the potter works up an identifiable object from her raw materials so the pulsar 'takes "shape" in and as of the way it is worked, and *from* a place-to-start with *to* an increasingly definite thing' (Garfinkel et al., 1981: 137, emphasis in original). Garfinkel et al. conclude that the optically discovered pulsar must be understood as a '*cultural* object, not a physical or natural object' (ibid.: 141), (emphasis added), in the sense that its reality cannot be divorced from the embodied details of the astronomical activities the scientists undertook on the night of their discovery.

In a far more accessible paper, Lynch and Edgerton (1988) report the results of research conducted several years later which looked more specifically at the factors which influenced scientists' decisions to generate visual representations. Specifically they sought to examine whether 'aesthetic' considerations play any part in contemporary scientific work, via a case study of the same scientific field – astronomy – which had witnessed rapid technological changes since the original discovery of the optical pulsar, through the introduction of digital and image-processing technologies. Interviews with, and observations of, astronomers at image-processing laboratories suggest that they are very much aware of 'aesthetic' considerations in that aspect of their research which is designed to promote or popularize their activities. In contrast the astronomers they interviewed maintained that there was an important difference between the production of what they term 'pretty pictures' for lay audiences and the real scientific work of representing the astronomical phenomena they are investigating. Lynch and Edgerton, however, argue that although the astronomers deny that they are influenced by aesthetic consideration in their scientific practice, they are nevertheless working with an older conception of aesthetics – that of 'perfecting nature through a crafting of resemblances' – as a constitutive part of their laboratory activities. But the meaning of aesthetics in this context, they suggest,

> is not a domain of beauty or expression which is detached from representational realism. Instead, it is the very fabric of realism: the work of composing visible coherences, discriminating differences, consolidating entities and establishing evident relations. These perceptual relations take place through a *crafting* of gestalt contextures, where relational elements in any configuration are manipulated through image processing machinery and software. This hands-on process of interpretation can be treated as an *art* situated within the performance of scientific practice. (Lynch and Edgerton, 1988: 212, emphasis in original)

More recently studies of scientific representation have taken a 'Foucauldian' turn to the extent that they have been concerned with identifying political aspects to the visualization of scientific activities. For example, Law and Whittaker (1988) examine the 'technologies of representation' which are employed by scientists writing about research into the phenomenon of acid rain for primarily lay audiences. In the document they examine – *Acidification Today and Tomorrow*, produced by the Swedish Ministry of Agriculture in 1992 – several of these technologies of visualization can be found which cumulatively work to produce 'simplification, discrimination and integration' of the phenomenon. The idealized photographs of unspoiled countryside – waterfalls, lakes, snow-capped mountains – which are found in the report serve, they argue, to generate an oversimplified view of nature which is spatially distinguished from 'the profanity of the text and its polluting human messages' (Law and Whittaker, 1988: 173). Second, there are a number of 'semi-naturalistic sketches' which are designed to provide a causal analysis of acidification but which, in ad-dition, present a simplified and discriminable view through the use of techniques of scaling which dramatically overemphasize certain elements in the process. Finally there are numerous graphs and charts throughout the report. One they examine shows the relationship between the pH level of the lakewater and the incidence of plankton – microscopic crustaceans which serve as the basis of the food chain. The graphic representation of these items in space and time serves to interrelate them in a simplified form but in ways which are very precisely defined. In short, through these representational devices of simplification, discrimination and integration, the process of acidification is rendered tractable and controllable. But this is achieved at a cost, for the representations 'are quite unlike those whom they represent'. Law and Whittaker conclude by arguing that such technologies of popular scientific visualization are inherently political in character in that they 'marshal, organize and purport to speak on behalf of objects that are rendered silent' (1988: 180).

In general terms, we can detect something of a shift in the studies of practices of visualization away from an ethnographic focus on the actual production of scientific artefacts within laboratory settings towards a more cultural-studies-inspired interest in the deconstruction of scientific communications. Law and Whittaker represent a half-way house between an ethnomethodological approach and that of cultural studies. More recently the cultural studies type of approach has come to dominate the analysis of scientific representation, reading them for their ideological and gendered biases. A useful example of the latter can be found in Petersen's (1998) investigation of representations of sex differences in Gray's *Anatomy*. Petersen's research suggests that over the course of its 140 year existence this most influential of all anatomical texts has operated with an assumption of the normality of the male body against which the female has been compared and implicitly judged as underdeveloped, weak or faulty. Scientific drawings and diagrams, therefore, share the same patri-archal assumptions and cultural codes as the wider society. The irony is that although society has begun to change, the discipline of anatomy, it would appear, has been largely untouched by the wider public debates about sexual inequality and gender representations.

The analysis of video recordings of natural interaction

The final approach to the use of visual data can be found in the form of video recordings of naturally occurring interaction. We exclude from consideration here the making of documentary films which we regard as having largely the same analytical limitations as the documentary still-photography tradition. As we have noted, the use of motion cameras has often been cited as part of the enterprise of visual social science but it has never assumed the prominence that still-photography has enjoyed.[6] At least part of the reason for this is based on technological considerations. Although the roots of this tradition can be traced to the pioneering efforts of the founders of proxemics – the study of the ways that humans use space culturally – and the related field of kinesics – the study of body language and gesture – such as Edward Hall and Ray Birdwhistell, it is only comparatively recently that video recording technology has become user-friendly and affordable and consequently widely available for use by social scientists. But it is also the case that researchers have generally lacked any systematic means of analysing video-recordings and of incorporating video-based evidence into published form. The major innovation in this context has been the work of researchers in the field of conversation analysis[7] who have provided both an elaborate conceptual framework for analysing sequences of actions and, equally importantly, a transcription notation system which has allowed the details of interaction to be recorded and subject to repeated investigation. The use of video-recording today remains largely within the provenance of researchers working within conversation analysis, for whom an interest in the visual record of interaction has become a natural extension of the linguistic dimension. However, unlike the earlier linguistic work which focused on ordinary conversational encounters, video-recording of behaviour has been largely confined to workplace environments, particularly those involving the use of computers or computer-mediated forms of communications: police and other emergency service workers, air traffic and underground rail controllers (e.g. Heath and Luff, 1997). We do not propose to consider this research activity in any depth. The work is very much cutting-edge material and requires students to be familiar with the foundational concepts and assumptions of the conversation analysis tradition. However, we will make brief reference to the analytical precursors of contemporary video-based research – proxemics and kinesics – when we consider the use of the body as a living signifier in Chapter 6.

In this chapter we have attempted to familiarize students with the diversity of work which currently goes under the title of visual research. Our major concern has been to identify the potential of photographically based visual inquiries. Notwithstanding our appreciation of some aspects of the field, two reservations need to be made at this juncture. Firstly the use of photography by anthropologists, sociologists and ethnographers has generally led to an insular and theoretically uninspiring subfield. Visual inquiry has, for the most part, failed to connect with the wider currents in social theory in these disciplines. Photographs have tended to be used in a purely illustrative or documentary fashion. Sometimes it is hard to see how academic uses of the camera have progressed much beyond the photo-essay of the Sunday newspaper supplements. Can it be coinciden-tal that the work held in highest regard by the general academic com-munity which has employed photographs – that of Bateson and Mead, Goffman, Hall, etc. – has not been by a self-proclaimed visual researcher? We would suggest not. It is precisely because these figures came to visual research from outside the camp that they had clearly defined theoretical agendas. It is this grounding in social theory which gives their visual work an audience and intellectual weight.

Our second reservation is that visual research – in all its manifestations – has been common-sensically equated with and confined to the study of images. As we have noted in earlier sections of the book, issues relating to observability, space and the visible material world in general provide fertile avenues for visual inquiry. Our intention in this book is to address these two deficiencies. In moving beyond the image in general, and the photograph in particular, we will argue that visual research can become a powerful and theoretically driven dimension of social and cultural inquiry. The next chapter begins this journey.

Notes

1   Bourdieu et al. (1990) capture this tension in photographic practice in their designation of photography as a 'middle-brow art'.
2   For example the principal journals for the publication of research using visual data – *Visual Sociology Review, Visual Anthropology, Visual Sociology* and the *International Journal of Visual Sociology* – are all based in the USA.
3   Becker's article is invariably cited by those whose work involves photo-graphic data. A measure of its perceived importance can be gauged from the fact that it was subsequently republished a year later in the arts and photog-raphy journal *Afterimage*. Becker also includes it in his 1986 collection *Doing Things Together*.
4   Contra Scott, Walter Benjamin attempted to make just such a distinction by shifting the concept of authenticity into the aesthetic domain. Drawing on his own critique of mechanical reproduction, Benjamin (1985: 250) distinguishes between the 'picture' characterized by 'uniqueness and duration' and the mass produced 'copy' which embodies 'transience and reproducibility'. Using these criteria Benjamin sees artistic photography and early portraiture as somehow more thoughtful, authentic and original than the kind of shallow images distributed through the mass media.
5   For a recent interpretation of the sociological and regulatory significance of the profusion of such 'signs of prohibition' see Hermer and Hunt (1996).

6   It is interesting to note that in the final section of his – largely overlooked – preliminary comments to *Gender Advertisements* (1979), Goffman alludes to the possibilities which video technology can bring. Goffman refers to the existence of a 'class of behavioural practices' which are particularly suited for image analysis. He refers to these practices as 'small behaviours'

> whose physical forms are fairly well codified even though the social implications or meaning of the acts may have vague elements, and which are realized in their entirety, from beginning to end, in a brief period of time and a small space. These behavioural events can be recorded and their image made retrievable by means of audio and video tapes and camera. (Tape and film, unlike a still, provide not only a recoverable image of the actual activity in question but also an appreciable collection of these records. More important, audio and video recordings of very small behaviours facilitate micro-functional study, *that is an examination of the role of a bit of behaviour in the stream which precedes, co-occurs, and follows*.) (Goffman, 1979: 24, emphasis added)

We can observe here a very different attitude on Goffman's part to the methodological dictates concerning the exploration of naturally occurring forms of social interaction from that which he has conventionally been associated. See, for example, the references to his methodological 'sleight of hand' in Schegloff (1988).

7   For a useful introduction to the conversation analysis tradition see ten Have (1998).

3

Two-dimensional Visual Data: Images, Signs and Representations

This chapter will:

- consider the ways in which two-dimensional images can serve as data for social and cultural inquiry in addition to their conventional use as 'texts' for interpretation
- discuss the ways images can be investigated using both quantitative and qualitative techniques
- continue to move beyond the reliance of visual research on photographic images by exploring the use of some less commonly researched media texts such as cartoons, comics and headlines
- show how students can become critical media consumers by decoding and radically altering the meanings of advertising messages
- broaden the theoretical foundations of visual research by discussing the ways in which two-dimensional visual data can be subject to both semiotic and ethnomethodological investigations.

In the previous chapters we have argued that visual research should advance beyond its preoccupation with images. We now lay ourselves open to a charge of hypocrisy by turning, in the present chapter, to consider this very topic. However, there are a number of additional points that need to be made here which serve to differentiate our efforts from those of self-proclaimed visual researchers. In the first instance, the use of photographic images – the subject of the previous chapter – will be de-emphasized, and we will devote much more attention to other examples of media texts[1] as well as forms of visual data which are not part of the mass media, such as directional signs and maps. Collectively we refer to these forms of data as 'two-dimensional', although we shall have occasion to qualify this designation later in the chapter. Perhaps more important, however, is the analytical stance we adopt in relation to these data. Although we will consider the prevailing semiotic approach taken by most media studies work, which treats images or signs as 'texts' which can be interrogated for cultural or ideological themes, we also want to see how they can be approached rather more sociologically. This means, in the case of most of the examples from the media, to look at the ways in which they might serve as indicators – that is, as sources of concrete visual information about the abstract concepts and processes which are central to understanding everyday social life. Another alternative, which we shall also examine, has been taken by ethno-methodologists who have used visual and media materials as sites for the explication of common-sense reasoning. Here the focus is not so much on the discovery of the hidden cultural meanings that might be assigned to texts or signs by the analyst, but rather on the ways in which ordinary actors use or make sense of this visual information in the course of their everyday practical routines.

Getting away from the semiotic paradigm, however, is not as easy as it might seem, precisely *because* the kinds of two-dimensional images on which we want to focus have invariably been artfully constructed as things which call for or invite interpretation. Common sense seems to tell us that it is more natural to think of items such as photographs, advertisements, cartoons, or signs as things which are meant to be decoded. Their use as indicators of underlying concepts and processes of social life is less obvious. This situation is exacerbated when one considers that the prevailing interpretive approaches to the analysis of visual materials tend to be restricted to a relatively small number of examples, which works against the discovery of generalizable information. Paradoxically, it is the more neglected quantitative tradition of content analysis of visual material, where sample sizes are generally far larger, which provides the best opportunity to investigate structural categories and processes. Accordingly we begin our discussion by looking at studies which exemplify this methodological approach.

Investigating two-dimensional visual material: quantitative considerations

Perhaps the principal advantage of quantitative visual research is the historical depth which can be obtained in an inquiry. Richardson and Kroeber's (1940) investigation of changes in women's dress over a period of three centuries stands as one of the most remarkable instances of scholars using historical resources to the utmost benefit. The study has an additional feature: despite being a quantitative study it was carried out by anthropologists – including one who was a leading exponent of the discipline at that time – and published in a mainstream anthropological journal. No one would dispute that women's formal dress fashions have altered over the centuries. Skirt length and width, waist position, depth of décolletage and so on, have all undergone changes: these sorts of movements are precisely what we mean by the idea of 'fashion'. However, it is not at all obvious to think of fashion changes as following an identifiable historical sequence. Richardson and Kroeber set out to investigate this proposition using visual materials: pictures or images of women attired in formal dress over a period of some 332 years between 1605 and 1936. To these images they applied standard content analysis procedures, only in their case the content was visual and the information collected took the form of a standardized series of precise measurements of the various dimensions of the clothing.

From where did they obtain these images? Obviously there is no single source which they could consult, and so their sample had to be drawn from several different locations. One of their primary sources was the various European fashion magazines and journals – *Vogue, Harper's Bazaar, The Ladies National Magazine, Galerie des Modes* – and these provided the period between 1787 and 1936 with the most complete record. Prior to this their collection of images had to be drawn from more irregular sources: engravings, lithographs as well as the works of some of the leading contemporary artists and painters (e.g. Velasquez, Van Dyck, Reynolds, Hogarth, Watteau). In this way they were able to assemble a more or less continuous record of a changing fashion style – that is, something governed by aesthetic considerations alone, given that the design of evening dress has no apparent 'utilitarian motivation'. Contemporary quantitative researchers might question their reliance on these data sources but this would be mistaken given the thrust of Richardson and Kroeber's inquiry. After all, painters and engravers were the image preservers of their day in exactly the same way that photographers are now. Whilst they may have represented their subjects in stylized or conventionalized poses, there is no reason to assume that they did not faithfully record the dimensions of their clothing.

Thirty-six years after their research was published, Robinson (1976) undertook a similar quantitative investigation of changing fashion, this time looking at the variations in men's growth of facial hair. Robinson modelled his inquiry often with explicit reference to the earlier study and, indeed, found some striking similarities between them as we shall see. For his data Robinson used photographs of men who appeared in the *Illustrated London News* over a 130 year period (1842–1972). The images were coded to identify various forms and combinations of facial hair: sideburns, sideburns and moustaches, beards, moustaches alone and clean shavenness. Robinson noted that the men who appeared in the *Illustrated London News* would have been members of the social and cultural elite and so his findings were not necessarily generalizable to all sections of (British) society. However, a compensating advantage was that the sample he obtained would have been very similar in terms of occupation, social status, income and age.

None of the authors included examples of the images which served as their respective databases. Glancing through their articles it would be impossible to tell that they were based on the analysis of visual materials. Each presents the results of their research in the form of summary statistical tables and time series figures which show how the various fashions have changed. We do not have the space to report all of their findings, but there was a surprising similarity between the cycles which characterized the changes in dress style and those relating to the facial hair of men. Richardson and Kroeber found that the basic dimensions of European female dress 'alternate with fair regularity between maxima and minima which in most cases average about fifty years apart, so that the full wavelength of their periodicity is around a century' (Richardson and Kroeber, 1940: 148). Robinson found that men's facial hair changes underwent similar cyclical changes and observed a 'remarkable correspondence' between the width-of-skirt wave reported by Richardson and Kroeber and his own finding concerning the frequency of beards. The two time series measurements are shown in Figure 3.1.

When seen in this way, the changes in fashion appear as eminently Durkheimian social facts rather than as the product of individual whim. Richardson and Kroeber in fact compare the cyclical changes in fashion to long-term economic trends. Both of these exhibit a 'stateliness of march' in which 'as far as individuals are concerned, the total situation seems overwhelmingly to indicate that their actions are determined by the style far more than they can determine it' (Richardson and Kroeber, 1940: 149). Finally they speculate that these changes in fashion may be linked to the incidence of some underlying cultural instability. During the three centuries they investigated, European women's dress could be seen as

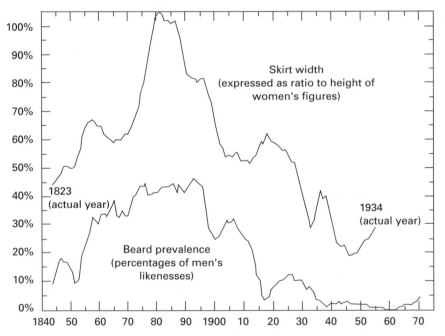

FIGURE 3.1   *Time series graph comparing width of skirts in images of women (1823–1934) and prevalence of beards in photographs of men (1844–1955), in five-year moving averages. Source: Robinson (1976: 1137)*

tending towards a particular ideal, one characterized by amplitude in most dimensions and scantiness in others. As these proportions are achieved, a period of equilibrium, stability, or low variability sets in. However, at other times these proportions are at the opposite extreme and there is an increase in their variability. What is intriguing, however, is that these periods of high variability also appear to coincide with periods of general social and political instability – e.g. the Revolutionary Napoleonic and World War eras. Richardson and Kroeber comment on the relationship between these factors in a manner which is remarkably similar to Thomas Kuhn's (1970) later observations on the development of scientific knowledge.

> Sociocultural stress and unsettlement seem to produce fashion strain and instability. However, they exert their influence upon an existing stylistic pattern, which they dislocate or invert. Without reference to this pattern, their effect would not be understood. ... The explanation propounded is not that revolution, war and sociocultural unsettlement in themselves produce scant skirts and thick and high or low waists, but that they disrupt the established dress style and tend to its overthrow or inversion. The directions taken in this process depend on the style pattern: they are subversive or centrifugal to it. By contrary, in 'normal' periods dress is relatively stable in basic proportions and features: its variations tend to be slight and transient – fluctuations of mode rather than changes of style. (Richardson and Kroeber, 1940: 149–50)

What are the lessons we can draw from Robinson's and Richardson and Kroeber's inquiries? Most important is the realization that visual material can be subject to rigorous quantification as long as the coding categories that a researcher employs in the investigation of this material are transposable across the entire corpus of data which are collected. In both of these studies, coding categories – aspects of the body or clothing to be measured or noted – were selected which fulfilled this criterion. A second issue concerns the advantages of obtaining time series data in an investigation. Whilst it may not be essential to cover historical periods as long as these, the kinds of social changes which can be investigated in this way may only become apparent when data are collected over a relatively long period of time. Finally and relatedly, their work suggests that the collection of quantitative data is an elegant way of making counterintuitive discoveries as well as proving hypotheses relating to these discoveries. Quantitative work thus opens up an entirely different vista on the use of visual material of which very few visual researchers have taken advantage. One researcher who has taken up this challenge more recently is Victoria Alexander.

Although she does not acknowledge either of the previous studies, Alexander's (1994) topic and her analytic approach are, nevertheless, remarkably similar: in what ways has the appearance of children in magazine advertisements changed over the course of the century? To research this issue Alexander follows the same quantitative path of content analysis taken by Richardson and Kroeber and by Robinson; however, she also makes a number of useful suggestions concerning the analysis of visual material which go beyond the reliance on this particular technique. Alexander suggests that the representations of children in advertising can be viewed as clues to more general societal attitudes concerning the importance of children and ideologies of child rearing as well as changing demographic factors such as the family size and fertility rates. Throughout the twentieth century, she notes, there has been a 'linear' trend in which children have come to be viewed as an integral component of 'the good life' and their place in the family seen as one of 'priceless love object' rather than 'economic contributor'. However, at the same time as this linear trend has developed, there has also occurred a number of cyclical trends regarding appropriate styles of child rearing which have oscillated between leniency and permissiveness on the one hand and more restrictive regimes on the other.

In the early decades of the twentieth century the Holt method, which emphasized the use of strict parental schedules in child rearing, was dominant. However, in the 1940s, with the publication of Dr Benjamin Spock's *Baby and Child Care,* a far more permissive and indulgent child-rearing regime came into being. Finally, a perception of the importance of children to society can also be gauged from changes in the overall birth rate during this period. Birth rates dropped during the 1920s and 1930s but increased rapidly in the period after the Second World War – the baby boom era. More recently, though, the birth rate declined in the 1960s and 1970s as female participation in the workforce increased. On the basis of these trends Alexander develops a number of hypotheses concerning the appearance of children in magazine advertisements. For example, she suggests we might expect to find the following:

- that as children become more central to society they will appear proportionately more often in advertisements;
- they will be more likely to appear in advertisements for adult products as a way of enhancing the appeal of the advertisement;
- and finally there should be an increase in the number of advertisements which feature adults and children interacting.

These hypotheses were explored by examining advertisements appearing in six general-audience magazines which collectively spanned the twentieth century and were found to be confirmed. The details of her findings are of less concern to us here, however, than the suggestions she makes concerning the analysis of visual information, which have relevance beyond the quantitative paradigm. We have already touched on Alexander's first point, which concerns the importance of researchers using systematic coding and sampling frames in their inquiries. Too often those who investigate visual material do not attend to this basic issue and consequently face criticism that their data are selective and their findings therefore invalid. Alexander notes that this is a charge which has been levelled against Goffman's use of advertising images as sources of gender display, although subsequent replications which have used more rigorous selection procedures (e.g. Belknap and Leonard, 1991) have largely confirmed his findings. Second, she argues that researchers must try to ensure that they have some understanding of the representational conventions which apply to the visual materials they are studying. Grasping these conventions is crucial to an understanding of the meanings that can be extracted from these materials. There are no fool-proof methods for achieving this but she suggests that one way might be to compare the evidence from the visual domain with that of a different cultural index such as literature. For example, in her own research she argues that the changes in the visual representations of children in advertisements can be more credibly viewed as genuine reflections of actual changes in adult–child relations given that such changes are also consistent with cyclical changes in child-rearing literature.

Alexander's third comment is possibly the most useful because it points towards a rapprochement between quantitative and qualitative methodologies. She argues that because most forms of visual data, including advertisements, are based on stereotyped conventions, they should be thought of as something which can offer us insight into the idealized character of relationships between groups or institutions rather than as an accurate source of information about behaviour or lifestyles. Essentially this is a call for a structural approach to the analysis of visual data: in other words to focus not so much on the overt content of advertisements but on the messages which can be gleaned from the interactions or relationships which they depict. Whatever meanings visual materials might carry are more accessible using this approach and consequently 'structural analysis is a vast improvement over simple content analysis' (Alexander, 1994: 760). Researchers, she argues, need to bear in mind that advertising images are purposeful creations and that they invariably carry much that is distorted:

> We all know that real women do not swoon in ecstasy over clean floors, nor do real babies care what brand of cigarettes their fathers smoke. The changing structural relationship between parents and children is more telling than the actual content of the advertisements. (Alexander, 1994: 760)

Quantitative analyses of visual data such as the ones we have been describing are generally outside the scope of an individual student project. However, they would be manageable if a number of students were to combine efforts, perhaps as part of an assignment for a methods class. As we have seen, the advantage of using visual data quantitatively is that much longer historical periods can be investigated using rigorous sampling techniques. We offer one suggestion for a group project which draws upon ideas from these three case studies – others could be readily identified.

BOX 3.1   CHANGES IN BODY SHAPE PROJECT

Feminists have argued that the increasing incidence of eating disorders, such as anorexia nervosa and bulimia, amongst young women has intensified in the last decade or so in part due to the unrealistic expectations concerning body size, which are disseminated by the mass media. To support this hypothesis they point out that contemporary representations of women in magazine advertising features models with much more slender bodies than was the case with their counterparts in the 1940s or 1950s. However, these claims have generally not been documented in a systematic empirical fashion. Drawing upon Richardson and Kroeber's methodology this issue could be quantitatively investigated by recording actual measurements of the bodies of the models.

For the project you would need access to a publication source which spans a reasonable time period and which has a continuous record of publication. Several of the better-established women's magazines would fit these criteria. Following Alexander's comments about the need for a systematic sample you would need to ensure that you obtain a sample of pictures from the magazines which span the years chosen for the project. A sample of, say, 50 pictures from each decade going back to the 1940s would be sufficient. Once you have obtained your sample then follow the same procedure that Richardson and Kroeber undertook. For example, obtain details of the bust, waist and hip measurements, etc. of women who appear as models in advertisements. Ideally this would be carried out on models for swimwear, but women modelling sports clothing or other more tightly fitting garments should also give you the same information. To compensate for the fact that the images are unlikely to be identical sizes, these measurements would need to be expressed as ratios to the overall height of the model as well as their relationship to each other.

Once you have obtained these measurements then plot them on a time series graph. If the feminist argument is correct then you should expect to find a decline in body size over the period studied. More detailed records might allow you to test the hypothesis that this intensified during the late 1970s or 1980s when many new publications for young women emerged on the market. An even more sophisticated research design would involve researching changes in the reported incidence of eating disorders from medical sources and then plotting this information alongside your body size data. Ideally here you would want to see the two graph lines diverging: that is, the incidence of eating disorders would show an increase at the same time as the advertising models in the images became thinner.

Qualitative approaches to visual analysis

Alexander's call for researchers to pay attention to the deeper structural messages which can be gleaned from visual data points towards a more interpretive or cultural studies type of perspective and yet, overall, her approach remains firmly within the quantitative camp. Trevor Millum's (1975) investigation of representations of women in print advertisements is an exemplary case of a researcher who has tried to combine qualitative and quantitative approaches on a more or less equal basis. Millum was researching this topic before the cultural studies paradigm became fully developed and so the categories and concepts which he used for the analysis of the images of women now appear rather dated in the face of the more specialized vocabularies which media and cultural studies disciplines have developed (we deal with this on pp. 66–69). We consider the analysis of advertisements at a later point in the chapter, so we will not dwell on Millum's work here. However, a number of other researchers have drawn upon his classificatory system for the analysis of visual materials in other domains. Hilary Graham (1977) has utilized his work in her own investigation of images of pregnancy in antenatal publications.

Graham's particular focus is the differences that can be observed between the images found in Health Department leaflets and brochures, and the photographs which are used to illustrate the more popular birthing books. She illustrates her article with a typical example from each of these categories. Her argument essentially is that the drawings in the leaflets represent the institutional or medical view of pregnancy where the mother-to-be is framed as actively engaged in the business of 'having a baby'. In contrast the photographs in birthing books show a more passive, or contemplative, view of pregnancy as a time of special significance for the woman. To document these differences Graham employs the categories that Millum had first developed: *nucleus, mood, setting, props* and *character* of the actor. Photographs of pregnant women tend to use well-known devices such as cropping, focus, camera angle which together create the nucleus – the element which is foregrounded – and the mood for the photograph. Expectant mothers typically appear in the photographs in side profile emphasizing the changed contours of their body. Moreover, photographs are frequently cropped to focus attention on the abdomen and shot in soft or subdued light. Settings for the photographs are invariably outdoors, whereas institutional or domestic settings such as kitchens are generally avoided. The outdoor settings allow for various props symbolizing nature and health to be included. Finally the female models who appear in the photographs have a uniformity of age, race and status as well as standardized appearance in hair styles and clothing.

In contrast to this idealized view captured in photographs the drawings contained in the leaflets present a much more functional view of pregnancy. Settings for the drawings are typically medical – doctors' surgeries or hospitals – and the props – stethoscopes, prescription pads, etc. – are more utilitarian. The mothers-to-be in turn appear as practically attired for the occasion on hand – visiting the doctor, exercising, or resting; compared with the photographs the figures are 'stiff and lifeless' evoking a notion of correct posture for pregnancy. Overall Graham suggests that drawings

> locate pregnancy in a world of impersonal and institutional relationships, where notions of femininity are notably absent. Instead, settings, props and actors are used to emphasize not her mystic and emotional qualities but rather her physiological role as the vehicle of reproduction. (Graham, 1977: 32)

Graham concludes by suggesting that these contrasting images of pregnancy can be read as visual evidence of the contemporary philosophy concerning antenatal care. On the one hand the model suggests that the doctor has granted considerable leeway to the woman and her partner over the emotional and relational aspects of the pregnancy (the photographic message). However the doctor is seen as retaining ultimate control over the management of the more central medical aspects and, by implication, control over the woman's body (the drawings).

The analytical categories which Millum developed for his investigation of magazine advertising photographs are just one example of the ways in which visual researchers have tried to deal systematically with the question of the content of visual materials. As we saw in the previous chapter this issue has been more pressing amongst the more theoretically influenced interpretive approaches which have come to be referred to as cultural studies, than in the older North American schools of visual anthropology and sociology. The type of photograph that generally attracts the researcher's attention in this more recent genre of analysis is not so much the ethnographic picture that will sit in an archive, but rather pictures that have attained distribution in the public sphere. Of particular interest are photographs which have been published in magazines and newspapers and have been seen by millions of viewers. This is because such media forums are not only an indicator of shared beliefs and ideologies, but are also presumed to have considerable influence in shaping them.

Over recent years the new field of cultural studies has developed an extensive toolkit of concepts for analysing images. These concepts come from fields as diverse as anthropology, sociology, psychology, film studies and literary criticism. A basic working knowledge of these is essential not only for thinking about images, but also writing about them. The following paragraphs will give you an introduction to some key concepts, which are set in italic type. In published analyses these are often complemented by other vocabularies such as those of marxism, feminism, queer theory and ethnomethodology.

Binary oppositions – these are concepts or signifiers which are arranged in pairs but opposed to each other. Common examples are man:woman, light:dark, right:left. Often there is a hierarchy involved in the binary opposition. In each of the pairs above, for example, the first term tends to be valued more than the second. Binary oppositions can play a crucial role in shaping the ways we read an image and our emotional and intellectual responses to it. In the picture of the policeman being kicked (Figure 2.2) the binary oppositions are between the policeman:protestor, victim:aggressor and law-and-order:mob.

Frames – these are the contexts within which an image, or part of an image, is presented to the viewer. Because interpretation involves relationships between the part and the whole (the hermeneutic circle) these frames often have an impact on how an image is read. Institutions like art galleries provide one kind of frame. As the inventors of the 'readymade' found, we see items like chairs and wine racks differently once they are removed from everyday life and placed in such a context. Other kinds of frames are the cultural packages that help us to deploy conventions and common-sense understandings to decode a particular visual item. We will probably read the image of a naked female body one way if we encounter it in a pornographic magazine and another way if it is in a book of lesbian–feminist photography. This example points to the close links between 'frames' and 'genre' (see below). Text can also be used to frame or 'anchor' the meaning of an image.

Genre – this refers to the categories that we use to classify cultural objects into groups with similar properties or themes. We can think of genres such as 'news photography', 'sports photography', 'fashion photography'. We can also think of genres in terms of the mood, style, or narrative they convey. We can think of 'heroic', 'romantic' and 'comic' images and of 'humanist', 'documentary' and 'dramatic' photography. Each genre tends to be driven by its own codes and conventions. Understanding these can provide a clue to interpreting individual images.

Identification – this refers to the ways in which people 'relate to' a particular image. Just as we tend to relate to the hero or heroine of a novel as we read it, so we can identify with a particular person or group of people in an image. Subject positions often play a major role in this process. Many successful (and ideologically powerful) images work by establishing identification between viewer and those depicted in the photograph. In the picture of a policeman being kicked (Figure 2.2) the reader identifying with the police officer will be more likely to oppose the demonstrators and their cause.

Narrative – this involves a storyline. This can be achieved through a series of images (e.g. a comic strip, photos arranged chronologically in an album) or else can be projected onto a single image (see discussion of the SafeCampus poster below) by imagining what has happened in the past and, perhaps, what is going to happen next.

Reading – this is the process of decoding the image. Whilst this may seem straightforward, the ability to correctly read some kinds of images (such as religious art) can take years of socialization. It is important to recognize the massive role that common sense plays in readings of images in everyday life. Advertisements often play on this, by providing subtle clues that people have to use to figure out what is going on. Sociological research into 'media effects' suggests that people may read the same image in divergent ways, often depending on their identity, their life experiences and the subject positions they adopt. Whilst there may be a *'preferred'* or *'dominant'* or *'hegemonic'* reading which is intended by the author or reinforces a prevailing ideology, *'oppositional readings'* can be made of the same text. These might contest the dominant meanings of the image. *'Divergent readings'* differ from oppositional readings in that they may not confront the dominant reading in a direct political way. Instead they might 'miss the point' of the image.

Signifier/Signified – these terms refer to the sign and its referent and can take various forms. One common typology was provided by Charles Peirce, a founding figure in the study of semiotics. An *iconic* representation is one motivated by direct resemblance. An icon is usually a copy of the real object, such as a photograph of a person or a model of the Eiffel Tower. An *index* has a direct connection with the thing it represents. This often involves *synecdoche*, where a part of something stands for the whole. The Eiffel Tower, for example, might be used to symbolize 'Paris', or a smile to represent happiness, or holding hands to represent being emotionally connected. A *symbol* has a link to its referent that is purely arbitrary and a matter of cultural convention. A red rose, for example, symbolizes love or passion. Most photographs are icons in that they are scaled down, two-dimensional copies of reality. They may, however, involve other kinds of signification and so become quite complex to interpret. Imagine a photograph showing two people sitting on a bench in a park holding hands. One is holding a model of the Eiffel Tower and the other a bunch of red roses. As this is a picture of a real scene that really happened (even if with models), the photo is an icon of people sitting on a bench holding hands. However there is more going on. The icon of the Eiffel tower operates as an index of Paris. The smile operates as an index of happiness. The roses operate as a symbol of love. Putting these together we can quickly build up an interpretation. The two people are a couple (the hands), they are in Paris (the model Eiffel Tower), they are in love (the flowers) and very happy about it all (the smile). Such an image might be found in a tourist brochure promoting Paris as a romantic holiday destination, or perhaps (if they are heterosexual) in the couple's honeymoon photo album.

Subject position – This is, roughly speaking, the identity that is invoked in a particular image. In an image of a woman with a child, the subject position of 'mother' is probably central to interpreting the role at work in the image. If the same woman is positioned at a board room meeting, we might think of her as occupying the subject position of 'executive'. Determining the subject positions at play in a picture is often central to interpreting its meaning. Screen theory also speaks of the importance of subject positions for the reader of the image. They do this by influencing the kind of *gaze* that is used. We might read a given image in different ways according to which of our identities (gender, race, age, occupation, etc.) we foreground. Some images try to provide a subject position for us, although it may not be one we adopt. Robert Doisneau's picture of lovers kissing (Figure 2.3) situates the viewer as the non-gendered occupant of a Parisian pavement cafe. This gives us a status as participants in the scene rather than voyeurs and allows us to imaginatively project ourselves into another time and place.

Advertising, part one: the SafeCampus poster campaign

We can apply these concepts to an in-depth analysis of a poster designed to publicize safety awareness at our own University. As we noted in Chapter 1 we were not given permission to use the posters which had been developed by the University safety committee, and so we have produced our own poster which is modelled on the original and which features similar conceptual messages (and our own students who were delighted at the prospect of appearing in an academic textbook). The poster we produced for our campaign – 'SafeCampus' – is featured in Figure 3.2. The picture's presentation as poster (as opposed to being an image in a book or photo album) provides a *frame* which tells us that public information is contained in the image. We can then read the picture for that information. As Barthes and Benjamin would point out (see p. 49) the accompanying text and SafeCampus logo are also important frames. By highlighting issues of threat and safety they work to eliminate other potential readings of the picture (e.g. the people have turned round to greet a friend who is running after them) and foreground a message about danger on campus. This reading is facilitated by our knowledge that the poster is in the wider *genre* of posters and billboards that convey messages about public health and safety. We know, for example, that we are not supposed to be reading the image for aesthetic pleasure or as a commercial advertisement. There seem to be four *subject positions* involved in the picture. There is that of the SafeCampus escort (guardian), that of male student, female student and that of the person they are looking at. The SafeCampus poster attempts to position the viewer in this fourth subject position – that of potential stalker or rapist. This creates an implied *binary opposition* between the 'good citizens' and 'evil people'. The tension between this subject position and our real status as a law abiding person causes us to reflect on our vulnerability and creates unease. By occupying this position, if only for a split second, we take on the *gaze* of the predator. In other respects the poster is remarkably free of typical binary oppositions. The male and female students, for example, are depicted in a way which de-emphasizes sexual difference. This possibly reflects the values of the liberal campus audience for whom it is intended. The poster contains a strong *narrative* element which, in the *preferred reading*, runs *something* like as follows. The people have been walking across campus. They have been stalked. There has been a noise, maybe a sudden cough or the sound of a twig breaking. They have just turned round in alarm, but the SafeCampus escort stays cool. They are safe. Various *signifiers* are at work in the picture to try to anchor the image. The casual clothing and backpacks are *indexes* of a broader student status and lifestyle. They mark out the two people facing the camera as 'ordinary'. The grass and leafy trees suggest this is a typical suburban or rural campus. These signifiers help the intended viewer (presumably also a student) to *identify* with the people in the photograph. The expressions on their faces are an index of an emotional state – they have been startled and are alarmed. The SafeCampus Escort appears athletic. Her radio, track pants and sneakers are also indexes. They mark her out as a person who is in continual contact with the authorities and ready for action. Finally the upturned hand beneath the logo symbolizes care and support in western culture. This tells us something about the organizational mission of SafeCampus: it is an informal and user-friendly service and not a militaristic security operation.

Considerable common-sense knowledge is required to make this *preferred reading* of the image. We need to draw upon a pre-existing understanding of the danger of predatory assault, the nature of SafeCampus

FIGURE 3.2 *'SafeCampus' advertising poster. Protect yourself*

and how to contact them (the poster doesn't provide these details), the conventions of clothing and facial expression, the conventions of the poster format, etc., in order to work out what the poster is about. The poster might be criticized on the grounds that it is too ambiguous and allows *divergent readings* to be made. Certainly this might be the case for new, non-English speaking students who might lack the cultural knowledge required to understand the poster. We asked a cross-section of people about the poster, and many said that they weren't quite certain what it was all about. Gay men might read the man in the SafeCampus poster as homosexual and identify with him as a potential victim of 'gay-bashing'. Such a reading would be consistent with the *preferred reading* but is unlikely to occur to heterosexual males. Having never felt threatened on campus, they may be puzzled at the presence of a man in the picture and wonder why he feels the need to be protected by a woman who is smaller than himself. The grassy, well-lit setting may be interpreted as being pastoral. This may lead to the viewer missing the cues about danger. There is little sense of threat in this environment. The facial expressions of the students are ambiguous. They may be indicating surprise rather than fear, as if they have been startled by a friend who is running after them. One viewer of the picture expressed concern that the students had turned round but not the SafeCampus Escort: 'It suggests they are incompetent. The students have heard footsteps, but the escort is oblivious to the danger.' Finally the accompanying text can be read in various ways. 'If not you, then who?' and 'Who? Me!' are shorthand for something – but what? If the viewer gets the preferred reading they might flesh these out as: 'If you don't use a SafeCampus Escort, then what kind of dangerous character might take advantage of you?' and 'Who is in danger? I am.' But other readings are possible. One person we spoke to thought it was a recruiting poster for SafeCampus. His reading was thus: 'If you don't volunteer to be a SafeCampus Escort, then who will do the job?' 'Who should be a SafeCampus Escort? I should.' Strongly oppositional readings of the text are also possible. When asked to talk about the poster, one male student's first response was to point to the SafeCampus Escort and say: 'She looks attractive, but perhaps she's a lesbian. She's got some kind of uniform and is in a position of authority. They like that sort of thing.' Here the poster was read as a gallery of physical appeal and deviant sexuality. Whilst oppositional readings are usually made by those on the left (e.g. see the exercise on advertising later in this chapter), in this case an *oppositional reading* had been made by taking a progressive image and reading it using a conservative and sexist gaze. Another person started laughing when shown the poster, suggesting – we think tongue-in-cheek – that it could be mistaken for an advert for a safe sex brothel. This could be seen as an example of a *divergent reading*, one which applies a completely different frame to the poster.

The ability of an image to be read in such divergent ways means we

FIGURE 3.3   *'SafeCampus' advertising poster. Drink smarter not faster*

FIGURE 3.4   *'SafeCampus' advertising poster. You are not alone*

BOX 3.2   READING POSTERS EXERCISE

Examine the other SafeCampus posters (Figures 3.3, 3.4). Write about them in a similar way to the example above. Try to explain the message of each picture and how it 'works' or doesn't work to achieve its goal. Note also the ways in which the interaction between the text and the image changes according to the reading you make. When you have finished this activity, ask various people to explain each poster to you. Did they make the same readings as you? Why / Why not? Do you notice any patterns in the responses that might be explained by gender, age or some other demographic characteristic?

have to be cautious in assuming images have fixed meanings or ideological effects just because we 'experts' are able to read these into them. Many images will mean different things to different people. Finding out why can tell us a lot about the ways in which images generate meanings in our society.

Advertising, part two: do-it-yourself

In David Lodge's (1989) novel *Nice Work*, there is a passage in which Robyn Penrose, lecturer in English Literature at Rummidge University, and Industry Year scheme 'shadow' for Vic Wilcox, Managing Director of Pringle's engineering firm, engages in a semiotic decoding of a cigarette advertisement billboard in an attempt to persuade Vic of the advertisement's underlying sexuality. Vic is outraged at Robyn's suggestion that the photograph of the purple silk cloth with its single slash symbolizes the female body and genitalia and that the advert consequently appeals 'to both sensual and sadistic impulses, the desire to mutilate and penetrate the female body'. For Vic it is simply a picture which represents the name of the cigarette brand. Why then, Robyn retorts, did the advertiser not use a picture of a roll of silk cut in half? Because, she continues, it would look like a penis cut in half.

> He forced a laugh to cover his embarrassment. 'Why can't you people take things at their face value?'
> 'What people are you referring to?'
> 'Highbrows. Intellectuals. You're always trying to find hidden meanings in things. Why? A cigarette is a cigarette. A piece of silk is a piece of silk. Why not leave it at that?'
> 'When they are represented they acquire additional meanings', said Robyn. 'Signs are never innocent. Semiotics teaches us that.'

'semi-what?'
'semiotics. The study of signs.'
'It teaches us to have dirty minds, if you ask me.' (Lodge, 1989: 220–1)

Lodge's choice of Robyn, a practising semiotician, to represent the university Arts and Humanities community is timely. The analysis of advertisements is probably the single most commonly occurring activity amongst media and cultural studies researchers who focus on two-dimensional images. Works such as Williamson's (1978) *Decoding Advertisements* and – although we have questioned its relevance to advertising – Goffman's (1979) *Gender Advertisements* have received canonical status in the literature. Williamson's work has become the template for those who work within the semiotic tradition, whilst Goffman has also received attention from quantitative researchers. It is not our intention to present a comprehensive account of these research traditions.[2] Instead we want to consider advertising as a practical activity in which students can engage and by so doing learn about how advertisements 'work'.

Robyn may have had more success in her exposition of semiotics by inviting Vic to construct an advertisement of his own, better still one which destabilizes an existing advertisement. We have found this tactic to be immensely useful with our own students. For several years now we have provided students in our 'Media, Culture and Society' course at the University of Queensland with the opportunity to become practical semioticians/advertisers through project work which involves groups of students decoding an advertisement and then devising a new advertisement which destabilizes or transforms the underlying cultural 'myths' which serve as the foundational interpretive resources. The advertisements we use are taken from the 'Diamonds are Forever' series which have been widely appearing in the weekend newspaper colour supplements. We have found these to be particularly useful teaching devices because the connotations and mythological elements they portray – the commodification of romance, heterosexuality, marital stability and harmony – are at the very heart of our cultural understanding of gender relations.

The generic format for the advertisements has altered little since their inception – essentially the use of chiaroscuro to display the brilliantly reflecting diamonds in vivid contrast with the muted, dark hued background. In some versions the background appears only as velvet cloth on which the diamonds rest; in others a variety of incongruous objects – arrows, chess pieces, wallets, chocolate truffles, clothing – are included on which the diamond jewellery has been strategically draped. In these cases, a brief written text apparently serves to disambiguate the juxtaposed signifiers but becomes itself an additional signifier adding to the complexity of the advertisement. Earlier in this chapter we looked briefly at the foundational concepts in semiotics: signifier and signified. Another, related way of looking at the distinction between these is by referring to the process of signification or the ways in which signs function in culture. As we briefly saw on pp. 46–48 this process is usually broken down into two levels:

1. *The first level of signification – denotation* – the simple, obvious, literal or common-sense meaning of a sign. At this level the sign is self-contained.
2. *The second level of signification – connotation* – meanings that occur when denotation interacts with the dominant cultural values associated with the sign and the attitudes, feelings and emotions of audiences/users. Connotations are ideological and mythological in that they (re)present cultural values as being natural when they are actually socially constructed.

In the advertising project, our student groups are required to perform two main tasks. First, a conventional decoding of the original advertisement by indicating:

- the major signifiers at the level of denotation
- the major signifieds at the level of denotation
- three different myths at the level of connotation, and how each of these correspond with 'reality'.

Second, the construction of a new advertisement which serves to denaturalize and/or destabilize the original advertisement whilst at the same time preserving elements of the original so that there is some visual or textual continuity between them. In defence of the new advertisement the students are also required to explain

- what their recoded advertisement is intended to connote
- what guarantees they can give that their recoded advertisement will be interpreted by an audience(s) in the way they intend
- whom they would get to publish and/or distribute it.

In our discussion we shall focus more upon the possibilities concerning the recoded advertisements, as this is likely to be the aspect which students find the most challenging. However, it is important to stress that success here first requires an accurate interpretation or decoding of the original in order to identify the mythic elements to be destabilized. If this is not done then the new advertisement may run the risk of becoming a parody or a simple inversion rather than a reconfiguration that destabilizes or opposes the original mythical elements. One of the noteworthy features of this sort of project research work is that, despite often starting with an identical original advertisement, each of the new advertisements is invariably different. This outcome in itself serves admirably to convince students as to the inherent instability of signs and perhaps a grudging

FIGURE 3.5   'Diamonds are forever' advertisement

respect for those advertisements which do manage to achieve a degree of semiotic 'closure'.

Two of the original 'Diamonds are Forever' advertisements are shown in Figures 3.5 and 3.6. In Figures 3.7 and 3.8 we present examples of the kinds of destabilizing advertisements which our students have devised.

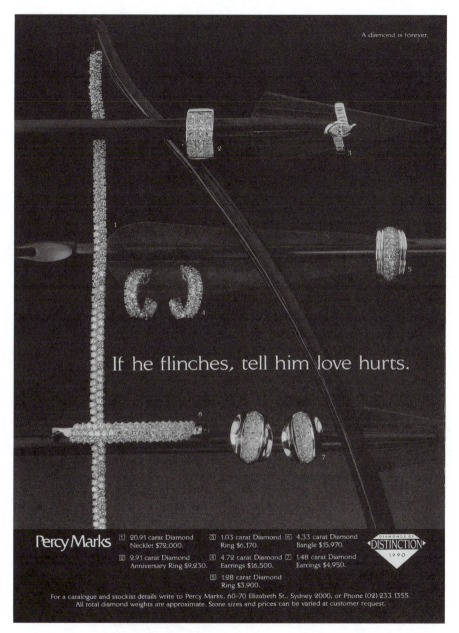

FIGURE 3.6   *'Diamonds are forever' advertisement*

As can be seen, the destabilizations have taken different routes: one via a theme of female independence and empowerment, and the other through a challenge to the theme of 'compulsory heterosexuality'. These destabilizations have been derived from the dominant myths that each group has identified. In 'You want to see more than just a twinkle in his

FIGURE 3.7   *Student-produced advertisement destabilizing Figure 3.5*

eye' (Figure 3.5) the theme of female sexuality has provided the pivotal focus. The signifiers in this advertisement, in addition to the jewellery – the black stiletto shoe, the black lace item of underwear and the crucial anchoring text – have been decoded as signifying a sexual encounter. More specifically the nature of the encounter is connoted as involving a

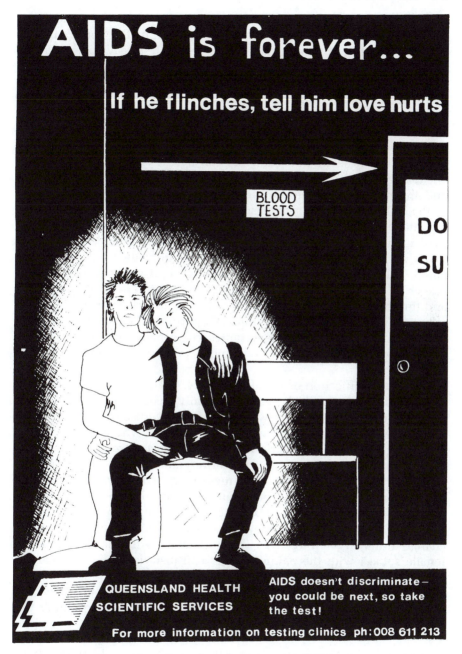

FIGURE 3.8 *Student-produced advertisement destabilizing Figure 3.6*

seductive female sexuality (undressing, disrobing – a striptease?) while simultaneously implying male dominance in the form of the masculine gaze. These particular connotations are, in turn, underpinned by a series of cultural myths concerning sexuality: the commodification of female sexuality and the idea that women's sexuality is male-defined and male-dependent. According to this dominant cultural 'myth' women are not seen as in control of their sexual destiny; they are passive objects available for purchase by men, with diamonds serving as the currency in these transactions. Women's aspirations and desires are thus trivialized, satisfied (here the myth connects with another, racist myth – 'the primitive savage' etc.) to trade their independence and identity in return for shiny objects.

The corresponding new advertisement (Figure 3.7) has elegantly destabilized these mythic elements through a crucial change to the anchoring text – 'You want to see more than just a twinkle in the sky' and the provision of supporting signifiers drawn from a non-sexual context. The new advertisement seeks to promote positive and empowering images of women's identity and ambition. The use of a female astronaut as the key signifier connotes that women can be achievers in their own right, moreover in domains that have traditionally been male dominated. The new anchoring text now subtly implies that women are no longer to be seen as the objects of male gaze but are actively looking and finding out for themselves. Although the advertisement – designed to be publicity for the 'Women's Equal Opportunity Project of the Department of Education' – does not guarantee a career as an astronaut, it probably serves its purpose to attract more women into tertiary science courses.

The commodification of female sexuality, of course, implies a regime in which heterosexuality is seen as the only basis of sexual expression and it is this 'mythic' element which the new advertisement in Figure 3.8 has worked to destabilize. In contrast to Figure 3.7, where changes to the anchoring text were necessary to convey the destabilization, Figure 3.8 retains both the original text in its entirety and aspects of the original signifiers. The resulting dramatic reworking of the myths which the new advertisement connotes has been achieved through a paradigmatic shift in the interpretative context. The crucial component in this shift is the re-keying of sexuality, which is neatly accomplished through a change in the targeted 'reader'. The original advertisement addresses a female subject with the painted finger nail just visible on the shaft of the second arrow appearing to signify a form of female 'empowerment'. This image is tempered by the cultural availability of cupid's bow and love-securing arrows, and it is this mythic element underpinning the advertisement which generates similar connotations to those in Figure 3.5.

The new advertisement transforms these dominant myths, particularly those concerning the commodification of heterosexual romance. Whereas in Figure 3.6 the female reader is enjoined to persuade her reluctant male partner by appealing to the price of 'true love', in Figure 3.8 the gay couple are shown as prepared to endure a rather different form of sacrifice for the sake of their relationship. Here the 'flinching' has no financial basis but is at the prospect of a (albeit minor) medical procedure which common sense deems necessary. The destabilization is enhanced by a number of stylistic features. The dark setting of the original denoting luxury and sophistication has been transformed into the stark bleakness of the medical waiting room where the couple wait anxiously for their tests. The decorative, bejewelled arrows of the original advertisement have become a functional directional sign. Analytically, perhaps the most salient feature of the new advertisement is that it reverses Barthes' dictum about the necessity of a written text to anchor a polysemous image (see p. 46). In this pair of advertisements the text is constant and it acquires its (different) meanings through the changing images with which it is juxtaposed.

Cartoons and comic strips

Although photographs and advertisements have received a good deal of attention from media scholars, their visual 'poor cousins' – cartoons and comic strips – have been largely neglected. In part this stems from their non-realist character and their humorous or satirical intent when compared with

---

BOX 3.3 DESTABILIZING ADVERTISEMENT PROJECT

The procedure we have outlined could be replicated using a number of different types of commodity. In the past we have found that advertisements for tobacco products, alcohol, motor cars, toiletries and so on, are also useful sources to work with. To a certain extent the health warnings which cigarette packets are now legally required to carry represent a partial 'official destabilization'. That is, the government now wants its citizens to be reminded that cigarettes also 'mean' lung cancer and emphysema in addition to meanings such as 'status', 'sophistication' 'ruggedness' and so on which the cigarette companies would like us to associate with their products. However, such health warnings hardly amount to a new advertisement of the kind we have discussed.

In the case of the commodities listed above, although the underlying connotations will, of course, vary depending upon the product concerned, similar processes of interpretation and destabilization can be brought to bear to transform the original advertisement. As in the case of the student examples we have been discussing, see if, contra Barthes, you can create a new advertisement which retains the caption or text from the published advertisement but which radically alters the meaning you assign to the text.

the more overtly 'political' newspaper photograph or the commercially driven advertisement. Whereas newspaper and magazine photographs have frequently been the targets of critical media researchers who have sought to document their perceived ideological frameworks and/or omissions, cartoons have generally only attracted more occasional interest. In addition to the common-sense view of the cartoon as a vehicle for humour or satire (e.g. Morris, 1992), cartoons have also been explored as sites of stereotyping, overt racism, or ideology (Alba, 1966; Coupe, 1966; Nir, 1977; Streicher, 1966; Walker, 1978). To a large extent, however, contemporary cartoons in the western media no longer display these features – although atavistic reminders of such practices were evident during the media coverage of the 1991 Gulf War in relation to the representation of the Iraqi leader, Saddam Hussein (see Gulf War cartoon project below).

The relative lack of attention paid to cartoons as media texts is unfortunate given that the historical record that is available in relation to cartoons can sometimes be more complete than for photographs. Many important magazines of social and political commentary founded in the nineteenth century (e.g. *Punch* in the UK, *The Bulletin* in Australia) relied on cartooning as their preferred visual medium well into the twentieth century. As we shall see shortly the cartoon record available in these publications provides a rich seam for investigation for visual research. A second reason why visual researchers should take more interest in cartoons is that they are arguably images to which readers pay more attention than to other media visual material such as advertisements. Generally speaking people do not purchase a newspaper to read the advertising, but the daily cartoon is invariably one of the first things to be noted.

In the last decade or so cartoons and comic strips have begun to receive more attention, particularly from feminist communications researchers who have argued that they are important sites for reinforcing stereotypical gender assumptions. Much of this work fits in to the quantitative paradigm outlined earlier involving the systematic coding of relatively large samples of material.[3] Typical of many of these investigations is a paper by Chavez (1985), in the journal *Sex Roles*, which examines gender inequality as evident in a number of popularly syndicated comic strips. Chavez's research shows that men appear as characters in comic strips far out of proportion to their ratio in the population (a ratio of 569 men per 100 women in comic strips, compared with 93 men for every 100 women in the population). Men, moreover, are significantly more likely to be represented in work roles whereas women are more typically portrayed as wives or mothers; in addition they are featured in a much greater range of occupations than women. Gender issues also feature in a study undertaken by Matacin and Burger (1987) of sexual themes in cartoons appearing in *Playboy* magazine. In this case the authors link the occurrence of such media images to wider debates about the availability of pornography and its relation to violence against women. Using categories identified by previous researchers – seduction, coerciveness, naivity and body image – Matacin and Burger found that the *Playboy* cartoons in their sample were more likely to depict women rather than men as the initiators of sexual activity (seduction) although the difference was not significant. In contrast, when sexual activity was shown to be associated with some form of power or status difference (coerciveness) this was without exception a male phenomenon. When the theme of naivity was located it was women who were overwhelmingly depicted (90 per cent of occurrences) as sexually innocent or vulnerable. Finally when there was a difference in the attractiveness of the bodies (body image) then the man was significantly more likely to have the less desirable body. Research such as this cannot conclusively establish a link between a particular type of visual representation and equivalent 'real-life' behaviour but at a minimum it points to the presence of cartoons as one element in the social construction of gender roles and sexual attitudes.

One of the few quantitative investigations of cartoon content which does not involve gender and sexuality is the study by Penner and Penner (1994) which compares representations of homelessness in cartoons and comic strips. In their case, by building in a comparative component to their research design, Penner and Penner were able to link their findings concerning representation to wider debates about the factors shaping public opinion and the role of editorial influence in newspaper production. Drawing upon and extending a classification of societal responses to homelessness first advanced by Marcuse (1988) the authors develop three categories for the analysis of images of homelessness. The first, 'publicizing' refers to portrayals of the plight of the homeless which focus on the realities of their day-to-day hardships; when the government or politicians are enjoined to accept some responsibility for the problem then, secondly, the depictions are termed 'politicizing'. Finally when the focus appears to place the blame for their condition on the homeless themselves then the authors speak of 'neutralization'.

Penner and Penner also considered the factors which govern the publication of a cartoon as opposed to a comic strip. Comic strips, they suggest, are likely to have been selected by newspaper owners on a trial basis and then retained on the basis of readership surveys; consequently they are assumed to reflect, however indirectly, the attitudes of readers. In contrast they argue that the selection of a feature cartoon is much more a matter of editorial decision making from the pool of cartoons available for any given issue. In the face of information from opinion polls which suggests that the public (in America) have a generally unsympathetic attitude to the homeless, Penner and Penner are led to two hypotheses concerning the content of comic strips and cartoons. The first is that comic strips which include references to homelessness are more likely to draw on the theme of neutralization. Second, the editorial concerns for action and accountability which come into play when cartoons are selected suggests that these will predominantly invoke frames of publicizing and politicizing. An analysis of comic strips and editorial cartoons appearing in the *San*

BOX 3.4   GULF WAR CARTOONS PROJECT

The study by Penner and Penner suggests that cartoons provide an important site for exploring ideologies and justifications. Such research usually works best when the topic of investigation is limited to a particular cartoon issue – such as homelessness or gender roles. This project suggests that cartoons can also be used to explore ideologies surrounding particular events as well as those linked to themes. The 1990–91 Gulf War (between Iraq and a coalition of nations led by the United States) provides a useful research site in that it involved intense cartoon activity over a delimited time span about a controversial event. Debates about the war revolved around a set of issues. Advocates argued that the war was about preventing aggression (Iraq had invaded Kuwait) and that Iraqi leader Saddam Hussein was a dangerous madman who had to be stopped. Critics asserted that the war was really about oil, American military hegemony and maintaining US President Bush's domestic political approval. Which position did the US press endorse? Many left-wing writers and organizations have claimed that the media was a hegemonic instrument which supported US imperialism and which failed in its duty to be impartial and critical. Instead it reproduced official and nationalistic stories about the war and its necessity. Such ideas, whilst plausible enough, tend to be based on illustrative case studies and general impressions rather than systematic methods. One way to test these sorts of claims would be to conduct a rigorous study of cartoons. Collect Gulf War-themed cartoons for the duration of the conflict in a major US newspaper or magazine. Use a quantitative coding system to code:

(a) the image presented of Bush and Hussein, respectively (is this positive or negative? militaristic or peace-seeking? rational or irrational? honest or duplicitous?, etc.)
(b) the causes of the war (Saddam Hussein, law and order, oil supplies, American militarism, etc.)
(c) the date of each cartoon.

What are you able to conclude about the structure of the ideologies that supported the war? Did these change over time? Do your findings about cartoons suggest that the media presented a balanced view of the war, or were the beliefs of its advocates given more prominence, as the left-wing critics argue? The exercise could usefully be repeated using cartoons from the UK or Australia, which were also significantly involved in the Allied war effort, and also those from a country which participated with some reluctance in the war (e.g. Spain).

Francisco Chronicle and the *San Franciso Examiner* over a three-year period which featured homeless characters and symbols of homelessness gave strong support for both these hypotheses.

Whereas Penner and Penner argue that comic strips and cartoons can be useful in exploring differences between public opinion and the views of more powerful community groups, Morris (1992) has investigated how cartoons can be used to gain insights into the perceptions of ruling figures in different national contexts. In addition he explores three different models concerning cartoon satire: a 'low satire' model in which the cartoonist selectively targets particular individuals or political parties according to the political preferences of the newspaper owner; a medium satire hypothesis which regards democratic decision-making process as something which should be lampooned; and, finally, a high satire hypothesis in which cartoons are seen as mocking all forms of decision making and all forms of leaders. The cartoons in his study featured three types of leaders – politicians, civil servants and royalty (the British royal family) taken from Canadian, English and Welsh publications. Cartoons are understood by him common-sensically as vehicles for satire and he draws upon Goffman's (1974: 44) concept of 'keying' – the transformation of an activity into something else – as a way of making this more explicit. In the context of cartoon satire Morris argues that keying refers to 'the replacement of serious, constructive, economical work by activities which may look identical to outsiders but which insiders clearly understand to have quite a different purpose' (Morris, 1992: 255). So leaders are represented by the cartoonist as engaged in frivolous or pointless activity although they do not recognize this. By comparing cartoons from different countries Morris was also able to ascertain whether there was any difference according to the national background of the cartoonist when compared with the target of the satire. Leaders could be divided into two groups: 'ours' and 'theirs'; for example cartoons by Welsh artists of English politicians or by Quebecois artists of English Canadian rulers were identified as 'theirs'. His research suggested that cartoonists were significantly more likely to represent ruling figures from other countries more negatively. 'Their' politicians and royalty were satirized far more frequently than 'ours'. Overall, civil servants were the group least likely to be satirized through keying, followed by royalty, with politicians the least favourably depicted of all. He accounts for this apparent anomaly by suggesting that civil servant decision making is closest to that which is found within the business world – the domain least likely to be subject to keying in cartoons. Morris concludes by arguing that the results indicate support for the 'medium satire' hypothesis concerning cartoon practice.

Morris' research reflects the prevailing view of the newspaper cartoon as a vehicle for the dissemination of political humour or satire. In contrast we want to suggest that cartoons can be 'read' or investigated for a number of additional analytical ends. In particular, cartoons provide an intriguing 'window' for viewing the ways in which societies come to understand their economic and political processes. Economics and politics are without doubt the two spheres of social life which constitute the focus of cartoonists' attention, and the manner in which these spheres have been historically portrayed offers us important clues to the nature of the structural relations within them, which are not always articulated through other discursive forms. In short, one of the most informative ways of charting the changes in our thinking about what the economy entails, the prevailing canons of state economic policy and practice, the transparency of class relations within the economic domain, etc. is to examine cartoon representations of the economy.

In Figures 3.9 and 3.10 we present two contemporary examples of economic/political cartooning. Both exhibit the ingredients which have become the canonical themes in this genre of cartoon practice. They are nevertheless themes which are historically specific and it is possible to chart the emergence of these conventions reasonably precisely. The three themes are as follows:

1. the representation of the economy as an entity, thing, or person – in these cases as a 'boiling cauldron' or a 'stubborn mule'
2. the presence of the state, metonymically personified by the Prime Minister or other senior cabinet ministers – in these cases by the former Australian political leaders Bob Hawke and Paul Keating
3. the way the cartoon 'works' or generates its humour through the opening up of positions of relative epistemological advantage. That is, the cartoonist and the reader are shown as having access to a more

FIGURE 3.9   *Cartoon representation of 'the economy' by Alan Moir, published in the* Sydney Morning Herald *in the early 1990s*

FIGURE 3.10   *Cartoon representation of 'the economy' by Mark Lynch, published in* The Australian *in the early 1990s*

privileged view of the condition of the economy, which the principal actor in the cartoon – the state – does not enjoy. The state is thereby shown to be incompetent or at least in error as an economic manager, because of its inability to realize or grasp the true economic situation.

These three elements have become virtually the standard form for contemporary 'economic cartoons'. The point to stress, though, is that this particular set of conventions is a fairly recent development. In other historical periods, quite different systems of representation were utilized and it is possible to chart the way in which this state and 'thing-like' economy couplet emerged. In doing this we want to focus on two core issues:

1. the manner in which the idea of the 'aggregate economy' emerges as a thing as opposed to the older idea of economizing and the way in which the state is implicated as the principal economic actor
2. the way in which the cartoons utilize a series of core oppositions to generate their meanings.

Economically related cartoons utilize a set of binary oppositions, and it is variations in how these oppositions are collocated or combined which allows us to identify changes in economic thinking. The most important oppositions that can be found are as follows:

> nature : civilization
> brute forces : domestic order
> lack of control : excessive intervention
> role of market forces : role of government
> health and prosperity : sickness and disease
> realism : non-realism
> perspective of cartoonist : perspective of the actor

Previous research (Emmison, 1983; Emmison and McHoul, 1987) has suggested that there have been at least two distinct phases in the way in which the economic process has been represented historically through cartoons. These phases also extend to the appropriation of metaphors for describing economic life. In the first phase, which lasts up to approximately 1940, the idea of 'the economy' as an aggregate entity did not exist either linguistically or visually. Prior to the emergence of the 'thing-like' or aggregated economy, the idea of 'economy' was instead confined to the notion of wise or prudent expenditure: economizing. In its most politicized version this practice was underpinned by immutable laws – those of supply and demand – which economic subjects ignored at their peril. These conventionalized understandings are vividly captured in Figure 3.11. The issue of wage cuts came to the forefront in the years following the First World War, culminating eventually in the General Strike of 1926. The reigning economic orthodoxy was that market forces would and must prevail and that labour should accept a wage reduction and become again 'employable'. Here we see these market forces anthropomorphized into the prize fighter 'Economic Law' ready to step in on capital's behalf should this be necessary.

The main significance of this cartoon for our analysis lies in what it does *not* contain: the state. In this period of chronic economic crisis, the government remained quiescent and was able to legitimize its non-intervention by appealing to the prevailing neoclassical economic orthodoxy. All this was to change with the Keynesian inspired 'revolution' in economic thinking in the late 1930s. From this point on, the idea of an aggregated economic structure – '*the* economy' – and the crucial role which the state should play within this totality of forces and processes, became the new focus of economic theory, a situation which was eventually translated into new forms of cartoon representation. It is important for our argument to understand clearly what was entailed by this shift in economic theory. It is not the case that Keynes 'discovered' the economy but rather that, in pointing out the implications of the existence of a national economic structure, he gave the term 'economy' a new and decisive meaning. The emergence of the modern usage for 'economy' is bound up with the rejection of the assumptions of neoclassical theory in the 1930s which owes much to Keynes. For Keynes argued convincingly that the economic well-being of a nation could be vastly improved by the then heretical notion of acting in ways that had previously been considered *un*economical. The economic

FIGURE 3.11   *Cartoon representation of 'economic law' by Bernard Partridge, published in* Punch *magazine in 1921*

orthodoxy of the 1920s and 1930s, with its divination of the laws of supply and demand, could only conceive of individual economic agents, be they firms or people, subject to the market mechanism. Keynes' suggestion was that there existed a level of economic analysis other than this, in fact a national economic structure that was capable of being, and indeed should be, modified by government action. To facilitate the expression of this idea he begins to refer to '*the* economy' as a totality, as something more than the combined activity of the individual economic units. Whilst the Keynesian revolution in economic thinking cannot be reduced to a minor change in terminology, a change in linguistic usage was a necessary feature of the ideas he had developed. Neoclassical economic theory was built around the laws of supply and demand – 'the market'; in rejecting the assumption of the inviolability of this mechanism, Keynes replaced one reified notion with another. The whole economic structure – 'the economy' – became the new focus of economic wisdom.

This historical background to the emergence of the category 'the economy' provides a framework for a project which can explore cartoon representations of the economy in more detail. Although we have argued that the idea of 'the economy' in its modern usage is discursively available from the late 1930s, earlier research on the UK press (Emmison, 1986) suggests that cartoon images of the economy as entity do not appear until the 1960s. Is this finding generalizable to other countries? A project to investigate this issue is described in Box 3.5.

Ethnomethodological approaches to visual data: headlines, direction signs, maps

If cartoons can tell us a great deal about how we think about economic processes then it is also the case that other forms of visual material – or more specifically the way we use or interpret this material – can tell us a lot about our common-sense communicative abilities we rely on to navigate through everyday life. In this final section we want to look at some of the ways in which ethnomethodological researchers have gone about the analysis of visual data. We have briefly touched on ethnomethodological work on the practices of scientific communication, in the previous chapter. Here we want to look at some more everyday or mundane examples of how visual information has been explored from an ethnomethodological standpoint.[4] Ethnomethodology is concerned with 'the study of the common-sense reasoning skills and abilities through which ordinary members of a culture produce and recognize intelligible courses of action' (Heritage, 1989: 21). Although the greater part of work in the ethnomethodological tradition has been concerned with the use of these abilities as exemplified in conversational encounters and other forms of linguistic communication, ethnomethodological principles can be equally well illustrated by looking at how people make sense of visual information such as signs. Let us begin, however by considering an example which in some respects is situated halfway between the linguistic and the visual: ordinary newspaper headlines.

Like most newspaper readers we never consume the paper as if it were a novel, starting at the top left on page one and systematically proceeding to the bottom right of the last page. Instead we find ourselves scanning the paper in a more random fashion, taking in an overall impression of the major items before settling down to read in detail those stories which have caught our attention. Story headlines – together with such features as page location, the inclusion of a photograph, and relative type size – are the crucial resources in attracting us as consumers. Headlines succeed to the extent that they convey enough information about the story they accompany to attract the reader's attention whilst leaving untold – or perhaps ambiguous – sufficient details to warrant the reader's closer attention. The headline speaks to us: 'I'm going to tell you

BOX 3.5   CARTOON IMAGES OF THE ECONOMY PROJECT: A CROSS-NATIONAL COMPARISON

This project is designed to explore the issue of national differences in the representation of the economy. Does 'the economy' appear at different times as an object of cartooning in different countries and are there any differences in the prevailing image which is adopted – 'beast', 'machine', 'person' etc.?

- For this exercise you will need access to a library which houses periodical and magazine collections. For example, a comparison of the UK and Australia could be undertaken using the magazines *Punch* (UK) and *The Bulletin* (Australia). Magazines such as these were the predominant outlet for the cartoon, and it is only relatively recently that this function has been taken over by the daily newspaper. Moreover, each issue invariably featured a full-page 'editorial cartoon' which was targeted specifically at the current economic situation.
- To chart the emergence of the economy and changes in its cartoon representation, a sampling frame covering the years 1920 to 1990 would be appropriate. The sample of cartoons for investigation could be generated by taking an issue of each magazine every five years on a rotating monthly basis. So starting in January 1920 the next issue to be examined would be in February 1925, followed by March 1930, etc. By varying the month as well as the year you make allowances for any cyclical or seasonal variation in economic activity (budgets, etc.). If the issue you are examining does not contain an 'economic' cartoon, then select the next issue for the same month and so on until you have examined the entire month. If no cartoon is located then record a nil entry for that particular year.
- Using the framework of 'paired oppositions' discussed above examine each of the collections of cartoons and establish when 'the economy' as an entity first appears and what form the entity takes.
- A related issue concerns the representation of specific economic processes or categories: 'inflation', 'the dollar', 'the deficit', 'the recession'. When do these start appearing and what representational form do they take?

something about my story. I can't tell you everything and you must come and read it for yourself.'

Seen in this way the headlines constitute condensed descriptions of social life, in which actors, their doings and their circumstances are combined. As readers we draw upon our 'common sense knowledge of social structures' (Garfinkel 1967: viii) to locate the elements of a recognizable scene, albeit one which requires us to undertake further clarification or elaboration. Let us move straight to an example: a headline taken from our local paper, the Brisbane *Courier Mail*:

Rapist gets $161,620 for reduced sex life

We have here a dramatic, but by no means structurally atypical, example of the attraction that headlines possess. A recognizable description of a socially organized activity has been presented but in a form that is inherently ambiguous or puzzling. We cannot immediately connect the events that are depicted in such a way as to account for their concatenation and we are thus drawn into the story to solve the puzzle. But to read the headline as even containing a puzzle requires us to invoke an analytical apparatus which has so far been unexplicated. What is the nature of this apparatus? To help answer this question we must turn to the ethnomethodological perspective, in particular Harvey Sacks' work on the organization of descriptions.

Sacks: membership categorization devices

In the early phase of his investigations into the organization of conversation, Sacks (1972) focused on the way that descriptions that people produced of their activities and the scenes and circumstances they encountered, were recognizable *as* descriptions by others. Sacks argued that one consequence of our successful socialization within a culture was that we acquire an elaborate 'inferential machinery', a set of devices, rules, maxims and so on which we invoke in a taken-for-granted fashion to make sense of the social world and bring off social interaction. Sacks begins with the observation that every member of society can be described in a diversity of ways. For example the same person could be referred to, depending upon the context, as a 'female', 'sister', 'mother', 'teacher', 'tax-payer', 'school lunch volunteer', 'football supporter', 'music lover' and so on. Of rather more interest to Sacks, however, is the ability we possess to 'sort' or 'classify' these various categorizations when we encounter them in visual form (as in newspaper headlines or advertising billboards) or in spoken form (e.g. conversations, sermons, medical consultations, interviews). Here Sacks introduces the idea of a 'membership categorization device' (MCD) or simply a 'categorization device' as a crucial resource in our sense-making abilities. An MCD is a collection of categories which 'go together' in some discernible way together with various rules for their application. Perhaps the simplest MCD is that of 'sex' which contains the two categories 'female' and 'male'. The most basic rule of application, he argues, is that the categories which constitute each MCD are mutually exclusive in the sense that if we 'hear' someone as belonging to one of the categories then we know that they cannot be described by one of the other categories in the collection. Hearing that someone is a 'sister' then we know that they cannot also be a 'brother'; moreover, it is not even necessary for the actual category to be used in a description for we have ways of working out what the appropriate category is as we shall see shortly.

Two further rules of application Sacks refers to are the 'economy rule' and the 'consistency rule'. By the former, Sacks means that in making reference to a person a single category from one collection *may* be sufficient or adequate to describe that person: we do not need to know that someone is a 'mother' *and* a 'tax-payer' to have them adequately referenced; either one of them will suffice as a person description. By the latter rule he wants to argue that, where it is possible, we try to invoke the same MCD when we encounter a description in which more than one person is being referenced. To use Sacks' own famous illustration, in a description which makes reference to a 'baby' and a 'mother' it is natural to 'hear' the two categories as belonging to the same MCD, in this case that of the family.

Some MCDs – family being a case in point here – have an additional quality which intensifies the effect of the consistency rule, namely that they possess what Sacks refers to as a team-like or 'duplicatively organized' structure. What is important about such MCDs is that they have a discernible number of possible incumbents for each of their categories which allows us to arrive at a sense of the social relations such categories may embody. A 'family' for example, has typically comprised only one 'mother' and 'father' and at least one child. The fact that an increasing number of 'families' do not possess this structure today does not invalidate this point at all, for the very designation of these families as 'single parent families' reflects the way in which their departure from the duplicatively organized structure is noticeable or accountable.

Sacks next introduces the concept of 'category bound activities', the idea that certain actions or types of behaviour are common-sensically 'heard' as performed or enacted out by particular category incumbents. So, for example, 'rape' is seen as a male activity, as to a certain extent is criminal activity as a whole (Harris, 1977). Think of how routinely a suspect in a crime case is referred to as 'he' despite no knowledge of the gender identity of the criminal having been established. More generally, our knowledge of activities and the ways these are common-sensically linked to particular membership categories provides us with a resource for making assessments as to the moral character or appropriate behaviour of individuals or even just their social identity when this is unknown. So the activity 'crying' is commonsensically 'heard' as performed by a baby and carries no evaluative overtones. But if this or a similar activity is carried out by an individual far senior within the 'stage of life' MCD (adolescent, teenager, adult, etc.) then the knowledge that this behaviour is 'category inappropriate' may be used to sanction that conduct. We might challenge the person to 'stop acting like a baby' or to 'grow up'. Alternatively if a toddler or young child demonstrates an unanticipated degree of bravery or responsibility (taking medicine, having an injection) then we can praise them for 'being a big girl'.

This inferential machinery which Sacks first documented has been shown to be a powerful interactional resource by researchers in a range of settings. Wowk (1984), for example, has shown the way in which a suspect under interrogation in a murder case constructs an account of his victim's character and conduct in such a way that she could be seen as at least partly responsible for the events that led to her death. Importantly, Wowk shows how the suspect accomplishes this 'indirectly' by attributing to his victim activities which he hopes the police interrogator will 'hear' as common-sensically tied to a particularly 'morally deviant' category of female. And in a medical context Silverman (1987) has demonstrated the artful way in which parents of diabetic teenagers draw upon alternative depictions of appropriate parent–offspring relationships, on the one hand stressing parental supervision and on the other hand stressing teenage autonomy, in their attempts to rebut charges from the doctor of excessive or inadequate tutelage.

We are now in a position to return to our headline example and consider the way in which this 'inferential machinery' can help us understand its construction and the ambiguity it poses for us as readers. The core of the ambiguity lies in the linkage of the category 'rapist' as someone who is also a recipient of court-awarded damages for sexual impairment. The category of rapist is common-sensically understood as someone who is a perpetrator of sexual violence and aggression, as someone who is normally punished rather than rewarded. But our inferential machinery makes the headline even more puzzling. Through our invocation of the consistency rule we see these two events as connected in some determinate way: that the damages the 'rapist' has received are somehow contingent upon circumstances surrounding an act of rape. We cannot readily conceive how this connection could have occurred and are drawn to the story to resolve the mystery.

In fact the 'mystery' is readily solved in the first paragraph of the story, where we read that the rapist was also a 'road accident' victim and it is this incident which lies behind his sexual impairment and the court's award of damages. The full story also reveals that the individual concerned could have been adequately referenced by any one of seven possible identities: 'man', 'armed robber', 'prison escapee', 'fitness enthusiast', 'road accident victim', 'husband' as well as 'rapist', but clearly it is last of these which provides the newspaper subeditor with the most 'newsworthy' possibility and the reason for its selection. We can glimpse here something of the working ideology of newspaper journalism, which is the achievement of newsworthiness through creative juxtaposition of categories and activity descriptions even to the extent of creating 'category puzzles': constructing headlines in such a way that, in themselves, they are not transparently obvious descriptions. The exercises in Boxes 3.6 and 3.7 are designed to provide students with greater familiarity with Sacks' MCD machinery as well as some critical skills in confronting media texts.

BOX 3.6   HEADLINE ANALYSIS EXERCISE 1

The following three headlines taken from Australian papers provide further examples of category puzzles.

'Terrorist in top security jail is expecting a baby'
'Baby to sue granddad over father's death'
'Jury acquits husband in penis-severing case'

For each headline indicate

- What identities and/or MCDs have been used (OR are discoverable through analysis) in the headlines?
- How do the 'economy rule' and the 'consistency rule' influence our reading of the headlines?
- What common-sense understandings are made possible by constructing the headlines in these particular ways?
- What is the precise nature of the 'category-puzzle' created in each case?
- How do these headlines demonstrate the *newsworthiness* of the stories they head?

Now repeat this process for two further headlines collected by yourself

BOX 3.7   HEADLINE ANALYSIS EXERCISE 2

This is a variation on the previous exercise which requires the participation of the entire class or at least a group of students.

- Divide the class into two groups
- Provide one group with a headline (but not the story)
- Provide the other group with the corresponding story (but not the headline)
- Ask the first group to sketch out the story which they think would have accompanied the headline
- Ask the second group to devise the headline which they think would have introduced the story
- On completion of these tasks discuss which group found their allotted task the 'easier' and which was more 'successful' in supplying the missing component

Signs, maps and everyday direction finding

Ethnomethodology's innovative approach to common-sense reasoning can be further demonstrated by looking at how it deals with more overtly visual material such as signs or maps. Ethnomethodology is dismissive of cultural studies approaches to such visual material, on the grounds that these approaches are invariably speculative rather than grounded in the details of the phenomena under investigation. As Miller and McHoul have recently argued in their call for EMICS – 'an ethnomethodologically inspired cultural studies'

> cultural studies can benefit most from beginning with actual cultural texts in their ordinary historical and everyday places *before* political and theoretical speculations are brought to bear upon them, *before* they are turned into mere artefacts of social criticism. (Miller and McHoul, 1998: 180, emphasis in original)

An example of just the kind of problem that Miller and McHoul identify can be found in Gottdiener's (1995) recent 'socio-semiotic' analysis of real-estate signs. For Gottdiener, that signs are erected for the practical purpose of giving directions and information to people who may wish to enter the new housing market goes entirely unnoticed. In a typical cultural studies 'move' Gottdiener is concerned solely with identifying what he perceives to be the 'ideological codes' which are contained within the signs. Four such codes are discovered: a 'naturalist anti-urban', a 'topographic/geographic', an 'English gentrification' and a 'neo-Fordist'. But it is not clear how these codes were arrived at, whether they are applicable to all other real-estate signs or just the ones in the region he studied (the Los Angeles basin), let alone the more basic question of whether ordinary persons also recognize these codes. But it is precisely these sorts of 'positivist' charges which speculative cultural studies, in its refusal to engage with the phenomenon, leaves itself open to.

Contrast Gottdiener's investigation of signs with the ethnomethodological approach taken by Sharrock and Anderson (1979) in their examination of directional signs in a Medical School complex. Signs in themselves, they declare, are of no sociological interest: rather it is the ways in which they are interpreted and the ways these interpretations occasion practical courses of action which deserve attention. Sharrock and Anderson illustrate their analytic interest in directional signs by showing how 'an ordinary user' of the premises in which they were located might conceivably use these signs in negotiating their way around. They argue that the interpretation of signs is an irremediably practical and local matter. Signs are not observed in isolation but in particular contexts and in particular sequences. Finding our way around a building is, quite literally, a procedural affair. Visitors to the hospital may need to follow the directions of several information signs before arriving at their desired destinations. In this process, although signs are encountered 'one at a time', the sequences in which these occur are equally important in conveying information about places or locales.

Sharrock and Anderson present their data (photographs of the signs) in the order in which they encountered the signs as they navigated their own way within the medical school. In this manner they try to recapitulate the practical reasoning which would be employed by users of the hospital. For such people the signs comprise a series in which some are encountered 'earlier' and some 'later' according to their relative placement from the entrance to the building. They argue that the relationship between the signs is governed by a 'tree structure' such that signs encountered earlier in a journey are understood as being 'higher up' the tree structure and therefore conveying information which is less discriminating. For example, one of the signs in their series (example C) contains information about the direction of 'lecture theatres' in general, whereas a later sign (example D) provides information about a specific numbered lecture theatre. However, first-time patrons of the building – people for whom the signs are most relevant – cannot see the tree structure as such. Instead such users treat the signs as 'being part of a prospective, unfolding series' in which there is an anticipation that if the general direction given by an earlier sign is followed then we can expect to come across further signs which take us successively closer to our destination. It is the implications of this sequential structure that suggests to them that

> The business of 'reading signs' is an embedded activity. . . . As an activity, it involves a highly particularized and localized kind of work, such that we read *this* sign in *this* way because it is *here* and because it is next to *this other* thing. (Sharrock and Anderson: 90, emphasis in original)

Figures 3.12, 3.13 and 3.14 present typical directional signs which can be observed at the University of Queensland campus which illustrate many of the points that Sharrock and Anderson make. Observe – a point which we have so far ignored – that the signs are what Sharrock and Anderson refer to as 'idiomatically expressive' in that the actual directions that are indicated by the arrows are not to be construed as the directions they intend to signify. So, for example, visitors to the University campus on encountering such signs will, we suspect, have no trouble in interpreting the upward arrows as indicating forward or horizontal movement up the adjacent steps into the building. Those specifically seeking the 'J M Campbell Room' (see Figure 3.12) or the 'Fryer Memorial Library' (see Figure 3.14) will, in turn, take the diagonal arrows to mean that their route will involve *in the first instance* a left and right turn respectively on entering the Forgan Smith building and that further signs will no doubt be encountered subsequently which will take them to their destination. Note also in Figure 3.12 the way in which the vertical placement of the various destinations on the sign is in the same order as they will be encountered in actuality.

Observe too, although this point is incidental to our analysis, the way in which the permanent University sign shown in Figure 3.12 has served as a host for a 'parasitic' sign which had been erected to direct visitors to a more distant part of the campus as part of a courses information day.

FIGURE 3.12 *Directional signs on a university campus*

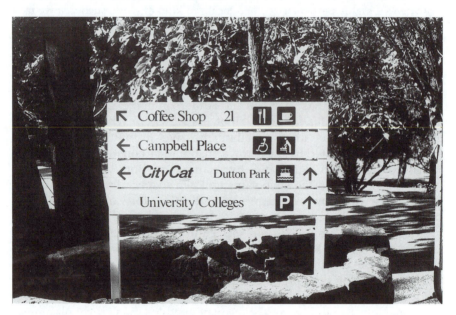

FIGURE 3.13 *Directional signs on a university campus*

The temporary sign mimics the shape of the permanent fixture and, in so doing, visibly acquires its meaning. The sign in Figure 3.13 shows how direction finding is facilitated by the inclusion of iconic motifs which indicate something about what can be expected if a particular arrow is

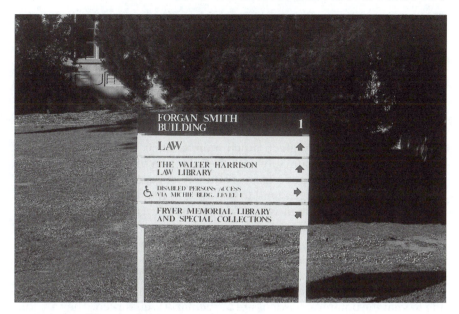

FIGURE 3.14   *Directional signs on a university campus*

followed. For example a visitor might be unaware that 'CityCat' was the name of the fast catamaran to the city or that 'Dutton Park' was the name of the conventional cross river ferry. However, the bold blue underscoring below 'CityCat' and its sloping typeface suggests speedy water transport whilst the choppy waves and tubby boat alongside 'Dutton Park' evoke a less glamorous aquatic experience.

The interpretation of directional signs such as these is, of course, not always successful. People can and do misinterpret signs, particularly if they are in a hurry or if they have more obvious practical matters to occupy them: for example getting to an appointment or lecture on time. Reading signs can, in part, be seen as a matter of economics: how long or how much effort should be spent in arriving at an unambiguous interpretation of its information.[5] But as Sharrock and Anderson note, the errors that people make when following signs have a 'recoverable' character:

> we can try the first thing that seems right, but if it doesn't work, then we can try something else and see if that will work, and if we experience a few failures, that doesn't do much harm or cost a great deal. Certainly taking a wrong turn in a building is often something that can easily be detected as an error, soon after it is made and rapidly recovered by a retracing of steps. (Sharrock and Anderson, 1979: 91)

But whilst this may well be the case for pedestrian direction finding, such practices are hardly likely to be of use to motorists. It is one thing to retrace ones steps but quite another to rectify a missed turn when one is at the wheel of a car on a freeway. Pedestrians can readily modify their routes, make abrupt turns, or stop dead in their tracks generally without any fear that such activities will occasion collisions with their fellows, but these are not options which are available to drivers. What we find, then, is that these contrasting 'logics of navigation' – finding one's way around on foot as opposed to finding one's way around by car – are reflected in different sign systems. Whereas pedestrians are given only general out-lines of where to proceed and must 'work out' the details *en route*, motorists are invariably given much more explicit visual information as to how to proceed, presumably with the intention of avoiding the kind of recoverable errors that pedestrians routinely engage in. The result is that key traffic directional signs tend to be iconic in that the physical layout of an up-coming road system is reproduced as a constituent feature of the sign itself. Figure 3.15 provides an example of such an iconic traffic sign. As can be seen the sign has been designed so as to leave little to chance. Motorists reading the sign are given explicit instructions on how to proceed, with the core feature of the sign mimicking the actual roundabout and the exit option routes they will shortly encounter. Motorists intend-ing to visit the botanical gardens are particularly well served. They are told which lane they should be in, they have their turn-off iconically marked and their destination is even colour coded (brown against the prevailing green background).

Ethnomethodological interest in sense making and direction finding has also extended to a consideration of the construction of maps. Psathas (1979), for example, has looked at the organizational features contained

FIGURE 3.15 *Traffic sign featuring iconic representation of road layout*

BOX 3.8 DIRECTION-FINDING AND COMMON-SENSE REASONING EXERCISE

The aim of this exercise is to make you aware of the vast amount of taken-for-granted common-sense reasoning which, ethnomethodologists argue, we rely upon in everyday life. The project requires you to find your way around a large complex such as a university but in a way which makes you self conscious of your 'way-finding' abilities.

From your university or college telephone directory select the name of a staff member you have no knowledge of and who works in a department at the university that you never frequent. As readers of this book are most likely to be in social science or humanities faculties, we suggest you opt for something like 'chemical engineering'. Beginning at the main entrance of the university your task is to locate the room of this staff member, using only the directional signs and maps (and, of course, your common-sense reasoning) which the university has erected.

It would help to take along a notebook and pencil with you to record what you do, and equally importantly, what you think about when you encounter a sign and act on the information you see. Most universities have a campus map at or near their main entrance, and so the first task would be to locate the building which houses your chosen staff member. Once you have located the building on the map and noted the general area of the campus in which it can be found (itself a task relying on a good deal of practical reasoning) then start your journey towards it. As you encounter signs which you deem relevant record them in your notebook, but also write down what additional information you are supplying which contributes to the direction-finding process. At first this may not be at all obvious but take it slowly and try to work out exactly what it is that you supply to make the sign 'work'. For example, we have already noted above that signs which point 'upwards' are common-sensically taken to mean go forward; signs which point diagonally at the entrance to a building typically require you to make a turn once you have entered the building and so on.

If you get 'lost' don't ask anyone for directions (although this is an eminently common-sense thing to do!) but retrace your steps to a place you are sure about. Eventually, we hope, you should find the building you are seeking, but this is not yet the end of the journey! You still have to find a particular numbered room in the building. Tacit common sense comes into play here: for example we typically read a number – e.g. '829' – alongside the staff member's name on the departmental directory board as indicating that the person will be found on the 8th floor of the building. Even finding this room once we have reached the 8th floor requires further tacit knowledge to determine the numbering sequence and the direction to be taken along the corridor.

At the end of your journey look at what you have recorded in your notebook and reflect on exactly how much information you had to supply. If all this 'additional' information had to be made explicit, then the university would be covered in a veritable forest of directional signs, informational boards and so on!

within maps which have been drawn to assist persons in finding a particular place – typically the home of the one who has constructed the map. Psathas' interest lies in how such maps can be investigated as sites of practical reasoning. That is, they can be understood as documents which both contain, and use as a resource, methods which are tacitly relied upon by persons who have to accomplish the practical task of getting from one place to another. Psathas finds that 'maps to our place' are never intended to be geographer's maps, 'drawn to scale' or objective. Instead they should be seen as 'maps with a purpose', this purpose being to show the way to a particular place. Such maps operate with a special sense of space. One of the tasks which the map maker has to accomplish is to get people 'onto the map', for such maps are always bounded by a real world beyond the map's space:

> The map begins and ends at its edges. The 'real world' within which its depicted places are depicted as existing is not claimed to end at these edges. There are connections to, continuations of, and extensions onto other roads, areas, and places from the roads, areas and places shown; but these other roads, areas, and places are not shown. (Psathas, 1979: 207)

'Maps to our place' may have multiple starting points, and so the core organizational feature to which all other features must be related is the destination. Places, streets, roads, bridges, junctions, etc. which are shown on the map are always in relation to this destination. So places are noted as being 'after' or 'next' in ways which indicate that the sequence in which they are noticed will be confirmation that one is still on the correct route. Distances on such maps tend not to be exact linear measurements but rather based on these sequential features. To have travelled the distance shown on the maps is to have passed certain streets, intersections or landmarks. Psathas concludes by suggesting that readers of these maps who identify the route to be taken as a 'set of sequential particulars' come to see this as a discovery:

> a discovery whose possibility is provided by the 'map itself', as though little or no work on the reader's part were needed – as though the maker of the map 'did it'. (Psathas, 1979: 224)

However, this is to underestimate the sense-making work which the reader herself must do. Methods of practical reasoning, then, are something which both map makers *and* map readers must unavoidably rely upon.

We conclude this discussion of the ethnomethodological tradition in visual research with an example of an analysis of a 'pictorial message' undertaken by someone seemingly far removed from the ethnomethodological school but whose comments about the image point in a surprisingly similar direction. We refer to the illustration which the National Aeronautics and Space Administration (NASA) included on one of its deep-space probes launched in the 1970s and the analysis of the message made by art historian Ernst Gombrich. The illustration in question is shown in Figure 3.16.

BOX 3.9 MAP-MAKING AND PRACTICAL REASONING EXERCISE

Psathas includes several examples of different 'maps to our place' in his article. A variation on the research he undertook would be to consider the organizational features of maps which are all designed to get people to the same place. For example, students could be asked to draw a map which shows how to get to a certain location – a central city building such as a post office or a hotel would be ideal. For the purposes of the assignment it should be assumed that the building can be reached by car, although the building in question may well be located in a pedestrian mall area. The map should be drawn so as to cover the route from each student's residential neighbourhood (this will mean a plurality of differences in how the question of 'getting onto' the map is accomplished) to the central location.

The map should also be designed to be read and understood by someone who is unfamiliar with the city and who therefore has no 'local knowledge' to draw on. If Psathas' arguments about shared common-sense reasoning are correct then we should expect there will be a great deal of variability in the places, landmarks, etc. which are included at the edges of the map (the area closest to the different residential locations) but that as the maps converge closer to the central city destination point then they should all begin to exhibit the same (or similar) noticings. In other words, from the multitude of features which could be included on the map, we should expect that only a limited repertoire will be used. If this does not turn out as expected then look for possible reasons as to why. Standard sociological factors might come into to play here: for example do men include different features (sports stadiums?, petrol stations?) to women in the design of their maps?

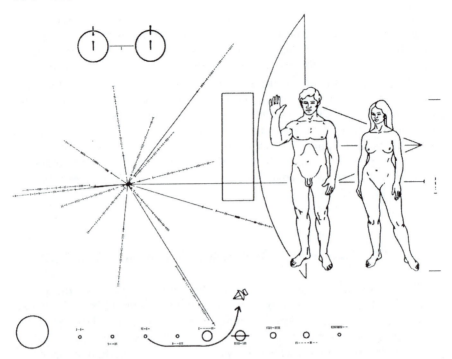

FIGURE 3.16 *Pictorial plaque from the NASA space probe, Pioneer. Source: Gombrich (1996)*

Gombrich's basic argument is that the pictorial plaque would fail dismally in its intended purpose: in short that it is not a good example of the kind of mutual common-sense or practical reasoning we have been discussing. According to press releases at the time of the launch of the probe, NASA included the plaque 'on the off chance that somewhere on the way it is intercepted by intelligent, scientifically educated beings'. The assumption was that these beings would easily be able to work out where the probe was from and gain some idea of the creatures who were responsible for sending it and their friendly intentions. Almost all the design features of the plaque, Gombrich points out, rely on the use of taken-for-granted knowledge which simply could not be assumed to be possessed by the inhabitants of planet Zogg or wherever else the probe ended up. For a start these beings would have to be equipped with sense organ 'receivers' (eyes) which respond to the same band of electromagnetic waves as ours. As for the human figures themselves, it is only our common-sense knowledge that feet are for standing on and eyes are for looking that allows us to see these as solid recognizable configurations. Our scientifically educated space creature, Gombrich comments, 'might be forgiven if they saw the figures as wire constructs with lose bits and pieces hovering weightlessly in between' (Gombrich, 1996: 54). The plaque even embodies conventional understandings about gender relations with the female figure positioned slightly behind the male and with her trunk angled towards him so that her right arm 'tapers off like a flamingo's neck and beak'.

The plaque has the human figures drawn to scale against the outline of the probe, but if those viewing it in deep space have a sense of perspective the craft would be conceived as much further back 'which would make the scale of the manikins minute'. As for the greetings gesture, 'not even an earthly Chinese or Indian would be able to correctly interpret this gesture from his [*sic*] repertory' (ibid: 55). Finally Gombrich notes there may well be confusion in distinguishing between the two diagrams – the first detailing the 14 pulsars of the Milky Way as a means to pinpoint the location of our sun, and the second which shows the planets of our solar system. Here the trajectory of the probe departing from earth and swinging into space past Jupiter is shown with a directional arrowhead, an entirely conventional symbol unlikely to be recognized by anyone who has never encountered a bow and arrow.

Conclusion

In this chapter we have tried to show how images and other forms of two-dimensional visual material can be subject not only to standard forms of decoding or interpretation, but also serve as tools for the investigation of concepts and processes which are at the heart of social science inquiry. Moving away from an interpretive framework, however, requires some effort precisely because the kinds of two-dimensional images we have looked at seem naturally to invite this kind of hermeneutic investigation. In the chapter which follows, where we turn to examine the use of three-dimensional objects as data for visual analysis, our task becomes a little easier. In general we think of objects as things to *use* rather than as things to be *read*. Whilst we will show that reading objects is a worthwhile task, we will also show how they can be appropriated for more traditional sociological ends. Finally the astute reader will have recognized that, although we have treated directional signs as another form of two-dimensional visual data, our investigation of these has, strictly speaking, exceeded their two-dimensional form to the extent that it has drawn attention to their practical uses in particular environments. In this sense we have already begun to touch on issues of spatial contexts and the interplay between settings and human movements as they impact on the visual. We return to this theme in Chapter 5.

Notes

1   It is not our intention to consider 'the media' in its entirety. This would be an undertaking beyond the scope of one book never mind a single chapter.

Accordingly we will have nothing to say about television, film or the visual arts more broadly as sources of information for visual inquiry. We recognize that some of the most influential work carried out by media researchers has been concerned with television content (e.g. Glasgow University Media Group, 1976, 1980) but, given that our focus throughout the book lies with research ideas which are accessible for students, this exclusion is justified. Research on film and television tends either to be the preserve of specialist departments with literary or cultural interests or else, when conducted by social science investigators, it requires expensive equipment as well as lengthy data collection phases (e.g. several months news coverage of an event like the Gulf War) which generally place this kind of activity outside the reach of undergraduate students. A useful recent, more modest attempt to deal with television content as part of an overall analysis of the visual media can be found in Hansen et al. (1998), chapter 8.

2   For a recent study of advertising which attempts to combine both the semiotic or interpretive and the more rigorous quantitative approaches, see Leiss, Kline and Jhally (1990).

3   A comic strip makes an unexpected appearance in Erik Olin Wright's recent book *Class Counts* (1997). Wright, the leading exponent of quantitative studies of class analysis uses an episode of a *Li'l Abner* comic strip from the 1940s which features the magical creature the Shmoo to illustrate a number of complex theoretical issues about the workings of class exploitation.

4   The most accessible introduction to the ethnomethodological perspective is still Heritage (1984). McHoul (1982) is more difficult, but the empirical work reported there has some connection with the themes raised in this section. The term, of course, originates with Garfinkel (1967).

5   Alec McHoul (personal communication) has pointed to an additional factor which may be responsible for people taking the wrong direction. He argues that one of the surest ways in which it is possible to identify someone as a 'visitor' to a building or locale is through the amount of attention that the person is paying to the directional signs. People who do not wish to appear as visitors, but who in fact occupy this status, may therefore avoid conspicuous displays of sign reading but at the cost of mistaking their way.

4

Three-dimensional Visual Data: Settings, Objects and Traces

This chapter will:

- introduce objects or 'material culture' as a resource for visual research
- suggest ways that interactions between people and objects can be explored
- consider the advantages of objects over texts within visual research, in particular the fact that stronger inferences can be made to populations than is the case with texts
- identify a number of everyday sites where objects can be studied, such as homes, cemeteries, toilets, museums and car parks
- discuss some limitations of a purely visual approach to objects.

The central theme of this book is the need for visual research to break free of the tyranny of the photograph. We began the move away from the photograph in the previous chapter by pointing to the research possibilities built into forgotten forms of visual data such as maps, signs, newspaper headlines and cartoons. With the exception of signs, these alternative forms of data are two-dimensional and share with the photograph a textual existence. In many cases they are also 'images' which we approached as things to be 'read', just like the photograph. In this chapter we push still further away from the photograph and orthodox visual inquiry in three ways. Firstly we introduce three-dimensional objects as a resource for visual inquiry. In so doing we move visual research away from the text and the image and towards the seen. Secondly, whilst we suggest the possibility for semiotic readings of objects, we will also argue that they allow a wider variety of inquiries to be grounded. In particular they can operate as unobtrusive measures of social processes and can allow inferences to be made to populations. Thirdly, in as far as objects are distributed and arranged in environments, rather than having a virtual existence on the page, questions of space and place become central to their understanding.

The semiotics of objects and beyond

The previous chapter explored the analysis of 2D data, partly in terms of semiotic approaches. In looking at news photographs, posters and at do-it-yourself advertising, we identified ways to decode images and work out how they operated as signifiers to convey particular messages. We begin this chapter by pointing to the possibility of decoding the 3D as well. The focus on advertising within Barthes-inspired cultural studies has become so ubiquitous that we often forget that in many of his essays he looked not at adverts and images, but at things themselves. Barthes was able to do this because he understood that mythologies were not simply layered on top of the 'real world' by *post hoc* advertising campaigns, but rather were built into the fabric of objects and practices. Their existence, consequently, was mate-rial as much as textual. A classical illustration of this position is Roland Barthes' essay on the (then) 'New Citroen'. Barthes was writing about the Citroen DS, a car with sleek lines that was technologically advanced for its time (the 1950s). He likens the car to 'the great Gothic cathedrals' and asserts that they are perceived as a 'purely magical object' which is con-sumed in image by the entire population. Barthes emphasizes the smooth-ness and shape of the car, and suggests its curvaceous glass contributes to a light, spiritual quality: 'Here the glass surfaces are not windows, open-ings pierced in a dark shell; they are vast walls of air and space, with the curvature, the spread and the brilliance of soap bubbles. . .' (1973: 89). He also points to a countering domesticity in the interior: 'it is now more homely, more attuned to this sublimation of the utensil which one also finds

BOX 4.1   DECODING CARS EXERCISE

Following in the footsteps of Barthes decoding the car is a worthwhile exercise for sharpening interpretive faculties. Select two contrasting cars (e.g. 4-wheel drive, luxury sedan, small urban car, etc.). Look them over thoroughly, inside and out. Write around two hundred words on each car. Try to discuss the following themes. What kinds of messages are you able to read into the materiality of the car? Which aspects of the car carry which messages? What kinds of larger mythologies does the car seem to tap into? To what extent have practi-cal imperatives (e.g. cost, functionality, legal requirements) compro-mised semiotic possibilities?

Note: You may wish to extend the project by comparing your analy-sis of the car itself to a further study of advertising that is used to promote it. Does the advertising suggest that your reading of the car was one that the manufacturers and distributors would agree with?

in the design of contemporary household equipment. The dashboard looks more like the working surface of a modern kitchen than the control-room of a factory' (ibid.). Nonetheless, the overall impact of the New Citroen is to 'actualize . . . the essence of petit-bourgeois advancement' (ibid.: 90).

Barthes' essay on the New Citroen, then, demonstrates the availability of objects for semiotic analysis. But it also points beyond this. Hidden away in the essay are clues suggesting that we might be able to do more with objects than with 2D texts. One of these is to observe people in inter-action with objects.

> In the exhibition halls, the car on show is explored with an intense, amorous studiousness: it is the great tactile phase of discovery. . . . The bodywork, the lines of union are touched, the upholstery palpated, the seats tried, the doors caressed, the cushions fondled; before the wheel, one pretends to drive with one's whole body. The object here is totally prostituted, appropriated. . . . (1973: 90)

Interactions with objects, then, are a source of visual data from which we can make inferences about social life – in this case the popularity (or as Barthes would have it, ideological success) of the Citroen DS. It is also important to remember that the car does not exist in a vacuum. Objects are always positioned in particular spatial contexts – in this case the exhibition hall where touching is permitted. Spatial settings, then, are of great importance in understanding objects and their relationships with humans. Elsewhere in *Mythologies* we find other hints at ways objects can be used in sociological analysis. In his essay on children's toys, Barthes claims that artisanal wooden toys are superior to bourgeois manufactured toys. They are organic and human rather than soulless and sterile. In building this argument he points to the qualities of wood itself, which 'does not break down; it does not shatter, it wears out, it can last a long time, live with the child, alter little by little the relations between the object and the hand'. Here Barthes prefigures another source of visual data we will explore in this chapter – the study of traces. Just as the wear and tear on a wooden toy betrays a history of use (and presumably enthusiasm), so does more general wear and tear allow inferences to be made about social activity.

In this chapter we will pursue these themes – the semiotics of objects, the importance of settings, the visibility of human interactions with objects and the ability of objects to record traces of human activity. Our general concern is to suggest that objects can operate as indicators of wider socio-cultural processes and therefore serve as tools for a theoretically informed exploration of social life.

Four advantages of objects for sociological research

As Barthes' work suggests, not only can objects be read or 'decoded' in much the same ways as their two-dimensional cousins, but also they offer other, equally exciting possibilities. To begin with, we can tell very little about social processes by observing someone reading. It is for this reason that media studies scholars have often turned to audience ethnography in order to work out the impacts that particular texts might be having. In contrast, people do things with objects which are witnessable to a pair of open eyes. They pick things up, they carry them, they wear them, they drop them, they wash them, they polish them, they tread on them and so on. All of these activities provide fuel for visual sociology. Importantly they allow us to develop behavioural measures. That is to say, they allow us to make inferences based upon what people actually do. Studies of two-dimensional texts (by contrast) generally allow us to study cultural beliefs systems and ideals as abstractions, but are of less use in exploring what really happens on the ground.

The sheer visibility of many objects is another bonus for the researcher. If we walk down a typical suburban street we will not be able to determine much about the reading habits of the occupants of each of the houses we pass, or how they view advertisements. Nor could we determine their sexual preferences or whether or not they are stamp collectors. To explore such issues we would need to intrude on their lives with an expensive and time-consuming interview or survey. There are, however, some things that we can deduce purely by using our eyes. Many objects are difficult to hide. And many activities leave behind them traces which are difficult to obscure. In that same street we can easily observe gardening styles, whether the residents drive foreign cars, and whether they have a satellite television dish. These may sound like trivial issues, but each of these can serve as an indicator of a broader social process of significant theoretical interest. Cultural assimilation can be examined by looking at whether migrants have adopted native gardening styles. Foreign cars are an indicator of globalization. Satellite dishes tell us something about media exposure and cultural consumption.

The great bonus of these very visible sources of information is that they allow us to explore social life covertly. Because respondents are not necessary for many kinds of object-centred inquiry, the usual problems of normative responding (telling the researcher a socially acceptable answer) are not present. Whilst ethnography or interview research is sometimes required to flesh out the meanings of objects and improve our inferences, we can often get by without it. As such, the study of 3D data is ideal as a source of what is generally called 'unobtrusive measures'. Many of the projects suggested here and in the remainder of the book fall into this category of research where we can collect data about social life without directly involving respondents in the research process. In some cases, however, we might suggest that you talk to people. This will allow them to explain the significance of objects and their locations, permitting the researcher to augment explanations and test whether speculative inferences are valid.

A final bonus with objects is that they are generally more 'democratic' than much published data. What appears in texts (2D data) is often the work of intellectuals and experts like journalists, photographers and advertising executives. These people can be thought of as an elite, and their output as a reflection of their particular concerns, values and world views. Many objects, by contrast, are intimately related to everyday experience and everyday practical activity. They often provide a better indicator of the lifestyles, choices and experiences of ordinary people.

People and objects

Before moving on to look at some of the more exotic forms of material culture, it is useful to begin by looking at ordinary objects and everyday settings. Objects are not just 'things', rather they are reflections of the wider lives of communities and individuals. This point has long been made by anthropologists with an interest in material culture. According to one authority, the concept of 'material culture' suggests 'a strong inter-relation between physical objects and human behaviour' and in particular the 'culture behind the material' (Schlereth, 1985: 3). The corollary is that far from being dull and uninteresting, artefacts can tell us a great deal about individuals and collectivities.

To date, the validity of studying material culture has been recognized for the most part by anthropologists and archaeologists. Attention from sociologists, cultural studies scholars and others has been slight. As a result much of the existing literature is of only marginal interest to those interested in studying complex industrial societies. Anthropological concerns, for example, have led to a particular consideration of the relationship between objects and their makers. This focus on the craftsperson and on handicrafts, mirrors the centrality of pre-industrial societies to mainstream anthropological research. There is also a strong tradition in the study of material culture which looks at objects as indexing a disappearing or long disappeared way of life. The concerns here, which closely parallel many approaches to photography, are centred on heritage preservation, documentation and archive management (e.g. Quimby, 1978; Schlereth, 1985). Another use of objects can be in the field of cultural history. The anthropologist might study household furniture over the centuries in order to make inferences about, say, sleeping patterns in the family. These sorts of historical concerns are usually (but not always) of limited interest for the wider community of researchers within social and cultural fields.

For these reasons we ignore most work in the field of material culture. We do not attempt to provide an overview of the field or discuss its merits or its leading theorists. Nor do we introduce the dense and theoretically challenging philosophical debates within the field about the ontological and epistemological status of objects.[1] Rather we try to suggest ways in which objects can be incorporated into small-scale visual research. We draw upon a variety of work which has used material culture as a way of tapping into the social and cultural processes of complex, contemporary societies. As the projects we suggest will make clear, we are also interested in exploring material culture less as a way of documenting a society-wide 'way of life' (as in traditional anthropological studies of material culture), and more as a means of exploring differences between groups and individuals. We begin this task by looking at the study of objects in ordinary settings.

Classifying everyday objects

Many systems have been proposed for classifying objects. These can provide a handy starting point for the analysis of material culture. Harold Riggins (1994: 111–15) provides a useful and extensive (if somewhat arbitrary and common-sensical) set of general conceptual tools for this purpose, albeit one framed primarily for the study of household objects. The advantage of Riggins' typology, as we see it, is that it was developed with the analysis of contemporary societies and everyday settings very much in mind. Just looking through the list provides a powerful reminder of the varieties of objects and their centrality to our lives. Core concepts are marked out in italics.

Intrinsically active refers to objects which are intended to be used or handled (e.g. a spoon). *Intrinsically passive* objects are intended for contemplation or decoration (e.g. a small sculpture). Riggins argues that many objects are not used in these intended ways. An antique spoon might form part of a collection, whilst the sculpture might be used as a paperweight. Hence we need to distinguish between *normal use* and *alien use*. The former refers to the intended use of an object at the time it was designed or made, whilst the latter refers to an unorthodox or unintended use. A screwdriver, for example, might have a normal use of driving screws, and an unintended use as a wedge for keeping a door open. Looking at alien uses can provide an insight into people's ability to improvise and to deploy objects in creative ways. *Status objects* work as indicators of social status, whether deliberately or not. Some objects (e.g. cars) are more easily interpreted as status objects than others (e.g. screwdrivers). However, it is important to note that status is always relative to a reference group. A high-quality screwdriver from Sheffield might be a status object among a group of professional builders. *Esteem objects* reflect personal self-esteem. Riggins argues that these fall into two classes. Some reflect intimate esteem, such as a wedding photograph or a Christmas card. Others reflect public recognition, such as a framed university degree or a sports trophy. *Collective objects* demonstrate wider social ties, such as national flags or religious artefacts. *Stigma objects* are associated with embarrassment, the socially unacceptable, or the marginal. These are often hidden out of public view in private or backstage areas. In the context of the home, examples might include medical supplies, dirty laundry and dishes, sex toys and pornography. *Social facilitators* are items which foster social interaction, such as a pack of cards. *Occupational objects* are generally tools linked to some trade or profession. *Indigenous objects* are locally made and reflect local themes, whilst *exotic objects* (e.g. holiday souvenirs) are from far-away places. *Way of production* distinguishes hand-made from machine-made objects. Riggins suggests that in western societies the former are often considered to be of special value and can provide a useful topic for generating interview data.

Aside from classifying objects themselves, Riggins also suggests we need to look at the *display syntax*. This refers to the ways that objects are organized in relation to each other. *Highlighting* is a process which involves some objects being positioned in ways which attract maximal attention, whilst *understating* is the contrary. In general, objects which are highlighted are more valuable or esteemed than those which are understated. We can also look at objects in terms of *clustering and dispersing*. The meanings of these terms is for the most part self-evident. Clustering is often a good indication of a belief that a number of objects somehow belong together in a set, or that they have some common significance. This might be the case with a 'collection'. *Status consistency* and *inconsistency* deal with the extent to which items in a room or other setting belong together in terms of financial or cultural capital. If we visit a stately home or palace, we often find high levels of status consistency. The eighteenth century four-poster bed is complemented by the Chippendale chairs and the portrait painting by Sir Joshua Reynolds. In most settings, however, we find a mixture of objects of differing status. In a typical student share house, for example, we might find expensive musical instruments, a good stereo and some high-brow novels, but also trashy old furniture and non-matching kitchen ware from a Salvation Army thrift shop. These sorts of inconsistencies often provide important clues about people's interests and priorities. The example of the student share house brings us to the issue of the *degree of conformity*. This looks at the extent to which a room or setting corresponds to shared, conventional notions of the appropriate in terms of order, colour, form and setting. Defining this can be difficult, especially in a postmodern world where there are said to be multiple taste communities. What is conformist for one group might be unorthodox for another. In counter-cultural settings, the traditional bourgeois house might be the nonconformist option, whilst furniture made from recycled logs and mud-bricks might be the norm! Still, thinking through these sorts of issues can provide a source of insight into priorities and values. Finally, Riggins speaks of *flavour*. By this he refers to the 'general impression' or 'atmosphere' given off by a setting. A chrome and glass office might have an up-beat, contemporary, corporate flavour, whilst a wood and leather office might speak of tradition and trustworthiness. Whilst the concept of flavour is often rather subjective, it can speak volumes if pursued in ethnographic research. For example, Stimson's work on the General Medical

Council's Disciplinary Hearing room, discussed in Chapter 1, is very much about 'flavour'.

Objects, settings, inferences

Riggins' typology suggests that objects allow inferences to be made about people, places and purposes. In everyday life we do this all the time. We might avoid parking in a street littered with burnt out cars and drug needles, as we infer it is crime prone. In a strange town we might go to the coffee shop with the genuine Italian cappuccino machine on the counter. We infer that they take their coffee seriously. An enduring problem for studies of 3D data is to work out which kinds of inferences are valid and which are spurious. The exercise in Box 4.2 should get you thinking about the process and the ways that your common-sense knowledge must inevitably become involved in helping to interpret objects and settings.

The exercise should alert you to the utility of observational data about objects and settings as a way of understanding and indexing values, beliefs and personalities. Even if you are conducting research informed by non-visual methods, detailed site descriptions such as the one in Box 4.2 can do a lot to add depth and character to your material. Having dispensed with preliminaries we are now in a position to look in more detail at particular approaches to objects and at particular research sites. Relevant studies of objects for visual research of the kind advocated in this book are diffuse and wide ranging with little sense of a common identity as a field. Consequently, organizing the literature is somewhat difficult. In the remainder of this chapter we suggest that 3D data can be explored in terms of the following interrelated themes.

BOX 4.2   DECODING ROOMS EXERCISE

Consider the following text. It is adapted from an Honours thesis by Cherie Millns (1998), one of our students. Whilst the real thesis contained contextual and historical information in this passage, here we have adapted it to contain only information that is visual. That is to say, information that anyone could derive simply from entering the room and looking around. As you read the description, make notes on the following points.

- Are you able to apply any of Riggins' concepts to the material?
- For each item of data, what kinds of inferences (if any) can you make about (a) what the room is used for, (b) who uses it, (c) what their values and beliefs are, (d) the 'flavour' of the room?

Complete your answers on a sheet following the example below. When you have finished, turn to page 116 and see if your analysis was correct.

Object	Inference
Computer	Technological skills
Red roses	Kitsch taste?

Site description

The room appears to be an office. There is plenty of 1950s style furniture. Each wall is painted a different, vivid primary colour. Next to the doorway sits a desk and ergonomic chair. On the desk is a high-powered computer. The computer is decorated lavishly with tinsel around the screen. Overhead on a brick red wall are numerous photos and postcards depicting Princess Leia from *Star Wars* and a kewpie doll along with snapshots of young women in silly poses. Along the right-side is a beige vinyl couch. There is a very large heart made of red plastic roses hanging above the couch. Placed strategically in front of the couch are two square, painted wooden coffee tables (one bright red, the other blue) typically holding all manner of bric-a-brac (grant applications, iced vovo [biscuit] packets, disks, books). Next to the sofa a small black metal bookcase holds magazines (*PC Today*, *Wired*, *Colours* – the Benetton magazine) and a CD-player and radio. CDs range from 'loungey style' (lounge music, i.e. 1960s swing, aeroplane music, bossanova, jazz), to 'funky trance-techno-drum'n'bass', to smooth mellow folk.

The facing 'Blue' wall is lined with a refurbished formica kitchen hutch, holding various assorted books (web design, graphic design, feminist theory, art and architecture, whole books dedicated to fonts and typographic style, 1960s cookery and etiquette books), food utensils (kettle, cups, coffee plunger and herbal teas), and snacks. Next to the kitchen hutch is a small grey filing cabinet, upon which a laser printer squats quietly. A formica table (operating as a desk?), ergonomic desk chair and computer takes up the rest of the wall length. A scanner, modem, zip drive, answering machine, and telephone also find their home here. The wall above the computer is spotted with a list of things to do, written on cards with golden wings, flying up the wall: 'world peace', 'write grant application' and so on. A round metal rubbish bin sits at the end of the desk. The far end Clover Green wall is dominated by a large window overlooking the city (only the grungy parts: mostly pubs and carparks) which allows streams of sunlight to enter the room, particularly during the afternoon.

ANSWER TO EXERCISE IN BOX 4.2.

The room was used by a community-based feminist web site design team which tried to provide a women-centred environment in which young women can become technologically competent in the male-dominated world of computing. The computer etc. document this technological activity. The shabby decor, poor location etc. reflect lack of money, as do the grant applications. The choice of photos, furniture, dolls, etc. shows the group's Generation-X style sense of irony, the CDs their eclecticism. The books and female icons suggest a feminist orientation. It is an interesting thought-experiment to compare this informal setting to one that could be found in a mainstream computing environment, either in a corporation or a university.

- *Cultural consumption.* The concern here is with the ways things can be used to indicate social status, cultural belonging and taste preferences. By looking at objects and, to a lesser extent, the ways people interact with them we are able to make inferences about how they see themselves and about their levels and forms of cultural capital.
- *Personalization.* The focus in this case is on the creative ways in which mass-produced objects are transformed to display individuality and identity. There are strong links with studies of cultural consumption and with symbolic interactionist traditions.
- *Use.* Objects can be used as objective and unobtrusive indicators of social activity. We can either directly observe people using objects, or else look for clues that they have been used. Studies of 'traces', for example, look for the marks people leave behind them on objects in their everyday lives.
- *Culture, knowledge, belief and ideology* can be investigated by exploring the ways that social values, discourses and epistemologies are encoded into objects and can be read from them. Semiotic and interpretive methods are central here.

The remainder of the chapter explores these four inter-related themes via a series of sites and research projects.

The home

One of the earliest and most important ways of exploring material culture in a sociological manner came with studies of consumption. A founding contribution was Theodore Veblen's (1912) writing on conspicuous consumption. Veblen noticed that people made use of the observability of objects in their everyday lives. He showed how artefacts of material culture were often deployed in an overt display as a way of attesting to social status. Things, in short, were useful as status markers. French sociologist Pierre Bourdieu (1984) has provided perhaps the most important contemporary project in this tradition. Bourdieu's work points to the ways that people's cultural consumption is structured by class location. A growing ethnographic tradition has followed Veblen and Bourdieu's footsteps, and has taken everyday objects in the home as a key tool for exploring taste and consumption. We exemplify some approaches to the home with an unlikely resource – the television.

Television   Television provides arguably the most important arena of cultural consumption in the modern world. Certainly data from survey research shows that watching television is the most popular leisure activity (e.g. Bennett, Emmison and Frow, 1999: ch. 3). Finding out what people watch, and how they watch it is a topic that has been very common in cultural studies. One thinks of research using audience ratings to measure trends in viewing, or of ethnographies which explore the various ways in which viewers have 'decoded' programmes from *Dallas* to the News. Needless to say expert readings of television and films programmes (which usually aim to detect ideological bias) are also a common type of research. Such research is clearly about the visual, although these kinds of projects use methodologies (surveys, focus groups, the analysis of moving images) which are beyond the scope of this text.

With all this attention on the television programme, it is easy to overlook the fact that television is also open to a different kind of visual inquiry, one that looks at the 'hardware' of television rather than the 'software' of content. Relatively little attention has been given to the television as a physical object and to its place in the domestic setting (Morley, 1995: 180). Yet the television is, in a sense, an object of consumption in and of itself regardless of what one watches. One can study that consumption without even knowing what programmes people watch. David Morely suggests that once this divergent perspective is taken a number of issues arise:

- the meanings of the television (e.g. the big-screen, high-definition TV, as a status symbol)
- the spatial arrangement of the living room (e.g. the television replaces the hearth as the 'sacred' focus of the space)
- the visibility of the television (e.g. is it proudly displayed or hidden away in a cabinet)
- the 'domestication' or 'personalization' of the television set (e.g. placing photos, ornaments on or around the set)
- the movement of televisions into other parts of the house (e.g. the kitchen, the bedroom), indicating a more 'informal' attitude to viewing.

Any one of these factors can provide fertile ground for visual research. The following two projects draw on Morley's proposal that we shift our orientation from the programme to the object.

BOX 4.3 TV SATELLITE DISH PROJECT

This project explores the intersection of cultural consumption with class. Following the introduction of satellite television into Britain during the late 1980s, consumers were confronted with a choice. Satellite television offered a larger selection of movies, sport and other programming. The down side was that consumers had to pay several hundred pounds for a receiver dish and a monthly fee for a black box to decode the signal. Consequently some people opted for satellite TV, whilst others chose to use only free-to-air television. Are there any social correlates to this decision? Which kinds of persons made which choice? Many commentators claim that, paradoxically, it was poorer people who opted for satellite television and that the dishes were mushrooming up in Britain's council (public housing) estates rather than in its leafy suburbs. Because such an image could deter advertisers, Rupert Murdoch's Sky Channel began a campaign, claiming that it was not just 'council-house television' (Morley, 1995: 187). Is the equation of satellite television consumption with low social status a fact or a mythology? One way to find this out would be through expensive survey research. An easier way is simply to go out and look for the dishes. The exercise works as follows. Select a lower socio-economic status (SES), a middle SES and an affluent SES neighbourhood in a nearby town or city, preferably one consisting of separate dwellings. Using a street index randomly select a sample of streets from each suburb. Walk along each street counting the number of satellite dishes and the number of dwellings. Divide the number of dishes into the number of dwellings to get a satellite-dish ratio for each of the sampled streets. Compare the ratios over the various kinds of suburbs. If you like you can use some simple statistics to see if the differences between neighbourhoods are statistically significant.

Note: In some countries cable television has become more popular than satellite. If cable connections have been strung onto existing phone lines or power lines it is still possible to conduct the same exercise. Where they run underground this project might be impossible to conduct. Back in the 1950s, one could have undertaken a similar exercise to find out who had a television by looking for antenna on the roof of the house.

Pictures and photographs Pictures and photographs are, like television, usually treated as 'texts' which have to be read by art historians and cultural studies scholars. They can, however, be looked at in a much more matter of fact way by shifting the focus from decoding 'hidden' content and reading them as a text, to looking at manifest themes and also exploring the

BOX 4.4   THE TELEVISION AS ICON PROJECT

The differential uptake of satellite television in the UK suggests that there are class divergences in attitudes to television. It has often been suggested that working-class orientations to television are different from those of the middle class. One way to explore this issue is by looking at the physical location of the television. In a study of television in Brazil, Leal (1990) observed that working-class Brazilians saw the television as a status marker and as an indicator of having 'arrived' as a member of a modern society. They tended to position it at the focal point of the living room, and in a position where it could be seen from the street. By contrast, middle-class Brazilians tended to locate the television in less visible locations, perhaps because it is associated with populist entertainment. For the middle classes, then, television is a kind of guilty pleasure of which one should be ashamed. Is this also the case in other countries? One way to find out is to visit various living rooms and see. Because gaining access to people's houses is difficult, and may be dangerous, we suggest using a snowball sampling technique. Start with a friend or relative and ask them to nominate other participants, and so on. As people become less familiar to you, you may need to make a preparatory phone call before you visit. Make an estimate of the size of the television, whether there is a surround-sound system with large speakers etc. As an indicator of SES, make an estimate of the value of the house. If the situation Leal describes pertains, then there should be a negative correlation between SES and the conspicuousness of the television. Middle classes might be expected to have a small and discrete set, whilst the less affluent can be expected to have a large set with visible home-theatre 'extras'.

Note: If you wish, you can conduct follow-up interviews in order to determine things like viewing patterns and attitudes to television. This will add depth to the study. The other themes noted by Morley in the list above might also provide the basis for investigations of a similar nature.

social and spatial correlates of their display. A project by David Halle (1993) exemplifies this possibility. In his study of New York housing Halle explored interior decoration in houses of upper, middle and lower classes. One of his most striking findings was that across all groups the landscape was by far the most common form of picture, making up around one third of all pictures prominently displayed on walls, outnumbering even pictures and photographs of family members. In terms of content the pictures overwhelmingly depicted calm and tranquil settings. Rarely could one detect a snowstorm blowing, a volcano erupting, or a river rampaging through rapids. When questioned respondents said they liked pictures which made them feel calm and tranquil. Halle argues the such pictures reflect a contemporary orientation to nature as a domain of leisure, and of the home as an escape from the busy outside world. Another feature of the pictures was that they rarely included people, unless they were of past settings. This again reflects a set of cultural beliefs which suggest that the enjoyment of nature is at its best when it is a private experience. Whilst there were these commonalities across classes, Halle detected some differences between groups. Higher-status households were more likely than lower-status households to have pictures which depicted the past and which depicted foreign settings.

Halle also looked at photographs in houses. The vast majority of these were of family members. Photographs of non-kin were extremely rare. Photographs were also overwhelmingly informal in terms of composition, setting and clothing. Whereas a couple of generations ago most photographs would have been taken on a special occasion by a photographer, Halle found that casual family snapshots were most likely to be displayed. Often these were clustered together on crowded mantelpieces or pinned on boards in a montage. There was, however, an apparent taboo on large, portrait photographs of the adults in the house, reflecting a belief that to display a picture of oneself on one's own wall would be egotistical. According to Halle, the content of these photos reflected wider social shifts. They mirrored the rise of informality and privacy in American social life. Halle's work, then, suggests that pictures and photographs can

---

BOX 4.5   PICTURES AND PHOTOS IN HOUSES PROJECT

A possible limitation of Halle's study is that it was conducted in one part of the United States, for the most part in 'typical' family dwellings. Whilst this allowed him to make close comparisons of class differences, it did not permit him to look at other issues. Interesting questions remain about the generalizability of his findings to other settings. Identify either a non-Anglo ethnic group or a non-traditional household (e.g. student share housing). Use a snowball sample to recruit new participants. This means starting with people you know and asking them to nominate others. Some softening up by phone or letter may be required before you visit strangers. As you visit each house make a list of the themes of each picture and its location in the house. Are the patterns of picture and photo use the same as among Halle's New Yorkers? In what respects do they differ? Why might this be? What can you conclude about the significance of Halle's results? Do they tap into a global trend or just a provincial taste in one part of the United States?

be used to explore shifts in ideology about the meanings of the family and self.

The museum

Foucault's (1973, 1979) work suggests that in institutional environments we will find visual traces of power and discourse. Whilst this work is most obviously relevant to built environments, and will be discussed in more length in the next chapter, it has applications also to the analysis of ma-terial culture and its display. In this section we are particularly concerned with the semiotic analysis of objects and the ways they can be 'decoded' much as 2D texts can be. Museums provide an excellent venue for this kind of project. They consist of objects of some purported significance which have been purposively arranged and displayed in order to convey information. Thinking about why certain objects have been selected and which cultural meanings are embodied in the process of display can provide a wonderful resource for small-scale visual research.

Henrietta Lidchi (1997: 159) suggests there are several significant features to museums.

- *Representation* refers to the claims of the museum to reflect some larger order of phenomena in microcosm.
- *Classification* deals with the way that the museum divides its exhibits into distinctive themes, topics or classes of objects.
- *Motivation* refers to the purpose of the museum. Aside from the preservation of artefacts, this usually includes educating and informing a wider public.
- *Interpretation* is the function of museums to provide a coherent understanding of the purpose of its exhibits and to place them within a broader framework of meaning.

According to Lidchi, museum displays are about ideas as much as objects and can therefore be read or 'decoded' by the sociologist. By looking at the display of exhibits of an ethnographic museum, for example, we are able to learn a good deal about the various discursive frameworks which are at work, not so much in the society represented, as in the society doing the representing. She illustrates this theme with a discussion of the role of ethnographic artefacts and how this has changed over time. Pitt Rivers was a Victorian collector of archaeological and ethnographic items who subscribed to the hierarchical and evolutionary views of his time on the rise of 'civilization'. These suggested that more complex and 'superior' cultures had emerged from primitive peoples. Artefacts were therefore exhibited according to type (like animal species) and in ways which indicated increasing sophistication of design (like animal evolution). There might be a display on weapons, for example, which started with stone spears, knives and clubs and 'worked its way up' through bows and arrows to muskets and machine guns. This form of display was designed to allow ordinary Victorians to understand the process of social evolution and to read the location of their own society at its pinnacle. In particular, it allows us to understand the complex discursive formation involving science, evolutionary theory and colonialism that was at play in Victorian England.

In Chapter 2 we mentioned that concerns have been expressed about sociological photography as a form of surveillance and as a tool of power. As they are also involved in the process of social representation, it is no surprise that museums have also been subject to this kind of attack (Bennett, 1995). Ethnographic museums in particular have become very aware of criticisms that their forms of representation contain hidden bias and that they privilege the views of powerful groups (Clifford, 1995; Lidchi, 1997). They have also become very sensitive to claims of cultural and scientific imperialism and grave robbing. They have responded by changing some of their display procedures. Results have included:

- displays and exhibitions seeking to record and validate the material culture and life experiences of forgotten groups (e.g. display on women's lives)
- attempts to foreground the process of constructing an exhibit (e.g. a panel in which the curator explains the process of selecting items for display)
- greater attention to the political contexts (e.g. discussions of the detrimental impacts of colonialism, multinationals, genocide on a particular tribal people)
- efforts at cultural relativism (e.g. Coca-Cola cans displayed next to a traditional drinking vessel. Accompanying description draws parallels between them: 'Both are powerful symbols in their own society')
- pointing out the positive role of the museum in preserving cultural heritage (e.g. photos of museum staff working alongside indigenous people) rather than appropriating it.

To sum up, objects in museums, the patterns in which they are displayed and the discursive contexts in which they are placed have changed over time. Whilst ethnographic displays in Victorian museums reflected Darwinian ideas of progress, these ideas are now discredited. In many cases ethnographic museums displays now embody the kinds of discourses associated with postcolonial critical theory.

As the exercise in Box 4.6. demonstrates, public institutions can provide excellent research sites for visual researchers interested in exploring power, ideology and discourses through the analysis of displays, pictures and texts. Whilst museums seem to have attracted a good deal of attention in this postcolonial era, there are a number of other locations worth thinking about. Churches, town halls, national park centres, sports clubs,

BOX 4.6   ETHNOGRAPHIC MUSEUMS PROJECT

Visit a museum with ethnographic exhibits. Code any of the devices identified above as you observe them. In order to work out the kinds of impacts these displays are having, loiter near the exhibit (try to look like just another visitor). Using a notebook, collect qualitative information on the response of the public. What kinds of remarks do they make to each other? Do they seem to take an interest in the 'new' spin or do they tend to skip over these aspects of the exhibit? Are they more interested in the purely 'exotic' artefacts or in educational discussions on, say, Third World politics? You could also try noting the amount of time they spend at each display panel or area. Look also for age, ethnic and gender differences. What are you able to conclude about the success of the museum's policy in terms of the concepts of motivation and interpretation?

universities, art galleries, etc. will often have displays documenting their perceived role in society. These can be 'decoded' in much the same ways as museum exhibits. Which groups are represented in the displays and which are absent? How have new ideas and responses to the discourses of what is pejoratively called 'political correctness' been incorporated into photographs, models and mission statements? To what extent does the organization seem postmodern (like some museums) in its ability to question its own traditional *raison d'être*?

Statues and memorials

Statues and memorials provide one of the best resources for visual researchers interested in exploring the intersections of semiotics, power and ideology with material culture. This is because they are deliberately created to convey messages, often by dominant groups in society. Decoding these messages is an important sociological task, and one that can be done using similar conceptual resources to those used to study advertisements, paintings and other 2D data. Because they are displayed in public settings, statues and monuments provide a convenient and accessible resource for such activity (see Figure 4.1). This location, moreover, allows us to conduct observational studies which explore how people respond to them and what they might therefore mean. It is also worth remembering that many public monuments, memorials and statues are (literally) 'dated'. Thus, they can be used to index changes over time in cultural values and beliefs. Before proceeding to consider issues of codes and action it is worth remembering that statues can support more positivistic, less interpretive sociologies. This is demonstrated in the exercise in Box 4.7.

(a)

(b)

FIGURE 4.1   *Statues and monuments as indicators of social and cultural processes. These statues and monuments were all photographed in the Brisbane central city area and can be assumed to represent the values and priorities of Australian civic culture. Photo (a) depicts a tableau embodying many discourses of Australia's colonial past. The pioneer Andrew Petrie is being farewelled by his devoted wife and family as he departs on horseback on one of his explorations. His youngest son Tom is shown happily playing with Aboriginal children whilst the scene is being observed by an ex-convict whom Petrie had nobly freed. From a critical perspective it might be argued that the tableau endorses the patriarchal family and trivializes the oppression of*

(c)

(d)

Aborigines and convicts. Photo (b) celebrates the iconography of the rugged Australian male and the bonds of egalitarian mateship as the men chat around the camp fire. Women – other than monarchs – rarely have monuments dedicated to them. Where they do, as in photo (f) of pioneer trade unionist Emma Miller, the statues are in more peripheral locations – in this case the edge of a flower bed. Interactions with statues can also tell us something about the priorities of the general public. For example the kangaroo family (photo c) provides a popular photo-opportunity for locals and international visitors alike (photos d and e). By contrast, in the course of several visits to the city centre, we have yet to observe anyone being photographed with Emma Miller.

(e)

(f)

BOX 4.7   GENDER BIAS AND THE STATUE PROJECT

Feminists have long argued that the public sphere has been dominated by men and that women have been marginalized. Statues provide a way of testing this assertion. If feminist theory is correct, we would expect statues of men to outnumber those of women in public memorials. Using a city or town map, mark out the defined area of what you consider to be the city centre. Systematically survey the streets and squares in the area. Code the number of males and females in statues. If possible note who they are of (politician, military, etc.) and when they were constructed or dedicated. What are you able to conclude about:

1.   male dominance of the public sphere.
2.   the kinds of male who are considered 'important' in our society
3.   changes over time in the proportions of men and women who are commemorated.

Decoding and observing statues   Semiotic and observational studies provide one of the best ways of understanding monuments when they are used in combination. The study of the Vietnam Veterans' Memorial in Washington DC by Robin Wagner-Pacifici and Barry Schwartz (1991) provides an example of this kind of approach. For America, the Vietnam War was not only a controversial event, but also a defeat. Wagner-Pacifici and Schwartz argue this is reflected in the semiotics and phenomenology of the memorial. Instead of the usual heroic monument above ground, the Vietnam memorial is below ground. It consists of 'two unadorned black walls, each about 250 feet in length, composed of 70 granite panels increasing in height from several inches at the end of each wall to 10 feet, where they come together at a 125 degree angle ... the walls themselves are placed below ground level, invisible from most vantage points. . .' (1991: 393). Wagner-Pacifici and Schwartz interpret this design as drawing the viewer into a separate warp of time and space. In other words, the design of the monument works to cut people off from everyday life. They also see the wall as embodying 'femininity' with its 'womblike embrace of the visitor' and as challenging traditional masculine notions of the 'phallic' statue. Moreover, the design focused attention on the individuals who lost their lives rather than on their (tarnished) cause.

Protests about the wall came from veterans and others. They saw the list of names as like a list of traffic accident victims. They interpreted the black granite and the lack of traditional memorial referents as insulting and unpatriotic. Subsequently a flag and a realist statue of three soldiers were incorporated into the complex. Here again, however, we can detect ambivalence about the war. The statue shows soldiers who 'appear disoriented ... exhausted and confused'. The flag pole is conventional enough, but an inscription at its foot speaks of the pride of the soldiers in 'having fought in difficult circumstances'. This is an oblique acknowledgment of the controversial and morally contested nature of the war. The Vietnam Veterans' Memorial, then, can be decoded or read. It can be explored for themes and contradictions between themes. Wagner-Pacifici and Schwartz argue that one way to think about memorials is in terms of the genre they represent. A war memorial, for example, can be heroic or tragic. The Vietnam Veterans' Memorial seems to fall between both genre stools. Its semiotics is ambivalent, reflecting the multiple and contested meanings that people made of the war itself.

An instructive feature of Wagner-Pacifici and Schwartz's methodology is that they go beyond this semiotic level of analysis to look at how people responded to the memorial. Despite initial controversy and semiotic ambiguity, the memorial has proved to be incredibly popular. Many visitors leave behind a form of visual data: souvenirs and mementos. These are collected each day and stored in the Museum and Archaeological Regional Storage Facility. The most popular of these are small American flags set in the ground near the name that the visitor wishes to commemorate. Just behind these in terms of popularity are military souvenirs like badges, dog-tags, etc. This suggests that visitors were responding to the wall in traditional ways. Whilst it had been designed as an apolitical memorial to personal loss, its users wished it to be a conventional shrine. They wanted the fallen represented as genuine patriots, not as sad failures.

The case of the Vietnam Veterans' Memorial suggests the utility of a two-step approach to the visual analysis of memorials. First, semiotic decoding, second the analysis of how people interact with them. Whilst cultural studies work has a long history of research on the first dimension, the uses of monuments and statues have been less thoroughly explored. Perhaps future trends in memorials will bring attention to this neglected site of visual data. Whilst traditional memorials and statues were intended to be looked at with awe and reverence, more recently attempts have been made to stimulate interaction and intimacy. An example is the statue unveiled in 1998 near London's Trafalgar Square to celebrate gay writer Oscar Wilde. The statue is a granite slab in the form of a sarcophagus. It shows Wilde in a reclining position and 'invites passers-by to sit on it and engage in conversation with Wilde's bronze head and hands' (*The Times*, 1 December 1998). We may assume that if this sort of action takes place, then the statue is of some interest to contemporary people, and, indeed, that they feel some kinship or affiliation with Wilde. By observing interactions with the statue we could, then, make inferences about the acceptability of gay-ness in contemporary London.

One need not study monuments that are designed, like Wilde's, to foster interaction in order to explore this dimension. One may visit cemeteries where the famous are buried like Highgate Hill (Karl Marx), Forest Lawn

BOX 4.8   INTERACTION WITH STATUES EXERCISE

Return to the statues you identified in the previous assignment. Conduct observation at a number of them for specified time periods. Just sit near each statue and pretend to be reading the paper.

- What kinds of interaction do you observe (e.g. photograph taking, climbing, discussion)?
- Do certain statue-topics seem to generate more interaction than others (e.g. animals vs humans vs abstract)?
- To what extent does the design, setting and scale of the statue seem to influence interaction?
- Which types of people interact with which kinds of statues (e.g. adults vs children)?
- What, if anything, are you able to conclude about public interaction with statues? Does the semiotics or political message of the statue play a role, or do convenience and curiosity seem to be more significant factors?
- How do you classify the interactions (e.g. playful vs solemn)?

(various Hollywood Stars) and Père Lachaise (Jim Morrison, Oscar Wilde, the Communards) and look for fresh flowers or graffiti as a sign of endorsement. On a recent visit to a Paris cemetery one of the authors of this book visited the grave of August Comte and found no flowers or cards. What does this say about current interest in the founder of sociology! The project in Box 4.8 takes up this sort of theme, and explores interactions with statues and monuments.

The cemetery

Studies of cultural consumption and of personalization suggest that identity is fundamental to the way we relate to material objects. Our identities are inscribed upon the objects we surround ourselves with. The inscription of identity can also take place literally at our next research site – the cemetery. Cemeteries can provide an underutilized and unobtrusive measure of various social processes. We can, of course, classify grave stones in various ways. Materials (marble, sandstone etc.), decoration (plain, with pictures), forms of writing (gothic, roman), complexity (vaults, railings). These sorts of features allow Anthony Synnott (1985) to claim that social divisions persist in death as in life. In his analysis of Montreal cemeteries, Synnott points to several ways in which cemetery organization can be read as reflecting wider social organization. Synnott found the following.

- Religious divisions separated the dead. Jews were buried in the Jewish cemetery, Catholics in the Catholic cemetery and Protestants in the Protestant cemetery.
- There were class distinctions among the dead. A number of features worked to reinforce these, including plot sizes, plot location, and monuments. The affluent tended to have elaborate mausoleums with brass doors, the middle classes statues, and the lower classes more simple grave stones. The welfare poor were buried in public cemeteries in unmarked graves. In general, affluent people were buried on top of hills, with poorer people in the dips and valleys.
- Ethnic distinctions could also be found. Chinese tended to be buried in one zone of the Protestant cemetery and Ukrainians in a large plot in the Catholic one. Many tombs were decorated in particular ethnic styles. The Irish, for example, might have a Celtic cross on their grave.

Synnott's analysis is largely descriptive. However, the kinds of features he identifies can be used to explore wider sociological themes than one might at first expect. Consider the project described in Box 4.9, which raises a host of possible issues for tombstone research.

Customizing anonymity: cars and houses

We live in a world where the vast majority of objects are mass-produced. The dominant perspective for approaching this fact in sociology has been critical theory. Writing in the 1930s Walter Benjamin (1973) commented on the alienating qualities of 'mechanical reproduction'. A few years later his Frankfurt School colleagues Theodore Adorno and Max Horkheimer (1979 [1947]) attacked the 'culture industries', which they saw as producing standardized products (e.g. movies, popular music) aimed at the lowest common denominator. In the 1960s critical theorists like Herbert Marcuse (1968) spoke plaintively of the capacity of consumer goods to produce passive, shallow citizens – a 'one dimensional man' – obsessed with the acquisition of stereos, washing machines and automobiles. This all sounds very bleak. Yet when we look at ethnographic research we find that people are not simply recipients of mass-produced goods, they are also modifiers. A number of studies have pointed to the ways in which impersonal objects are adapted to express individuality or community.

Theoretical discussions of standardization, along with analyses of mass production, have often used motor vehicles as the paradigm exemplar of the anonymous consumer good. Henry Ford's Model T, in particular, was famously said to have been available in any colour, so long as it was black. Sociological discussions on the meanings of vehicles suggest that whilst they may be produced in uniform, rational ways, their consumption is often marked by efforts at 'personalization'. This concept refers to the ways in which people adapt their environment to suit their own needs and desires. In his study of motor bike gangs Paul Willis (1978) looked at the symbolic meanings of the bike. He pointed to the ways that bikes had been

BOX 4.9   ETHNIC GRAVES PROJECT

This project uses gravestones as an unobtrusive measure of ethnic integration. Theories of assimilation suggest that, over time, ethnic ties become weaker. Whilst first-generation migrants might hold strongly to their traditional culture, second- and third-generation migrants slowly shed ethnic identification and feel they are members of their host nation. Is this the case? One way to find out is to study tombstones. First conduct some library research to identify ethnic groups which are likely to have migrated to your area. Try to form some estimate of the date of first arrival *en masse*. Select a local cemetery and see if you can detect evidence of a significant number of burials for this group. Names on gravestones and biographical information will help (e.g. 'Luigi Baldini, Born Rome 1910, Died Melbourne 1950') as might inscriptions in the language of the group you have chosen. If there appear to be a number of burials, proceed to the next stage. Draw a sketch map of the cemetery and locate on it the site of the graves which you can identify as belonging to your chosen ethnic group. Colour code each grave site according to decade (e.g. 1950s blue, 1960s red, 1970s green). When you have finished look at the distribution of the graves for each decade. According to assimilation theory, there should be a trend towards dispersal. Just as ethnic groups move out of housing ghettos, we might expect ethnic graves to be increasingly dispersed among the general population of graves.

Notes: (1) This project might work less well when the migrant group has its own cemeteries. This is often the case if they have a distinctive religion. It works best when the migrant group shares a religion with a significant proportion of the host population. Catholic cemeteries are therefore often best for the exercise. (2) You can back up your argument with further measures of assimilation. A shift away from native language towards host language on gravestones would be one indicator. (3) You can extend the project by comparing the dispersal and assimilation patterns for more than one group, or by looking at rates of dispersal for nineteenth-century migrant groups as opposed to twentieth-century migrant groups. (4) Some commentators argue that we are seeing ethnic revivals. This means that people are rediscovering their ethnic 'roots'. Is there any evidence for this in your study? Are tombs from the 1980s, for example, more likely than those of the 1970s to have distinctive 'ethnic' features? (5) Another project along similar lines to this one might look for changes in sexism or family orientation. One could count and date inscriptions along the lines of 'Jane Doe, beloved wife of John Doe'. These identify women in terms of their relationship with a man. It would be interesting to see if these have declined over time. One could also compare these sorts of inscriptions across religious denominations. Are Catholics more 'sexist' than Protestants?

customized to fit the self-image of the rider and the collective identity of the gang. Leather tooling, laid-back seats, suspension and noisy exhausts made the bike as mean, masculine and threatening as possible. Studies of Mexican-Americans have drawn attention to the 'low rider' cars favoured by younger urban males. Such cars are typically large American models with expensive paint jobs, chrome wheels, massively powerful sound systems and 'hydraulics'. This last term refers to suspension which can be raised or lowered through the operation of pumps, allowing the body of the car to appear to jump. Such cars are typically used for display and the acquisition of prestige among peer groups rather than routine transportation (Cintron, 1997). According to criminologist Jack Katz (1988: 91–2), such vehicles can be read as reflecting the distinctive outlook and personality of their *cholo* owners.

> The low position of the cholo's aristocratic squat is repeated in the automobile esthetic of the low rider. By altering stock shocks and springs, cholos make cars ride literally low. . . . The overall effect is less an approximation of the advertised modern man in an up-to-date car than a fantasy image of a prince in a horse-drawn chariot, sometimes racing each other.

Analyses like these are in a similar vein to that of Barthes on the New Citroen, with which we started this chapter. However, there is a crucial difference. Barthes was concerned with decoding of the motor vehicle itself and tracing its links to bourgeois mass culture. The literature on customization, by contrast, tends to see the object as a tool with which to understand the owner, their creative activity and their (often deviant) value system.

Another arena for personalization is the home. In the contemporary world, relatively few people live in unique, architect-designed residences. Most people inhabit relatively uniform houses and apartments in developments and estates. Distinguishing oneself from one's neighbours and creating a sense of identity is important for most dwellers. Miller (1988) looked at residents in a public housing project and the ways in which they had transformed their kitchens. This could involve anything from hanging a few pictures and tea towels, to repainting to complete remodelling. Whilst class was more-or-less a constant on the estate, Miller detected ethnic and age differences in preferences for kitchen modification. It is a worthwhile project to replicate Miller's work in another setting (see Box 4.11).

An issue you may confront with projects which look at people's homes is the question of privacy. In order to collect data you have to intrude into people's lives. Some respondents might find your presence threatening. They may feel you are there to question or mock their taste. In conducting his own research on the home and its decoration, Riggins (1994: 102) found that his inquiry 'put the self-esteem of informants in jeopardy because of the intimate link which exists between the self and domestic objects. Any questions bearing on the latter are too easily construed as a questioning of

BOX 4.10   CUSTOMIZED-CARS EXERCISE

Studies of vehicles, like the ones mentioned above, have typically explored the spectacular modifications that are used to demonstrate subcultural membership. Most people, however, drive around in cars that look perfectly standard. Is this really the case? Detailed inspection will usually reveal some efforts at personalization. The most common include: stickers, upgraded stereos, after-market alloy wheels, seat covers, window tinting, sports steering wheels, etc. Are these efforts at personalization free-floating, or are they anchored in some kind of demographic?

Stickers provide perhaps the best item of data to explore. Since they are inexpensive, everyone can potentially use them to customize their cars. Moreover, you do not need expert knowledge to work out if they came from the factory or are an after-market addition, as can be the case with alloy wheels, stereos, etc. Select two or more shopping centres or car parks in areas which attract divergent class or ethnic dynamics. Sample about 100–200 cars in each. Walk around each car in turn looking for stickers. Make a note of each sticker, excluding ones supplied by the car dealer. Be certain to keep a tally of the cars without stickers as well. After completing the sample, devise a typology and classify each sticker into a type. Classes of sticker might include the political (e.g. Gore for President), the humorous (e.g. The Simpsons), affiliation with a club, school or college (e.g. Ridale High School), musical (e.g. Radio 4QR), personal names (e.g. the apocryphal Kevin and Tracey sun strip on the windshield), sports (e.g. Manchester United), the ecological (e.g. Save the Whale). You may well find other ways to divide up your data. Information on car age and car type might provide further clues as to the social location of the driver. A new BMW, for example, is probably owned by someone who thinks of themselves as cosmopolitan and fashionable. An old van, by contrast, is likely to be owned by a less affluent trades-person. Look for significant differences between your two samples not only in terms of the number of stickers, but also the themes they cover. Which population seems to be most attracted to personalization? What kinds of inferences can you make about the interests and concerns of each group that shape their personalization efforts? Who seems to be 'resisting' anonymous consumerism the most?

the former's social status and personal life.' In a recent tutorial in an introductory sociology subject, we found something similar. We asked students to classify activities and preferences into high and low cultural capital. Many of them were outraged when the tutorial group as a whole classed

BOX 4.11   MODIFIED-KITCHENS PROJECT

Identify a recent housing development or block of units where it is likely that standardized kitchens have been provided and where you know at least one person. Using a snowball sampling technique, try to get access to as many kitchens as possible. Ask a few basic questions about age, occupation, etc. of the occupants so you can build up a simple demographic profile.

Which demographics prefer which personalization techniques? Why did they make the choices they did? In order to produce more-interesting results, it may be a good idea to pick a research site with mixed ethnicity.

If you wish, a similar project can be developed looking at household appliances. Most of these come in standard black, white or silver boxes. Many of these are modified. On a fridge we might find postcards, magnets, or pictures. The television, as we mentioned earlier, might serve as a photo, plant or Christmas card stand. What kinds of changes can you detect? Who likes to modify these items of consumer culture? What kinds of conclusions can you reach about the ability of mass production to generate mass conformity in consumption?

Note: In order to conduct this project at a thesis level, it may be necessary to have a more rigorous sampling frame. Past experience suggests that a process of softening up is required to get access to homes in this way. Request letters on university letterhead signed by a professor are one way of improving response rates. A snowball sample is, however, convenient and should be sufficient for a small-scale pilot.

their favourite rock band or hobby as 'low cultural capital'. So be careful what you say and stress that you are not being judgemental.

If you feel uncomfortable dealing with people and entering their homes, all is not lost if you wish to explore modifications to the dwelling. If you look at the outside of the house you may well be able to conduct a quiet and covert study, taking advantage of the ability of 3D data to offer unobtrusive measures for visual inquiry. Windows and doors, paint schemes and renderings, ponds and plants, ornaments and gnomes can all be used to express individuality in the exterior of a property that faces the street.

Wear, tear and rubbish

As we noted back in Chapter 2, photographs often provide an excellent 'unobtrusive' or 'non-reactive' measure of social process. Perhaps the best

BOX 4.12   HOME EXTERIOR MODIFICATIONS PROJECT

Select streets in two contrasting areas and tally the kinds of changes you detect. Because changes in older property can often arise simply from wear and tear, try to choose newer housing developments where changes to the built fabric are most likely to be non-functional. In some cases building codes and residents' associations can limit the kinds of changes that people make. Mission Viejo in California is often studied by postmodern sociologists as an example of a community which revolves around a Spanish Mission theme. This up-market, suburban development has strict guidelines about design (must be Spanish in style) paint colours (must be white, pastel, etc.). Such places provide a challenging environment for the would-be personalizer. If you are able to locate such a place, it should afford an excellent location for detecting the subtle ways that people make a house into a home.

such measures, however, are not photographs. In some cases past behaviours by people leave behind them physical evidence which can be used as the basis for sociological deductions. Sometimes this evidence might be left behind deliberately, as is the case with graffiti, at other times it might be unintentional. Studies of traces and accretions focus on this latter type of data and use it to make inferences about human behaviour. According to Webb et al. (1966: 35) in their now classic text on unobtrusive measures, 'physical evidence is probably the social scientist's least-used source of data, yet because of its ubiquity, it holds flexible and broad-gauged potential'. Webb et al. distinguish two general types of physical evidence or traces. *Erosion measures* try to identify wear and tear on materials. As this chapter exemplifies, we tend to think of the study of objects as the study of things. The study of erosion measures reverses this. Instead of looking at what is there, we can look at what is not there. Specifically what has been worn away, scratched or polished by use. Take a look around any old building, such as a church or town hall, and you should be able to locate erosion measures like the following.

- Stairs are worn into a concave shape, due to millions of feet eroding the material at the centre.
- Door handles and stair rails have been polished by thousands of hands.
- Ceramics in the toilets will have been worn and stained by thousands of gallons of urine.
- Key holes will be scratched as keys are scraped around in search of the lock.

Accretion measures are deposits of material that have built up over time as a result of human activity. It seems to be rather harder to think of accretion measures than erosion measures. By far the most frequently used accretion measure in sociological research is garbage. Traces like these provide a wonderful unobtrusive measure of use. Archaeologists in particular are skilled in using traces to make deductions about life in past societies. For example, a worn kerbstone might allow some kind of inference to be drawn about the volume of traffic on a Roman road. An Ancient Egyptian knife that is barely used might have been ceremonial, or intended for display rather than for day-to-day use. Making use of traces and accretions in this way is often likened to the work of a detective attempting to make sense of what has gone on at a murder scene from the various bits of physical evidence that remain.

Traces can be looked for on a remarkable variety of research materials, including movable objects. Second hand cars, for example, are often 'clocked'. This means that an unscrupulous dealer will wind back the odometer and fool the customer into thinking they are buying a car with less mileage than it really has. If you think this might happen to you, then a study of traces could be of use. Indicators of wear can include pedal rubbers, carpets, the driver's seat cloth, scratches, dents, sagging door hinges and sun-faded paint. Whilst seat covers and floor mats might have been used in the past, and body and paintwork can be fixed up, pedal rubbers are almost never changed. So beware pedal rubbers which don't match mileage!

The used-car example should alert you to one other problem with traces. This is that they can often provide only a minimal indication of use. When items are replaced (e.g. tyres) signs of previous use might be obliterated. When they are repaired (e.g. dents) it can often be difficult to detect the trace, although such evidence (if visible) is an excellent sign of use. When protected (e.g. the floor mats) true levels of wear will be under-recorded. It is important to bear these possibilities in mind when

BOX 4.13   THE USED-CAR EXERCISE

This exercise is of limited sociological value, but might save you from getting ripped off and is a good party trick. Arrange to see a number of cars belonging to friends, neighbours and relatives. Using a ruler, estimate the amount of wear on the pedal rubbers and make a note of the mileage. Usually sample on the edge nearest the gas pedal, as it's here that most people press. Try to develop an indication of how many thousand miles are required to create a millimetre of wear. To evaluate your measure, test yourself on cars whose mileage you don't know. Once you are confident in your ability, amaze your friends at a party. After placing a bet, have them cover up the odometer while you pretend to inspect the car using 'psychic forces'.

evaluating evidence from trace studies, especially those involving the built environment.

Webb et al. (1966) and Alan Kazdin (1979) provide a number of further examples of how useful erosion and other unobtrusive measures can be. The following suggestions are adapted from their text. Because these all deal with physical traces, issues of meaning and interpretation can be put to the side. Whilst commonly discussed as 'qualitative methodologies', these sorts of projects really work best when simple counts or scales are used to provide a more objective level of wear and tear. If necessary, follow-up interviews and observation can be used to address issues of 'why?' and 'who?' which are difficult to tap with a purely observational study of this kind of data.

- At the Chicago Museum of Science and Industry the floor tiles around an exhibit of live and hatching chicks needed replacing every six weeks. The tiles normally lasted for years in other parts of the museum. Webb et al. suggest that through such a measure we could test the hypothesis that 'dynamic exhibits draw more viewers than static ones' (1966: 37). In order to test this sort of proposition one would simply need to compare the amount of tile wear around the two classes of exhibit.
- The wear on library books affords a measure of their popularity. In order to validate this measure, wear could be compared with the library records of withdrawals. Obviously, older books would have more wear, so age would need to be taken into account in developing your measure. It is also possible to look for signs of use in individual pages. Books in university libraries often contain underlined passages where students have (illegally) marked sections they consider useful for study. Other sections of texts also seem to attract more attention than one might expect. When one of the authors of this book was undertaking his anthropology degree he noted that, in ethnographies by classical anthropologists like Malinowski, sections dealing with sex and sexual life to be more worn than others. The implication would seem to be that students had taken rather more interest in the sexual practices of 'exotic' peoples than in their kinship systems! Social science encyclopedias (and others) offer an opportunity to study which topics and thinkers are 'hot' and which are 'not'. Whilst it is difficult to evaluate absolute levels of interest, it should be possible to trace the relative impact of theories. One could compare, for example, interest in 'Foucault' with interest in 'Habermas' to work out who is winning the battle of ideas at a particular institution. If it is possible to locate older copies of encyclopedias which have been shelved and are rarely used, one could then think about establishing a longitudinal data set. If entries on 'functionalism' are dirty and thumbed in the 1950s encyclopedia but clean in the 1990s encyclopedia, one might be

able to make some conclusions about the rise and fall of a particular social theory.

- Car radios are usually tuned to stations. By switching on the radio, one knows who has been listening to what. During the 1950s garage mechanics were enlisted to supply audience data by this means. Whilst more sophisticated measures are now available, this still provides a potential measure for the low-budget researcher. Webb et al. suggest looking at the dials of parked cars in your local shopping centre. This might prove ineffective given the widespread use of digital radios in cars today. An alternative method might be to enlist the help of a local hire car agency. You could provide them with your research findings so they might know where to advertise!

- Another project involving cars could look to see who is security conscious and who is not. One study showed that cars outside men's university dorms were more likely than those outside women's dorms to be left unlocked. The conclusion is that men seem to be less safety conscious than women. This study can be replicated by looking for steering wheel locks in different locations. Again, shopping centres in affluent and poor areas would provide one research avenue. But be careful you are not mistaken for a thief!

- The amount of interaction between people in certain locations can be traced by looking at the number of cigarette butts in the ashtray or on the floor, or exploring the amount of coffee consumed. Volumes of litter might also perform the same function. Contact between inmates of an institution and the outside world can be traced by looking at the volume of mail each receives.

Rubbish offers perhaps the best form of accretion data. There is a lengthy history of rubbish being used to gather information on consumption. Archaeologists have long had an enthusiasm for middens (ancient garbage heaps). From the contents of the midden we can work out what people ate in the past. From this we can sometimes make deductions about social structure. For example, to kill some animals, like the mammoth, collective hunting strategies would have been needed. If we find mammoth bones on the midden, this allows us to make certain deductions about the complexity of social organization in a prehistoric population, or perhaps its ability to use language to coordinate a hunting strategy. Rubbish research has a dedicated following in sociology too. People are generally careless with what they throw away, but careful about what they keep. As a result, things that are deliberately preserved are often doctored or edited to create the right impression rather like a memoir. Rubbish, on the other hand, is assumed to be of no interest to anyone. By looking at rubbish, therefore, we can often get a better idea of what is going on than by talking to people. These points are made clear in the case of alcohol research.

Research on alcohol consumption normally makes use of either surveys or diaries. These research methods are flawed. Participants in a study might be tempted to minimize their reported consumption in the search for social approval. They might forget to fill in the diary, or, in the case of the survey, have little idea when answering the question 'On average how many beers have you drunk over the last month?' (Can you answer this question accurately? Unless you are teetotal, how do you know you remember accurately?) An alternative approach is to look for physical signs of alcohol use. Rummaging through rubbish bins for beer, wine and spirit bottles provides an alternative measure of alcohol consumption at the community level (Webb et al., 1966: 41). According to Rathje (1979) an analysis of garbage shows that interview-survey data on beer consumption consistently underestimates true levels of consumption. Low-income households were prone to non-reporting and middle-income households to under-reporting. The project described in Box 4.14, which suits people who like getting dirty and smelly, builds on this sort of finding.

Graffiti

Graffiti forms a special kind of residue. It is something that people leave behind, yes. But, unlike other kinds of trace or residue, this is done consciously and intentionally with the hope that others will encounter it. Messages are encoded into graffiti using text or drawings. Graffiti is also, in some ways, a form of 2D data. It is a form of communication consisting of an image on a (usually) flat surface. In some ways it is also a property of places and spaces. It never exists on the page, but rather in particular spatial contexts. Consequently, we were uncertain whether put graffiti in this chapter or the previous one or the next. We eventually chose to treat graffiti as a 3D form of data because it exists *in situ* on objects. Locating and studying graffiti usually means moving beyond the library and the printed page, and engaging with the world of material objects. The physical location of the graffiti is important in understanding its context and intended audience. For this reason, studies of graffiti usually distinguish 'public' and 'private' graffiti. 'Public graffiti' are located where they can easily be seen by the passer-by. Examples include walls and underpasses. 'Private graffiti' is found in backstage places like toilets. Such graffiti is usually not intended for a general public audience. Graffiti studies has a long history in the social sciences. Aside from ethnographic research on graffiti subculture (e.g. Ferrell, 1993), graffiti can provide a nice unobtrusive measure of values, beliefs and communication styles. The following studies provide examples of the kinds of approaches that can be taken to looking at graffiti.

John Kloftas and Charles Cutshall (1985) conducted perhaps the most impressive quantitative study of graffiti we have encountered. They made a content analysis of graffiti collected from the walls of an abandoned

BOX 4.14 ALCOHOLIC RUBBISH PROJECT

Alan Kellehear (1993: 103) reports that a prospective liquor store owner spent some time rummaging in the garbage cans of an area where he was going to set up a business. The idea was to find out what his future clients were likely to drink. This anecdote draws our attention to the fact that social groups have different consumption patterns. For this study select two areas which differ according to some relevant demographic criteria (e.g. student suburb vs family suburb, working class vs middle class, 'ethnic' vs 'white'). Sample a reasonable number of bins in each suburb (perhaps 50 in each). Record the number and kinds of alcohol containers you find. What kind of conclusions can you make about the links between alcohol, taste and the independent variable you used to select the suburb? To what extent are your findings supported in the literature?

Notes: (1) With the advent of recycling bins this exercise should be easier and quicker to carry out than in the past. Simply look in the bottles section of the bin. (2) It is best to conduct the study on the morning of the day when garbage is recycled. (3) Wear protective clothing and gloves to prevent injury. (4) People may not like you rummaging through their garbage. It's probably best to work in pairs. Try to look efficient and business-like. Maybe wear a boiler suit so it looks like what you are doing is 'official', but, if questioned, politely and honestly explain what you are up to. (5) You may wish to establish the legality of this research before you start. (6) The project can be easily adapted to explore other issues. Exposure to globalization might be measured by looking for evidence of 'ethnic' foods in the bin. Levels of wastefulness can be explored by weighing the amount of uneaten (yuk!) food, etc., etc.

juvenile correctional facility in Massachusetts. Two teams of recorders transcribed verbatim data from walls. Each transcription was also coded as to location (e.g. individual cell number, corridor type). In total there were 2,765 items. The breakdown is given in Table 4.1, which also serves as a nice example of a coding schedule.

Kloftas and Cutshall note the high percentage of inscriptions which located people in terms of 'personal identifiers' (e.g. 'John from the Bronx was here'), and the large numbers of inscriptions which could be identified as 'teen romance' (e.g. love poems). Surprisingly under-represented in the graffiti was material of a sexual or racist nature or material dealing with drugs. Exploring the location of the graffiti also provided dividends. Material on cell walls that were visible to outsiders tended to feature tough

TABLE 4.1   *Types of graffiti recorded at an institute for juvenile guidance*

Percentage	Category	Description
35.7	Personal identifier	Names, names and places, initials
4.6	Group identifier	Group names, places, name strings
1.9	Slurs and insults	With names or place names
21.8	Teen and romance	Girls' names, hearts and initials
7.8	Criminal justice rel.	Police, crime and IJG, biography
6.6	Activism	Contemporary political slogans
1.3	Race	Praise, slurs, other references
1.5	Outlaws	Swastika, iron cross, etc.
1.1	Drugs	Drug names, slang, pictures
1.0	Sex	Sexual references, drawings
2.5	Religion	Religious symbols, references
2.0	Obscenity	Unconnected obscenities
12.3	Miscellaneous	Cartoons, song titles, doodles
100		
($n = 2{,}765$)		

Source: Kloftas and Cutshall (1985: 362)

and aggressive themes, whilst material on the other walls tended to be more contemplative. During their time at the institution the boys were moved through zones to areas with increasing privilege. Kloftas and Cutshall show that the themes of the graffiti vary between these zones. Identity-related graffiti was more prevalent in the first zone, suggesting a defensive reaction to the depersonalization of the 'total institution'. Whilst the proportion of personal identity graffiti decreased during incarceration, 'romance'-related inscriptions increased. This might reflect the impact of visiting privileges, with inmates turning to future plans as a coping strategy as the sentence progressed.

Whilst the study by Kloftas and Cutshall may be hard to reproduce, given problems of access to similar locations, it does contain three key lessons. Firstly, that graffiti can provide an unobtrusive measure of human responses to institutions. Secondly, it suggests the importance of coding graffiti into categories so that patterns stand out. Thirdly, it draws our attention to issues of privacy and visibility as central themes in visual analysis. Studies of toilet graffiti, or 'latrinalia', provide another hint about how to approach graffiti – namely to use it to look for differences between populations. Because toilets are usually single-sex environments, they provide a natural laboratory to explore how male and female cultures and communication styles might differ. Harold Loewenstein, George Ponticos and Michele Paludi (1982: 307) looked at restroom graffiti in a Midwestern American University. They found that women's inscriptions offered advice and considered issues like love and marriage. Men were more interested in sex, politics and competition. There were also linguistic differences. Linguist Robin Lakoff (1975) argued that men were more likely to use direct, forceful language and expletives, whilst women were more likely to be indirect and polite. This theory was confirmed by the content of the graffiti.

The research project of Loewenstein et al. (1952), then, seems to confirm popular stereotypes and academic research about women, men and language. It is not alone in doing so. Numerous other studies have found that men make graffiti to talk about sex and trade insults, whilst women offer advice (for overview see Bates and Martin, 1980: 300–3). John Bates and Michael Martin challenged these sorts of findings. They collected graffiti from the men's and women's toilet stalls in restrooms at the University of Massachusetts and coded them into 16 categories. Contrary to their expectations, they found that most of the graffiti was located in the women's restrooms, that women provided most of the sexual graffiti, and wrote more graffiti with a homosexual content than men. Other studies have looked to graffiti as an unobtrusive measure of attitudes to homosexuality (Sechrest and Flores, 1969) and as a way of exploring sexual differences between women and men (Kinsey, Pomeroy, Martin and Gebhard, 1953).

Ethnographic studies of graffiti artists suggest that they have an elaborate subculture, with its own rules about style, materials and sources of

---

BOX 4.15   UNIVERSITY RESTROOM PROJECT

One way to account for divergent findings in restroom studies is to think about the kinds of institutions where they were undertaken. We might expect some institutions to be more progressive than others, or to attract various kinds of students. On the face of it, it seems a plausible hypothesis that a Massachusetts University might be more progressive than a Midwestern University, or at least attract more progressive students. Does your university conform to the findings of Loewenstein et al. or to those of Bates and Martin? Investigating this issue might provide you with some indication of whether your institution is traditional in terms of the gender order, or progressive. Select three or four toilets around the campus and transcribe the graffiti. Ideally these should be in matched pairs (e.g. male and female toilets on the same floor of the same building). Code the data into themes and look for gender differences.

Note: This assignment can be modified in various ways. (a) You could compare two or more institutions in your city (e.g. a university and a technical college). (b) You could look for cross-faculty differences (e.g. are engineers more progressive than women's studies students?). (c) You might wish to conduct research with a partner of the opposite sex in order to avoid embarrassing or conflictual situations.

prestige. This subculture also designates suitable locations for graffiti. According to Jeff Ferrell (1993: 76), graffiti artists tend to restrict their 'tagging' to areas which are previously dirty and unkempt. It is considered 'uncool' to mark a statue or sculpture or to work in an area which is already beautiful and well maintained, such as a park or attractive city square. Writers who desecrate such locations are liable to be sanctioned by their peers. For this reason graffiti tends to be concentrated in certain spots which have already been heavily worked, confirming the motto that 'graffiti attracts graffiti'. Such locations are typically characterized by urban decay. The artists see their work as beautifying such places, or at least as adding interest to them.

Although graffiti is typically seen as a challenge or resistance to authority, sometimes it can take on a conservative character. The breakwater at Nambucca Heads, New South Wales, provides a good example of this (see Figure 4.2). This sleepy seaside town is a popular venue for family holidays, usually in a caravan or tent. It has become a tradition for families to paint one of the boulders on the breakwater and to record the years of their visits. Motifs include maps showing their home town, family or pet portraits, and poems about how much they like coming to Nambucca. The semiotics of the graffiti is conservative, reflecting the importance of family, tradition and community ties. In recent years religious and philosophical motifs have also become more popular. Whilst your own area may not have a Nambucca Heads, there is likely to be some conservative graffiti around. City councils often provide materials for youth and other groups

BOX 4.16 GLOBAL GRAFFITI CULTURE PROJECT

Ferrell's observations were made in the US city of Denver. We might question whether it has a wider applicability. If we are able to find supporting evidence for his proposition in other places and countries, this might suggest that graffiti writing has a shared global culture. Using a street plan, mark out an area of your city or town which includes both 'attractive' and 'run down areas'. Systematically survey the streets and code the locations of graffiti and the number of items at each spot. If Ferrell's findings in Denver are generalizable, we should expect to identify (1) more graffiti in the depressed area and (2) more locations with clusters of graffiti than places with only single items (3) relatively low levels of graffiti on statues, in squares and parks.

To what extent do your findings replicate Ferrell's argument? What kinds of exceptions and problems did you identify in conducting the project? Were there differences between types of graffiti and their locations, for example, between 'serious' artists and casual scribblers? Does there indeed appear to be a global norm?

(a)

(b)

FIGURE 4.2 *Examples of 'conservative' graffiti at Nambucca Heads, New South Wales. Many visitors to Nambucca Heads leave messages on the breakwater boulders which are similar to those in photos (b) and (c). These messages reaffirm the values of the family and celebrate a sense of continuity with place over time. For example the Newberry family from Tamworth have visited the holiday destination every year since 1982 with only one exception. In photo (c) another family have recorded their feelings for Nambucca in a poem. Note also how in photo (b) the white space carefully painted by the*

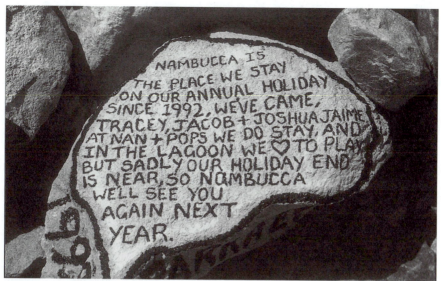

(c)

(d)

Newberry family to record future visits has not been occupied by graffiti from others. Ideas about 'stall defence' discussed in Chapter 6 might help explain this. Photo (a) suggests that even one-time visitors may be inspired to record a message. Photos (d) and (e) indicate the prevalence of religious and existential themes in recent messages. Finally photo (f) suggests that the Nambucca norms have been adopted by non-Anglo visitors. The inscription is dated – 1999 – and appears to include a reference to a beautiful red bird. Colourful parrots and lorikeets are common in the area.

(e)

(f)

BOX 4.17   BATTLE OF THE GRAFFITI EXERCISE

1. Locate places with conservative graffiti and code the themes of the murals. They might include things like local history, local community activities, the local environment.
2. Look around for unofficial graffiti in the same area. It might be sprayed onto the official mural. It might be hidden behind the wall. What themes are featured on the unofficial graffiti? These might be things like politics, sex, racism.
3. What are you able to conclude about official and unofficial graffiti, about acceptable and unacceptable forms of public discourse?

to construct murals and other pseudo-graffiti. Presumably they would withdraw support if the content offended public sensibilities.

Vandalism and litter

The analysis of visual signs is now a hot topic in the field of criminology and policing. Graffiti and vandalism are often lumped together as symbols of urban decay and as symbols of crime. Some people argue they are more than just a symbol, they are also a cause. According to scholars like James Q. Wilson, George Kelling and Catherine Coles, minor signs of disorder, like broken windows, are a visible sign that nobody cares (Kelling and Coles, 1996; Wilson and Kelling, 1982). Such signs encourage crime, generating a vicious circle. The result has been a worldwide advocacy of 'zero tolerance policing' in which minor misdemeanours are harshly punished so that streets are cleared of signs of disorder: squeegee bandits, loitering, skateboarders, graffiti, jay walking and so on.

As supporting evidence for their theory, Wilson and Kelling (1982) cite a study by the psychologist Philip Zimbardo. He parked a car in the street with its hood up and the licence plates removed. It remained untouched for weeks until he smashed part of it with a sledgehammer. Within hours the car was stripped, turned upside down and destroyed. The implication seems to be that visual signs of disorder attract further disorder. It is possible to test the broken windows hypothesis in various ways without damaging public property. A group of students could purchase an old car or bicycle and try to replicate these experimental and observational studies. A more modest, if less spectacular, experimental project is described in Box 4.18.

Conclusions

In this chapter we have suggested a number of ways in which three-dimensional objects can provide a rich form of visual data for sociological

---

BOX 4.18 THE LITTER BUG PROJECT

Does disorder breed disorder, as Wilson and Kelling claim? A cheap and relatively harmless way to find out is with litter. Select an area on campus or in your community and count the amount of litter you find early in the morning. Return in the evening and recount. On another day, clear away the litter early in the morning and at intervals during the day to keep the site clean. If the broken windows hypothesis is correct, less rubbish should be deposited on the days that you do the regular clean-ups than on an ordinary day (remember to include the rubbish you collect in your periodic clean-ups in calculating garbage totals). If you have time you can vary the study in subtle ways. Which kinds of rubbish act as the best stimulant to litter bugs. Newspapers? Fast food wrappers? Old household junk? Is there a linear correlation between the amount of rubbish at the start of the day and the amount at the end, or is the relationship more complex?

---

inquiry. We have argued that such objects can be 'decoded' and read in much the same ways as 2D texts. But we have also tried to do more than this. We have suggested they open up opportunities for a visual sociology which observes, describes and counts and makes deductions on the basis of these observations. As such the visual sociology of the 3D has a strong overlap with the literature on unobtrusive measures. The major advantages seem to be as follows.

1. In many cases objects of material culture, and traces can be used as objective measures of social process. They tap into 'actual behaviour, not reported or experimental approximations' (Rathje, 1979: 77). A physical trace or a material object is either present or it is not.
2. Objects and traces provide non-reactive and (often) unobtrusive measures. This has the advantage that the process of research is not confounded by respondents' behaviour changing once they know they are part of a study. Normal issues like interviewer bias, providing socially preferred responses etc. are avoided, unless we move on from the objects themselves to try to find out about their meanings.
3. Objects and traces are very often easy to quantify and classify, making comparative sociology and rigorous research design easy to conduct. This does not rule out interpretative sociology (decoding objects and their meanings), but it does add another string to the bow of the researcher.
4. Objects and traces are all around us. They provide a free source of data

for the visual investigator. All that is required is an active imagination which can work out how to mobilize them in a theoretically informed project and a pair of eyes to see them.

Having said this, it is important to record some of the limitations of this form of data. Following Alan Kellehear (1993: 107), Webb et al. (1966), Sechrest and Phillips (1979) and Rathje (1979) and our own thought, we can propose several common limitations that arise from the study of objects and traces.

- The selective survival of materials. Some objects are more durable than others and will last longer. Some things will be considered to be of value and will be preserved in archives, others thrown away and destroyed. The result can be a biased material record. Determining just how biased is often no easy task. Consequently, little is understood about the sources of error in unobtrusive measures.
- The material does not always tell us much about the population that uses it. Whilst we can make strong inferences about populations in studies of graves and households, in other studies this is much more problematic. When looking at traces, for example, it is not always clear who left the marks. We might notice a groove on a stair well, but was it formed by the action of men or women? And of what age? Graffiti writing is a semi-secret activity. We know what is said, but can rarely be certain just who is saying it. Here we may have to turn to the literature for information. Qualitative studies suggest most graffiti writers in the subculture are male and aged 15–24. We have to assume such people might have written the material we find in public spaces. But how can we know this? And are these the same people who write graffiti in toilet stalls? To what extent is toilet graffiti the work of a vociferous minority rather than an index of the attitudes of the majority? Problems become even greater when we want to make inferences about attitudes, beliefs and values on the basis of 3D data. It might seem plausible to common sense that dull-coloured cars indicate conservative attitudes, but validating this sort of measure would require considerable resources.
- The use of unobtrusive measures can sometimes lead to banal and largely descriptive inferences unless complemented by further study using traditional reactive measures, or by a strong sociological imagination. The trick with the study of objects and traces is to find meaningful links to wider social theory. Otherwise, who cares if people like interactive museum exhibits, or have tourism souvenirs in their living rooms? One way round this problem is to begin with a hypothesis derived from a theory and then think about how this can be explored using visual data and direct observation. We have suggested some projects in this chapter which attempt to do this.
- Emic/etic problems. This common issue in qualitative research relates

to the possibility of a disjunction between the researcher's under-standing or interpretation of an object (the etic perspective) and the member's understanding (the emic). Often we can resolve these questions by talking to people who use objects, and learning about the values they place upon them – but sometimes intractable problems can remain. Thanks to our cultural studies training we might interpret a particular brand of German motor car as a status symbol, or as a marker of a phallocentric authoritarian personality, but its user might see it simply as efficient, comfortable transportation with a good resale value. Who is wrong here, and who is right?

- In the study of traces, erosion and accretion, efforts at repair can obscure true levels of use. For example, over the years multiple attempts might have been made to repair a staircase, or carpets may have been put down to protect it. Such a process will make it difficult to detect true levels of use.
- Ethical problems to do with the invasion of privacy make some forms of unobtrusive research unattractive to some sociologists. It might be argued that garbage research, for example, involves snooping on people's private lives. When the study of objects takes a more open and explicit form these problems still persist. If we ask to enter someone's home and to talk to them about the meanings of the things they have there, are we not invading their privacy, even if they give informed consent?
- In many cases visual data are relics of the past. It is not always clear to what extent this provides an accurate picture about the present. To give an example, universities often have portraits of former faculty members dotted around in lecture rooms, reception rooms, etc. These are almost invariably stuffy portraits of older, white men dressed in full academic regalia who are trying hard to look serious and know-ledgeable. Do these data contribute an accurate representation of *former* ideologies and sexisms in universities, or present day ones?

Despite these limitations, the objects of our material culture deserve more attention than they have been given to date. We have suggested in this chapter some of their advantages relative to the two-dimensional data that is the stock in trade of visual researchers. The next chapter continues the move away from the 2D. We consider not objects, but rather entire settings. Our focus is on the places and spaces that we inhabit as members of our society. Like objects, these provide a data resource every bit as rich as the world of texts and images for researching the visual.

Note

1   These debates have traditionally been organized around scientistic and hermeneutic polarities and have reached their most developed state in the

discipline of archaeology. On the one hand it has been argued that objects contain objective information which can be retrieved using formal methods and advanced field and laboratory technologies. On the other it has been asserted that objects encode meanings which have to be retrieved through a process of culturally sensitive interpretation. More recent interventions from 'post-processualist' archaeologists have been influenced by postmodernism and highlight the indeterminacy of objects and the ways that their meanings shift according to the frames of interpretation that are applied to them.

5

Lived Visual Data: the Built Environment and its Uses

The previous chapter suggested some ways for visual research to move away from the study of the 2D image, towards the analysis of objects. This one continues the journey with analyses of places and settings – what we call 'lived' visual data in as far as our lives are inevitably conducted in and around such locations. We have already touched upon some of these: museums and houses have been shown to be places where one can conduct visual inquiry. Our concerns are differentiated from these previous ones in the following way. In the study of 3D objects our primary concern was with locations as spatial contexts for understanding objects. Now we turn our attention from objects towards locations themselves, moving for example, from the display of items in museums to the museum as a total environment. Objects tend to be things that people interact *with*. Here we focus on places that people interact *in*. As Rob Shields puts it, places like shopping malls are 'ensembles of objects' which 'are not arte-facts in the traditional sense but are environments which, once entered, enfold and engulf us. . .' (1994: 203). In approaching such places we will show that semiotic methods can be used; we can decode places because they are, in some ways, texts just like pictures and objects. They are designed to throw off meanings. As with 3D objects, we can also look at the ways people interact with them. The great differences with total environments, however, is that spatial considerations must come to the fore. Questions of motion in time and space, arenas of visibility and invisi-bility and the patterning of zones, objects and activities are central to the organization of 'lived visual data'. In assessing these sorts of things we can use methodologies ranging from direct observation in naturalistic settings to the study of architects' drawings.

In short, this chapter:

- shows how visual research can be conducted in the study of what Giddens calls the *locale*, a socially constructed and socially relevant space within which human interactions take place
- demonstrates how places and buildings tap into the cultures, values and ideologies in which they are situated
- suggests that observable movements of people in time and space can be used as indicators to answer sociologically informed questions
- points to the ways that issues of visibility and invisibility, privacy and publicness are often central to the organization of people, objects and activities in particular locales
- offers a number of locales such as museums, the home and the park as places for conducting research projects.

The chapter is organized into three sections. First we look at efforts to decode places. The focus here is on the locale as a signifier. Second, we explore how people respond to places and move through them. Third we examine some of the ways that visibility and invisibility are structured into built forms, influencing the arrangement of objects and human beings.

Decoding places

Museums, houses, shopping malls, offices, parks, streets and gardens are not simply functional structures whose built form reflects imperatives of utility and cost. Of course these kinds of factors come into play in influencing design, construction and decoration. But they are far from determinative. This fact becomes obvious when we look around the world. Housing styles, for example, vary radically between countries, even regions, yet we would be hard pressed to claim that any one kind of housing provides better shelter from the elements than any other. These kinds of differences can be attributed to varying 'traditions' as to what makes an adequate house. A more theoretically compelling approach, however, is to move beyond blanket terms like 'tradition', and explore in detail the ways that cultural systems are encoded into built fabric.

The house

Perhaps the most famous illustration of the power of theoretical insight to decode the dwelling is Pierre Bourdieu's (1990) classic essay on the Kabyle house (the Kabyle are a peasant society inhabiting the mountains of Algeria, North Africa). Originally written for a book in honour of Lévi-Strauss, this study provides a tour-de-force of structuralist thinking. Bourdieu studies the floor plan of the house, and links it with his ethnographic knowledge of Kabyle life to demonstrate that the house is structured by a number of binary oppositions. These link built form, gender roles, agricultural cycles, human reproduction and cosmology in complex ways which are difficult to summarize here. Bourdieu argues that 'the house is organized in accordance with a set of homologous oppositions – high:low:: light:dark:: day:night:: male:female:: fertilizing:able to be fertilized' (ibid.: 275). These oppositions structure issues like the placement of the loom, the storage positions of water and grain jars and the locations of activities like cooking, sleeping and sex. Grain kept for sowing, for example, is stored in the 'dark' and 'wet' part of the house. This is also where sex takes place. Women's activities are also associated with this part of the building: 'carrying water, wood, manure, for instance' (ibid.: 274). 'The dark, nocturnal, lower part of the house, the place for things that are damp, green or raw – jars of water placed on the benches on either side of the stable entrance or next to the wall of darkness, wood, green fodder – and also the place for natural beings – oxen and cows, donkeys and mules – natural activities – sleep, sexual intercourse, childbirth, and also death – is opposed to the light-filled, noble, upper part' (ibid.: 272). Bourdieu explains that the dry, light, upper part of the house is associated with 'culture', with fire, and the transformation of nature. It is here that guests are received. This is the more 'male' part of the house, the part that is more associated with the public sphere.

Bourdieu also argues that we can detect binary oppositions not only within the house, but also between the house and the world outside. Taken as a whole, the house is seen as the domain of women, whilst men belong outside in the fields. Men who spend too long in the house are liable to ridicule as a 'house man'. Biological activities – eating, sleeping etc. – are all conducted within the house. Whilst the organization of the Kabyle house, and its social meanings, might appear to be just the product of an undifferentiated 'tradition' or 'way of life' to an outsider, Bourdieu's detailed decoding shows it to be an environment through which we can read the deep structures which pattern Kabyle life as a whole.

It does not take much sociological imagination to realize that the kind of approach taken by Bourdieu can also be applied to Western housing. In *Myths of Oz* Fiske, Hodge and Turner (1987) decode the typical Australian suburban dwelling – in this case a showhome called the 'Rembrandt'. Entering the house they note divisions between kinds of people are encoded into the built fabric. At the entrance 'we are faced with a choice: left, right or straight ahead. To the left is the study and main bedroom – the most private area of the house. Even as viewers we don't turn left, so strong are the signals sent by the placing of walls and doorways. Straight ahead (with a further turn to the left) would be the family rooms – more private but not forbidden. To the right, following the natural curve initiated by our entrance is the "living room". . . . The three directions in practice classify three different kinds of person: non-family (to the right), family (straight ahead) and marital couple (left)' (Fiske et al., 1987: 33). The

built form of the Australian suburban house, then, encodes cultural distinctions about private and public space and about the family and sexuality. Through visual and spatial cues it works to channel outsiders into
the more 'public' areas of the private dwelling. Gender ideologies can also
be detected in the design. The open kitchen, they suggest, reflects the
changing status of cooking. Whilst in the past it was seen as invisible servants' work, today cooking is seen as 'creative' and the mother given more
centrality and visibility. The physical location of the open kitchen is also
noteworthy: 'The placing of the kitchen between the family meals area and
the visitor's dining area, and its openness, establishes the woman as the
mediator between the family and the guests, and suggests that children
only have access to the visitors and to the "dining area" through the
mother's grace' (ibid.: 35). Whilst changing kitchen designs reflect changing expectations about the women's role, in other areas the Rembrandt
demonstrated that norms had not changed. The entrance to the laundry
was invisible to guests, but 'convenient for the woman in the kitchen, and
a long way from the man's private place, the study' (ibid.: 35–6). Fiske et
al. conclude that washing was not only seen as women's work, but also
that (unlike cooking) it was seen as menial and not as creative.

   In an earlier chapter we looked at David Halle's (1993) discussion of art
in the home. His exploration of housing in working-class and middle-class
areas of the New York region provides another example of the ability of
visual research to decode social and cultural values. Halle used architects'
drawings and direct observation as his data. First he looked at upper-class
housing in Manhattan which had been constructed in the 1880s and 1890s.
In this earlier period the front of the house was important. Elaborate staircases and ornate front doors were a signal of wealth to the passer-by. Back-
yards, by contrast, were small, dark and dirty according to available
records and inferences that can be made from design. Halle shows that
today this emphasis has been reversed. Back yards are prized for their
privacy in the middle of the noisy city. Halle identifies two main types of
garden. The contemplative garden is adult oriented. It is carefully
designed (perhaps by professionals) and has plantings, and maybe a
bench and a patio. Child-dominated gardens are found in households
with young children. They typically have swings and other play equipment taking up much of the available room. Halle sees this trend towards
the active use of the garden as a symptom of the suburbanization of urban
life and as a reflection of idealized conceptions of nature and the 'country'
that are now very powerful (as we saw in the previous chapter he also
found these values embodied in art choices). Contrasting with the interest that residents took in the backyard was a comparative neglect of the
front of the house. In over a third of the houses the grand staircase entry
had been removed, with householders preferring to enter the house via
what had once been the servant's door. Inside the house, areas which had
once been occupied by live-in servants have been taken over for other
uses. Formal reception rooms had also been appropriated for day-to-day

156 RESEARCHING THE VISUAL

living. Kitchen areas had been moved closer to dining areas, with many houses featuring combined kitchen/lounge/dining spaces. This reflected the decline of the paid 'downstairs' cook. 'Dens' were prized as indoor places for recreation and reflected the significance of intimacy to the nuclear family.

Similar trends were evident in the working-class Greenpoint area that Halle studied. Ornate exteriors were a feature of original designs, and reflected a vigorous street-life. This has declined since the 1950s, with the advent of the automobile. This had made play and conversation in the street dangerous and unpleasant. By contrast, gardens at the back of the house (which had once been kitchen gardens) are highly developed as sanctuaries and as children's play areas. Inside the house, formal areas and rooms originally intended for boarders had been taken over as extra bedrooms and the kitchen had merged with the dining/living room.

In the suburban locations where Halle explored housing design, the same cultural patterns were evident. Only, as the housing was newer, it had been designed with contemporary social norms in mind rather than adapting to them over time through modifications. Thanks to larger plots, houses were typically set back from the road for privacy, reflecting the non-existence of street life in leafy areas. Houses had no servants' quarters, and, since the 1960s, kitchens had been merged with living areas, reflecting the disappearance of the family servant and/or cook. Gardens were once again the centre of much thought and effort. These were usually fenced in order to maximize privacy, keep in children and dogs, and to keep wandering children safe from pools. Vegetable growing was seen as a hobby rather than as a necessity as it had been in the past.

Halle concludes that themes of privacy (from outsiders and also non-family members living in the house), the use of the garden for leisure, and the importance of the nuclear family were reflected in the built environment of the houses that he looked at. These themes cut across divisions of class and housing location. Whilst Halle supplemented his inquiry with interviews and reference to historical materials, most of his findings were based on visual evidence alone. In his book he makes exemplary use of sketch maps to record the spatial characteristics of the houses and gardens he studies. Another point to think about is Halle's use of longitudinal data (in the form of changing house design, both interior and exterior) which help us to break away from common-sense thinking about the home and garden and to relativize our perspective. This in turn assists in highlighting contemporary social norms and values which would otherwise be hidden. The assignment in Box 5.1 attempts something similar.

The garden

Like homes, gardens also provide an attractive resource for the visual researcher interested in social semiotics. In discussing Australian suburban gardens of the 1950s, Fiske et al. (1987) point to the centrality of two

BOX 5.1   DECODING AND RETHINKING THE HOME EXERCISE

The studies discussed above alert us to a number of themes that are built into housing and which can be decoded from them: (a) appropriate gender roles and their status, (b) degrees of public vs private places, (c) categories of persons and places where they belong, (d) uses of space. These can easily be explored using direct observations conducted in the home.

1. Select a home that is known to you and construct a floor plan. Make notes on how the built form encapsulates established social values. You may be able to quantify some of these. The most private areas of the house, for example, might be the furthest from the front door.
2. Because concepts about gender, privacy, etc. are so deeply embedded in our common sense, it is a useful reflexive exercise to try to shatter these. Using another sheet of paper, redesign the home in a way that challenges these values and encourages new ways of thinking, alternative values and patterns of interaction. For example, you might wish to undertake your planning from a feminist perspective.
3. Consider which design is more 'practical'? To what extent do understandings of the 'normal' structure our belief that the conventional home is more practical: e.g. are communal, public, sleeping rooms only 'impractical' because of our established ideas about privacy?

Notes: A variation on part 1 of this project would involve a longitudinal design. It may be possible to locate floor plans covering a substantial time-period. You may be able to find these in builder's advertisements in newspapers, for example, or in architectural history books. In theory it should be possible to trace changing norms over these plans. Whilst these are 2D data, strictly speaking, they do provide an important resource for exploring built forms.

binary distinctions: public vs private and nature vs culture. The front garden, they argue, was organized primarily for consumption by those passing in the street. It was neat and tidy and surrounded by fences. It tended to feature exotic plants that required high maintenance, but was rarely used by the owners. The front garden, then, was coded as 'public' and as 'culture'. The back garden, by contrast, tended to be shabby with little attempt at gardening, but was more often used by the family for play or for hanging out washing. The back garden, then, could be coded as 'private' and as 'nature'. More recently, they note, attempts have been made to convert the back garden into an 'outdoor living area', with paving, pergolas and landscaping, whilst Australian native plants have been introduced into front garden areas, replacing European exotics. As a result the kind of binary oppositions they identified marking front and back have weakened, as have distinctions between the inside of the house and the garden outside it.

In a recent comparative study of British gardens in a typical middle-class suburban housing development, Sophie Chevalier (1998) makes use of similar conceptual devices to Fiske et al. For Chevalier, the garden is a location which expresses both local cultural values and universal cultural principles. It is a 'mediator linked to the natural, social and cultural environment' (1998: 48). In Britain, as in Australia, the front garden serves as an 'identity marker' which usually functions to reproduce the illusion of conformity. The back garden is a private/public space like the lounge – it is a private space, but one that visitors can expect to be allowed to enter. It is also, in many cases, a 'child dominated play area' in which children's toys seem to take up much of the free space. Notwithstanding children, the garden can generally be decoded as a 'garden of delight'. It contains plants designed to give pleasure, rather than plants that are useful, and serves to express the identity of the occupants of the house. One might also find toys and ornaments, fountains and bird houses. Chevalier also indicates affinities between the lounge and the garden and the 'bridging' techniques that people use to unite them conceptually. Gardens might be transformed into a kind of outdoor lounge through the use of furniture, and the lounge might be transformed into a kind of garden through the use of flowers or pictures of birds.

Institutions and public spaces

Whilst domestic spaces are a convenient resource for small-scale socio-logical inquiry, in the remainder of this section we wish to point to the opportunities for study that are available within larger lived environ-ments. Institutions like schools, hospitals and office blocks afford plenty of opportunity for investigation into the intersection of beliefs and dis-courses with built forms, especially in the case of longitudinal studies. Because the architecture of such places typically reflects forms of know-ledge at the time they were constructed (rather than just the whim of indi-vidual architects), we can use the visual/spatial information encoded into buildings to trace shifts in expert knowledge about things like education, sickness and efficient business practice. They offer, then, a different set of opportunities from studies of the home and garden, which tend, by con-trast, to give insight into norms of everyday life about which people are comparatively non-reflexive.

A study by Lindsay Prior (1988) provides an illustration of this sort of methodology in action. Prior asserts that 'the spatial divisions which are

BOX 5.2   DECODING GARDENS EXERCISE

Visit a number of gardens belonging to houses in your area. To what extent are you able to identify the kinds of cultural codes and patterns discussed above. Look for evidence of:

- bridging between indoors and outdoors (e.g. garden furniture)
- divisions between nature and culture within the garden (e.g. wild bushy parts vs formal lawns and borders)
- the kinds of uses that are made of the garden. Is it a 'garden of delight' or is it used for utilitarian purposes, such as the storage of bulky items, drying washing, or as an outdoor workshop. Are efforts made to hide these utilitarian activities?
- the labour that goes into maintaining or developing the garden

Draw a sketch map of each garden, like the one in Figure 5.1, and make notes. Refer to these later when writing up your results

Note: To convert this exercise to a more significant project you may wish to sample systematically across some kind of social cleavage. Class and ethnicity stand out as two potential variables which might predict people having varying attitudes to their gardens. In the case of migrants, garden styles can also be used as an indicator of assimilation. Migrant groups whose gardens correspond to the host-type could be considered to have taken on some of the cultural codes and values of their host society. In the case of class, one might predict more utilitarian garden uses amongst the poor, and a more elaborate 'garden of delight' approach amongst the affluent.

expressed in buildings can be best understood in relation to the discursive practices which are disclosed in their interiors' (ibid.: 110). He explores the relationship between changing medical theories of disease and care by looking at hospital plans and architects' drawings for infection wards in children's hospitals from around 1850 onwards. In effect this form of 2D data provides an insight into 3D built form. Whilst the use of such data is convenient, we note that the project could also have been conducted by means of direct observation of actual buildings. Prior discusses the way that the 'Pavilion' hospital of the nineteenth century was organized around the miasmic theory of disease. This held that disease arose from stagnant air and dark spaces. The circulation of air and light was held to be necessary to prevent illness. For this reason there were large spaces between beds in open, airy communal wards. Often there would be an outside verandah to which patients could be moved to facilitate the circulation of air.

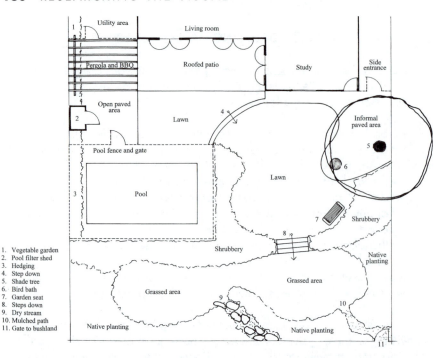

FIGURE 5.1   *Sketch plan of a typical Australian suburban garden layout. Maps such as this can highlight taken-for-granted cultural patterns in the use of domestic space. Notice the transition from culture to nature as we move from the top left of the plan towards the bottom right. There is a progression from orderly, linear, built environments towards disordered, planted spaces and finally a gateway onto untamed bushland. Observe also the presence of a transitional zone consisting of lawn, informal paving, shrubbery, bench and steps mediating this*

   In the latter part of the nineteenth century the germ theory of disease became more widely accepted. The result was that operating rooms were removed from ordinary ward space. The open-plan ward of the pavilion model was replaced by a new emphasis on separation and containment. Plans show that patients were to be enclosed in isolation cubicles, or separated by partitions. Windows were designed not to open, so as to prevent the spread of germs – a dramatic U-turn from the ventilation orientation of the miasmic theory of disease. The use of glass partitions and windows allowed observation (a central feature of hospital design; see below, p. 184) to continue. Prior argues that the shift from one kind of architecture to another was far from clear cut. There would often be a mixture of design, with some pavilion blocks and some isolation wards. He asserts that 'such a mixture of design reflects a conflation and confusion of two theories of disease' (ibid.: 97). By the 1920s new discourses about child health and development came into place alongside strictly clinical discourses. These argued that hospitals should not be too authoritarian or forbidding, but should provide opportunities for self-expression and social interaction among the child-patients. So around this time we can locate the introduction of the play room as a key aspect of ward design in children's hospitals. These were later replaced by play spaces, in which play was less isolated from day-to-day life in the ward. By the 1960s, the sick child was also being located within discourses about the family. It was being argued that steps should be taken to encourage parents to remain in the hospital and interact with the sick child. Earlier isolation of the child from the parent was condemned as 'madness'. It was claimed that the trauma of hospitalization would be reduced if the mother could spend more time with the child. Consequently, in plans from this time onwards, Prior is able to locate facilities for parents, such as the provision of a divan for sleeping next to the child. Concerns were also raised that the hospital needed to meet the educational needs of children and so these facilities were added. In conclusion, then, changing ward designs are indicators of changing discourses about the disease, nursing and the child.

BOX 5.3   INSTITUTIONS AND IDEOLOGIES PROJECT

This project requires you to copy Lindsay Prior's methodology. Locate an architecture or design journal (or series of journals) in your college library. These will often include designs from exemplary or award-winning buildings. Select a class of institution and try to find plans for this sort of institution over a time period. From the evidence on the plans, what can you conclude about:

- changing discourses about care and control
- the centrality and care of the body
- hierarchies and gender orders.

Using library research, try to link your findings to the literature on the kind of institution you have selected. For example, if you have been looking at schools, explore the literature on child development and the social construction of childhood like Prior (Alexander's work on children in advertising discussed in an earlier chapter also used this method). This will help you evaluate the kinds of inferences you made on the basis of the visual data alone.

Note: You could also conduct this project from direct study of real buildings. This is a viable option, but it is also one which might prove difficult in terms of gaining access. If you contact people like hospital administrators, school heads, etc. it might prove possible. Universities might also provide an option for this kind of research.

Public spaces   In concluding this section on decoding places and spaces we move from the 'private' and enclosed institution towards public spaces. These have the important advantage of being readily available for investigation. In most instances you will not need to ask permission in order to conduct a study. Over recent years shopping malls have become the most researched public space, replacing earlier Chicago School-type studies of the street and street life. Later we explore issues of behaviour in the shopping mall. Here we focus on decoding the built form itself.

Shopping malls are centres for the consumption and experience of signs by large numbers of people. Whilst there have been important precursors, such as nineteenth-century department stores and the arcades studied by Walter Benjamin, today it is the shopping mall which exerts probably the greatest influence on public retail spaces in developed nations. Malls arose out of suburbanization during the twentieth century. Whilst some can be found in city centres, many are isolated behemoths surrounded by residential areas. During the first part of the twentieth century, special shopping areas designed and run as a unit were first trialed. The 1950s saw the emergence of the fully enclosed shopping centre (Carr, Francis, Rubin and Stone, 1992: 71). These subsequently became places of interest in their own right, not just places for shopping. The major characteristics of the mall (at least in Western cultures) are given by Shields (1994). In general they have a variety of shops arrayed along interior galleries which terminate at one or more large department stores which are thought to 'anchor' the mall and attract shoppers. One might also find parking, offices, conference and entertainment facilities added to the complex. Malls have to fulfil certain utilitarian characteristics. There has to be a large floor area for the display of goods, ample parking, wide corridors and walkways to facilitate the circulation of shoppers and so on. Such functional needs are generally of little interest to the sociologist.

Of much greater interest are the stylistic trends embodied in shopping malls. Because malls are very much under the public eye, they need to appear up-to-date and need to work hard to attract customers from competing retail spaces. These factors, along with the large sums of money that investors have to hand, means that they are constantly being remodelled and redesigned. As a result they take on board cultural trends much more rapidly than other kinds of public space, such as parks and other kinds of (usually cash-strapped) public buildings such as hospitals. Over recent years the mall has become of theoretical centrality because of its status as a 'postmodern' environment. Much time and effort has been spent in writing about the mall as a crucial symptom of the stylistic and social trends that prevail in late capitalism. It is a useful exercise to decode the mall in terms of these postmodern features by contrast with the simpler malls of the 1950s. These consisted of rectilinear designs, where a row of shops linked two larger department stores (Shields, 1994;

Woodward, 1998). By contrast the more postmodern mall will much more closely resemble a theme park like Disney Land. In these we will be able to find:

- The availability of activities other than shopping. Typically the mall will be able to provide cinema, food and body-care services as well as retail purchasing opportunities. In postmodern jargon, the mall has become a 'de-differentiated' place, in which shopping is no longer separated from other pleasure activities. Indeed, the mall becomes a kind of total environment which meets all human needs for survival and amusement, rather like a space station.
- Theme-park like features. These can include fairground rides and activities and themed miniature villages of shops (often on a 'Main Street USA' or 'Olde England' plan). Jean Baudrillard's ideas of the simulacrum provide some purchase here. It is argued that the real, built world is being made up of copies of idealized myths. The most written-about example of such a mall is the West Edmonton Mall in Canada, which has a wavepool, hotel, skating rink, funfair, miniature golf course, copies of Versailles fountains and a re-creation of New Orleans Bourbon Street. And, by the way, there are also around a thousand shops!
- Non-linear floor plans. Instead of straight-line, modernist corridors which produce 'mall-fatigue', the trend is towards 'curvy' designs which invite exploration and discovery. These are sometimes considered labyrinthine and confusing.
- Entertainers like singers, jugglers, etc., attempting to convert the mall into a kind of fairground. These, along with the simulacrum features, contribute to the 'liminal' qualities of the mall as a carnivalesque fun-zone which is outside of ordinary life.

An unintended consequence of these kinds of changes has been that older malls have to update their image or risk being marginalized as unattractive places to shop. As Turo-Kimmo Lehtonen and Pasi Maenpaa put it in a discussion of trends in Finnish shopping malls, 'The marginalization of the old shopping centres is usually the outcome of the constant urge to novelty of a modern city development' (1997: 141). The next exercise examines this issue.

Shops   With the mall as a whole being theoretically the most intriguing aspect of the shopping centre for decoding, there has been a tendency in sociological research to concentrate on the woods at the expense of the trees. If we turn attention to shops and their design, we can also find fruitful material for visual research. Shops, after all, are oriented towards display. These displays can be decoded in terms of their semiotics and in terms of the techniques they use to stimulate buying. As Fiske et al. (1987: 109) point out, 'just as individuals construct their images within the similarity of

BOX 5.4   DECODING THE MALL EXERCISE

Select two or three malls in your area, preferably from different eras. Visit them and make notes on the activities, decor, themes, etc. Try to answer the following questions.

- Which of the malls appears the most dated. Why? Is there a correlation between your subjective perception of datedness and the quantity of postmodern features that are present?
- How have the older malls been modified to make them 'postmodern'? What lingering features can you detect which give away their age?
- Can you detect any evidence of the success or failure of the mall? – e.g. empty parking spots on Saturday morning. Some shops not rented out. Does this success or failure correspond in any way to the amount of postmodernism you detect?

fashion, so different shops construct their identity'. Working from within a critical perspective, Fiske et al. claim that 'class distinctions' can be identified in the semiotics of shops. The codes they identify run as follows:

- 'Democratic' shops have low priced goods which everyone needs. Examples include newsagents, chemists and hardware stores. They have 'leaky boundaries' and don't bother with windows, often having open fronts with shutters. Goods are often displayed on the pavement in front of the shop as well as within it. Such shops don't really try very hard to mark their own identity. With their displays they signal that they are open to all.
- 'Middle-class' shops are exemplified by medium-price fashion outlets. Although there may be a few racks out in the street, such shops make extensive use of windows and window displays. Such displays are often crammed with goods. Interiors are well lit and can be seen through the window to contain large quantities of goods. The key semiotic here is plenitude.
- 'Upper class' shops are, by self-definition exclusive. Such shops might sell designer fashion and accessories or else valuable *objets d'art* – paintings, antiques, etc. Windows, display racks and shelves have fewer goods on them, signalling limited supply and scarcity value. Lighting is subdued, with individual items spotlighted like museum exhibits.

Fiske et al. (1987) suggest that such shops will often be spatially separated in the mall. In multi-storey complexes the exclusive shops will tend to be located on the top floors. In city centres shops of a particular class will tend to cluster in particular streets. Exclusive shops, for example, are to be found in London's Bond Street and New York's Fifth Avenue. However, they suggest the practice is 'not universal and does seem to be implicated in the class structure of the community it serves' (ibid.: 110). In cities with strictly segregated housing markets and marked class dynamics, types of shops will tend to be separated from each other. In blue-collar cities, by contrast, the various kinds of shops will tend to be next to each other. Shields (1994: 205–6) reports a similar kind of stratification in the Rideau Centre, Ottawa. The lowest level of the mall has 'economy minded' service stores, whilst on the upper levels we find 'high-end' jewellers, shoe stores and speciality clothing shops.

In order to explore the visual universe of shops, one need not take a strongly semiotic approach like that of Fiske et al. One alternative is to look at the pragmatic strategies that shops use to increase sales. Many of these are plugged in retail sales manuals and in retail training courses. Specialists and consultants in these sorts of areas can make large sums of money by telling stores how to reorganize their built space and displays. According to *Choice* (Jan/Feb 1998: 9), the Australian consumer magazine, there are a number of basic things that supermarkets stores can do to increase sales. Most of these are designed to appeal to the visual field of the shopper, but without them noticing.

Store layout can be designed so that people encounter 'interesting' fresh food as they go in, rather than packets of dry goods. *Ambience* can be generated so that people feel that they are having a unique shopping experience rather than a boring trip to buy dogfood. Themes might include 'rural market' or 'village square', and might include the whole

---

BOX 5.5   SHOP STYLES EXERCISE

Visit your local mall or city centre armed with a sketch map (you may be able to copy this from a 'You are here' board). Mark on it shops which conform to the various semiotic codes identified by Fiske et al. Do you detect the kinds of clustering they predict? What kinds of factors might contribute to this? Think about the class structure of the client group for the shops. To what extent do class distinctions between the shops you study correspond to the semiotic codes identified by Fiske et al.? Remember their data was collected in Australia. It is possible that cultural differences might generate a divergent set of cultural codes in another country. Are other cultural codes more important than 'class' styles in shaping shop semiotics? It is possible, for example, that ethnic or environmental themes play a larger role in some shops.

store or just a part of it. *Music* (OK, it's not strictly visual data!) is selected so that there is an even tempo, so that it is non-threatening and so that it encourages people to feel relaxed, browse or linger. *Lighting* is manipulated in terms of colour, direction and intensity so that meat looks red, fruit shiny, fish bright and fresh and so on. *Shelf Location:* eye-level is the most attractive location for stock, so goods at a premium price will often be located there. In addition one can expect to find products aimed at children at lower heights. *Impulse buying* is encouraged by free demos and tastings, 'specials' at the end of aisles, and sweets and magazines at the check-out queue. These are placed in strategic visible locations and can comprise around a third of all purchases.

Open public spaces   When we think of public space, we usually think of outdoor settings like parks, streets and plazas rather than about indoor environments like the mall. Here we look at these kinds of 'common-sense' public spaces. In *The Image of the City*, Kevin Lynch (1960) argued that the physical attributes of public spaces provide visual and spatial cues and clues which structure its identity and link it to larger cultural or historical themes. Lynch suggested that in order to be effective a public space had to be *legible*. This means that it has to be decodable by ordinary people. After decoding they would be able to understand the place and the communal narratives that it taps into and also work out which kinds of behaviours are permitted and which are not. Often this legibility arises as the result of history and the gradual accretion of signs. An old fishing village, for example, might have the necessary boats, equipment and harbour to generate a distinctive sense of place without any conscious effort being expended on the task. Places like Trafalgar Square, the Champs Elysées and Times Square, to pick some examples at random, also have established identities and connections to the public life of the city.

In newer public spaces a sense of place might have to be constructed in more reflexive ways. Architects and planners are well aware that the most

---

BOX 5.6   DECODING THE SUPERMARKET EXERCISE

Visit your local supermarket and as you tour around note how many consumption-promotion devices you can detect. Do you see any evidence of them working to encourage increased consumption? How would you evaluate the relative importance of visual stimuli to those bombarding the other senses in the shopping environment?

Note: It may be instructive to try a location other than the supermarket. Traditional street markets and car boot sales may have a different visual logic.

successful public spaces are also those with a distinctive identity and will attempt to generate meanings and connections by manipulating the visible and physical environment. In this section we draw largely on a text intended for architects and planners (Carr et al., 1992). Public spaces that work must fulfil a number of criteria, many of these visual. Firstly, the place needs to mesh with local narratives and develop a symbolic identity. An example here might be a waterfront development which uses motifs which play on its former identity as a dockland or harbour. Public spaces which fail, by contrast tend to be marked by weak or self-contradictory visual cues. Carr et al. (1992: 191–2), for example, speak of Boston's Waterfront Park which was constructed in the 1970s and was intended to link the city to the water and celebrate its maritime connections. The design failed. Elements of design which had a nautical theme (e.g. play structures which looked like boats, marina-style lights and bollards) were contradicted by 'large lawn areas, mounding, heavy planting and wooden trellis' which 'give the park an almost suburban character that is incongruent with the urban waterfront location' (ibid.: 192). Much the same can be said for the Place de la Bastille in France. The storming of the Bastille is the location of what is arguably France's most significant historical event. In earlier work (Smith, 1999) we demonstrated that during its two hundred year history the Place de la Bastille has never been able to connect with these historical resonances. Today the walls of the old fortress have disappeared and apartments and roads have been constructed over some of its former area. A monument to revolutionaries situated in the middle space is difficult to reach, being surrounded by a multi-lane whirlpool of noisy and dirty traffic. In the case of the Place de la Bastille, Paris's urban planners have missed a golden opportunity to construct a public place by drawing upon its historical narrative. It has become a mundane or functional space rather than one of the major civic spaces within Paris.

The second requirement of a place that 'works' is that it allows intended activities to take place and signals their acceptability. In other words the place has to meet human needs. Carr et al. (1992) locate five kinds of reasons why people need public space: comfort, relaxation, passive and active engagement with the environment, and discovery. Each of these can be facilitated by the built environment, but in a more direct relationship to function rather than symbolic needs. In terms of *comfort*, relief from the sun and glare is important in hot climates, whilst access to the sun is important in cold climates, especially during winter. Shelter from rain and comfortable seating is also important. It is also important not to forget the need for clean and adequate toilets. *Relaxation* and resting can be helped by the provision of peace and quiet, plantings, and spaces to lie down and repose. Separation from automobile traffic and the use of water are also significant relaxers.

In terms of *passive engagement* with the environment, people like to have opportunities to watch others. Successful parks offer places where the gaze can be directed unobtrusively at others, for example at a cafe or from a terrace. Staircases, like the Spanish Steps in Rome, offer a particularly good vantage point for looking down on a world going by. Vistas are also attractive, for example a view over a river or lake. For *active engagement* the park needs to provide opportunities for meeting friends and hanging out, eating and drinking, walking, cycling, perhaps even shopping in market areas. *Discovery* is facilitated by the park providing opportunities for people to explore pathways and gardens. Changes in perspective offered by height can be particularly effective in promoting this sense.

A third requirement is that the space should provide people with a sense that they are welcome and safe. When public spaces are able to fulfil this need they tend to be successful. Evidence of use by 'undesirables' can lead to places developing negative meanings which discourage use by wide sections of the public. Urban areas marked by visual clues like graffiti, drug needles, or inhabited by suspicious-looking characters quickly become unattractive and take on negative meanings. The result can be a spiral of decline. As 'good' citizens desert these places, they become more and more attractive to 'bad' citizens and develop increasingly tainted meanings. Here again, design can be important. Where places are attractive and offer good visibility they will encourage 'good' citizens.[1] In an effort to turn bad places around, security guards are sometimes employed. These signal to the 'respectable citizen' that they are welcome. The issue of perceived safety is particularly significant for women, who are vulnerable to harassment or sometimes attack in public spaces. Studies suggest that women tend to be discriminating park users and tend to use the best-designed facilities (see Carr et al., 1992: 156). They tend to pick places which are more public, where other people (especially women) are around and where they cannot be approached from behind. Other, perhaps less dramatic, visual cues than drug needles and hoodlums can also tell people whether or not they should enter the public space. Expensive shops and cafes might suggest to some people that they are excluded. By contrast, affordable cafes send out a democratic message which will encourage patronage. Signs on park gates indicating attitudes to things like skateboarding, ball games and sitting on the grass also do more than signal permitted and non-permitted activities. They also suggest which kind of person can legitimately use the space.

What Carr et al. (1992: 144) call *visual access* to the public space is often vital in ensuring its appeal. This is the ability of potential users to see into the space from the outside so that they know it is safe and inviting. Public spaces surrounded by high fences, walls and hedges may deter users because they have little information about the character of the place and its occupants.

Another approach to the public space is to look at it in the way that we looked at the garden. Public spaces often work through binary opposition between nature and culture. Some, like city centre plazas, might be coded as being closer to culture, whilst others, like Central Park in New York, might be coded as being like nature. One might also find distinctions

BOX 5.7   SUCCESSFUL AND UNSUCCESSFUL PUBLIC SPACES EXERCISE

Select two contrasting public spaces in your town or city. One of these should be a place that is popular, the other a place that seems neglected or forgotten, but in other respects they should be sufficiently similar to permit meaningful comparison. Can you explain why these contrasting results have arisen? Look back to the discussion above and think about:

1. the ability of the place to connect with local events, environment history, or people
2. the ability of the place to meet functional needs (e.g. play spaces, seating)
3. the ability of the place to appear welcoming and safe.

To what extent does the visual play a role in each of these? Think here about issues like, gaze, vistas, visibility, signs and semiotics. To what extent do the needs of other senses contribute to the overall success or failure of the public space? Think here about issues like food and drink, exercise, toilets, noise.

within a single public space. Some areas might be more 'culture', like a formal fountain or formal garden, whilst other parts are more 'nature', like woodland or an informal grassy area. One can expect each of these areas to have their own codes of behaviour. Topless sunbathing, for example, may be permitted in the 'nature' area of the park but considered unacceptable in the 'culture' area. One can also look at the various ways in which 'nature' is made 'culture', for example by bringing picnic furniture, radios and sunshades and by colonizing an area in comfort for the afternoon (Fiske et al., 1987: 57).

Decoding the museum and art gallery

Just like homes and public spaces, museums, too, have a spatial and visual language built into them. This provides them with a definite character, signals appropriate behaviour and creates a 'learning environment'. John Falk and Lynn Dierking (1992: 85ff) point out a useful practical decoding of this in a book written for museum professionals. On arriving at the 'typical' traditional museum the visitor will often encounter stairs and Greek-style statues. These resonate with the concept of the temple, suggesting the museum is in some way a place of worship and also an elite institution. The visitor will then encounter a guard, and perhaps an x-ray machine indicating that the environment is one that is policed, where behaviour is watched and that treasures are contained within. Inside the museum the visual intimidation (at least of the novice visitor) continues with high vaulted ceilings, more stairwells and grandiose rooms. Falk and Dierking comment: 'Modern shopping malls, by contrast, are designed to be of moderate, rather than extreme, novelty, because places of moderate novelty have been found to be exciting rather than intimidating' (ibid.: 87). These visual clues feed in turn into visitor behaviour and attitudes. Research shows that people often find museums awe-inspiring, because they offer a connection with 'sacred' themes and things. Visitor behaviour reflects this, with people often walking slowly, talking in hushed tones and waiting patiently in line. Such behaviours seem to be common in sacred places – in Western culture at least (Smith, 1999: 19).

Much the same kind of analysis can be made of the traditional art gallery. Fiske et al. (1987) make a devastating, neo-Marxist decoding of the visual and spatial language of just about every major art gallery in Australia. The New South Wales art gallery is located in a grassed park called the 'Domain' which conjures up images of the British stately home, and is surrounded by other buildings dramatizing state power, such as libraries, the state parliament and war memorials. The modernist Australian National Gallery in Canberra physically resembles the neighbouring Supreme Court building and is situated in an area of public buildings and parkland. In Western Australia the art gallery is located in a run-down area, but is physically elevated above neighbouring buildings. According to Fiske et al., this 'imperiously imposes an official state culture upon the ethnic subcultures for whom the area was previously home' (ibid.: 149). The exterior of the buildings is bunker-like or Fork Knox-style, symbolizing hidden treasures, whilst inside these various buildings, 'the space is not unlike that of a temple or church' and 'evokes the effect of entering a cathedral' (ibid.: 150). We also find 'attendants dressed in uniforms like those of the police or army', whose function is to guard the art works from the public. All in all, then, Fiske et al. see the semiotics of art galleries as forbidding. It telegraphs their status as elitist institutions which do little to make the broader public welcome, especially the working class and minorities.

Today many traditional museums and art galleries have come under attack for these very reasons. Being under pressure to maintain government subsidies, they have had to respond by trying to attract a more numerous and more culturally diverse clientele. Consequently, many have attempted to change their image from being stuffy and intimidating to being exciting and welcoming. The visual and aural language of the museum can reflect this. At the Queensland Museum, for example, a pod of life-size whales suspended from the ceiling of the atrium serenades the visitor with piped clicks, groans and grunts. They probably still generate feelings of awe, but in contrast to monumental statuary it is a non-intimidating welcome. At a recent weekend visit to the Otago Museum in New

Zealand, one of the authors encountered clowns at the entrance and a rock band in an exhibition hall full of stuffed animals. Once again, this can be interpreted as an attempt to reverse an unappealing museum image. The clowns and the band work as visual (and aural) signifiers that the institution is democratic, contemporary and accessible to everyone.

Another way in which the museum can transform its image is with the display itself. Traditional museums have used a 'look don't touch' philosophy in which exhibits are protected behind glass and watched over by guards. Visitors in such situations are expected to behave in appropriately reverential ways and to demonstrate 'respect for the collection' (Falk and Dierking, 1992: 65). The trend today is towards a hands-on, interactive approach. Here behaviours like laughter and loud voices are permitted. A problem that museums often have is instructing visitors which exhibits are interactive and which are 'look only'. When the two kinds of exhibits are mixed, there is a risk of visitors touching the wrong things, or of feeling too intimidated to play with others. Visual cues have to be built into the landscape to indicate the status of the exhibit. These might include rope or glass barriers, written notices or iconic signs. Art galleries seem to have had a harder time coming up with alternative modes of display and information. Their response to accusations of elitism has largely been in terms of content. Blockbuster touring exhibitions of major (dead) artists like Van Gogh help attract the large audiences that make galleries appear popular. Displays by ethnic and minority artists enable them to claim that they are relevant to the experiences of 'ordinary' people.

Postmodern museums   So far we have been looking at largely conventional museums. More recently museums have been faced by a number of competitors who seek to challenge the idea that a museum should consist of

---

BOX 5.8   MUSEUMS AND ART GALLERIES EXERCISE: BETWEEN TRADITIONAL AND MODERN

This project is similar to the one involving public spaces that 'work'. Make a visit to your local museum or art gallery. Decode its visual language. How does the visual language of the institution signify its cultural identity and signal to patrons the appropriate ways of behaving? Next, watch the patrons. What evidence can you find that the museum has managed to successfully transmit this message? For example, how do people behave in the galleries? Do they interact with the interactive exhibits? Do they behave with appropriate decorum around priceless look-but-don't-touch artefacts? If the museum or art gallery fails in conveying its message, why might this be?

material objects complemented by written explanations. The most notable of these is the open air folk museum. These institutions can be considered postmodern in that in extreme cases they offer a simulacrum, rather like a theme park. In the case of the folk museum, elaborate efforts are made to recreate a past life complete with shops, banks and eateries and with real living people talking in supposedly old-fashioned ways. According to Tony Bennett, such museums seek to 'recreate the timbre of the everyday lives of ordinary people in past forms of community' (1995: 156). Bennett argues such museums are characterized by a number of features. They are 'theatrical' in that they often involve people in period costumes recreating everyday life in the past, pretending to be bakers, miners, shoemakers, etc. They involve 'miniaturization', with buildings compressed into a limited space so the visitor can experience an entire social world in a stroll. They exscript political realities, particularly those to do with capitalism. A display on work conditions in the nineteenth century, might place the blame on technology or the harsh qualities of pioneer life rather than the exploitative economic system. Signs of modernity, like public telephones or rubbish bins, are excluded or hidden from the visual field. There is typically a transition space, such as a tunnel or passageway between 'today' and 'then' . This makes it impossible to see one 'time' from the other. They are also dedicated to making money. Many of the exhibits are really shops aiming to sell merchandise to the tourist.

Bennett argues that the overall impact of the museums is apolitical. The message they transmit is a politically conservative one. Although they claim to present an accurate picture of the true past, they really disguise it. They tend to offer an idealistic vision of history. They neglect

---

BOX 5.9   FOLK MUSEUMS EXERCISE

Explore a local folk museum. How many of the features identified by Bennett can you identify in the visual landscape of the museum? Go on to decode the exhibits from a semiotic point of view. How is the past presented? Is it idealized as a 'golden age' of community and earthy toil? If struggle and hardship are presented, are they de-politicized? If so how?

Note: A particularly good place to do this might be a museum centred on industry, slavery, or crime. These purport to deal with aspects of a difficult past where exploitation and hardship went hand-in-hand. Bennett's observations are taken primarily from pioneer museums. These usually find it easy to evoke a *gemeinschaftlich*, cooperative imagery. Does his model hold up in more testing situations where outcasts and coercion are major themes?

struggle (except with nature) and tend to see past life as rural rather than urban.

Movement of people in time and space

In this section we shift from the decoding of environments to the study of how people interact with them. This entails a change in emphasis from semiotics towards observational inquiry. As with the previous section, although a camera could be used to collect information, this is not strictly necessary. In conducting a sociology of the seen, rather than a sociology of the image, notepads and coding sheets serve perfectly adequately in the majority of cases.

There is an extensive literature dealing with the gaze, visual display, built environments and human movements. This literature, in our view, plays an important role in our claim that a good deal of social theory can be recast as part of a tradition of visual sociology. One of the central concepts in this literature is that of the *flâneur*. This originated in the work of French poet Charles Baudelaire. The *flâneur* is an urbane urban spectator, wandering the streets at will in search of spectacle. The *flâneur* is no mere window shopper, enthusiastically participating in a consumer culture. Rather s/he takes an ironic, distant, aesthetic attitude to the commodities and street life on display. The concept has since been adopted and critiqued by theorists as diverse as Walter Benjamin, Richard Sennett and Mike Featherstone. In this ideological battleground the *flâneur* is displayed as either a disinterested bourgeois sensualist, or as a revolutionary whose everyday practice subverts and denies the dominant codes of the metropolis. More recently some cultural studies work has ignored the focus on reflexivity and phenomenological distance inherent in originating concepts of the *flâneur* and inaccurately applied the concept to designate zombie-like, automated consumer behaviour in the shopping mall (Woodward et al., 2000). Whatever path is chosen, the idea of the gazing individual navigating public spaces has become a motif in sociological theory.

Strikingly similar to ideas of the *flâneur* have been Simmel's thoughts on 'The Metropolis and Mental Life' (Donald, 1995). For Simmel, the city threatens to overwhelm the individual with sensory experience. The result has been a blasé attitude through which the individual provides him/herself with a protective shield. Contemporary work has also looked to the private sphere, treating the concept of the *flâneur* as a metaphor for a particular kind of gaze. Television, it has been noted, provides an ideal indoor environment for the *flâneur*. Flipping channels with a remote control becomes, in this scenario, the armchair equivalent of the *flâneurial* stroll.

As well as ideas about the gaze, ideas about navigation have also emerged from the *flâneur* literature as well as from a more positivist tradition looking at time–space geographies. Here the focus is on pathways, routines and spatial awareness. Baudelaire's Paris has been described as a kind of labyrinth through which the *flâneur* strolls, uncovering its shady, seedy, hidden underbelly. The *flâneur's* pathway is circuitous, accidental but s/he is driven by curiosity. The places visited are then reconstructed into a symbolic architecture of memory (Donald, 1995). Goffman's (1961) classic work on *Asylums* also carries this theme of voyages of discovery within the profane places. Inmates come to know and navigate their environment, discovering secret places outside of routine pathways and establishing covert and unauthorized uses of space. Jameson's (1991) work on postmodern architecture suggests that such competencies might become futile in the future. Jameson's point is that possibilities for the critical *flâneur* are radically circumscribed. Thanks to the allegedly disorienting properties of postmodern buildings like the Bonaventure Hotel, individuals no longer have the capacity to perceptually or physically navigate such spaces.

For all its promise of linking the gaze with the city and with movement, sociological work on the *flâneur* is often heavily theoretical. It is also overburdened with political interpretations. For some the *flâneur* is a victim of consumerism gazing in shop window after shop window, whilst for others s/he has become a kind of ironic anti-capitalist moving anarchically through the city. Such ideas reached their peak with Guy Debord's (1958) idea of the *dérive*, a kind of drifting movement in which one moves around the city from situation to situation, going with the flow. Debord saw such a form of motion as a refusal of the rationality and ordered control characteristic of life in capitalist modernity. Such theoretical work, then, sets the scene for this section, in which we try to map out some more empirical and sociological, rather than metaphysical, ideological and phenomenological approaches to human and crowd movements. We suggest such a topic belongs to visual analysis for two reasons. Firstly human movements are directly observable, and therefore are available to visual methods of inquiry. Secondly, visibility and responses to visual cues play a central role in directing such movements and controlling human behaviour.

Movement in the museum

We have already looked at ways to approach both museum exhibits and museums as a whole. Now we return to this research site to discuss how people move through the building. Designers of museum exhibits are often very conscious of the movement of people. This may be because they wish to avoid jams, but is more often because they wish to structure a learning experience. Skilful museum planners use a number of findings about human movement to good effect. According to David Dean, an experienced museum director and academic, there are a number of 'shared behavioural tendencies' that people have which are modified by societal or cultural preferences. Dean argues that 'to create effects, move people and attract attention it is normally wiser to play upon natural tendencies rather than oppose them' (1994: 51). Many of these human preferences seem to be based on visual and spatial perceptions that people have. Dean claims that:

- If all other factors are equal, people will turn to the right.
- People tend to stick to the right wall, ignoring exhibits to the left of their line of movement.
- The first exhibit on the right side will receive more attention than the first one on the left.
- People tend to spend more time at displays located at the start of an exhibit than towards the end.
- People dislike entering areas without visible exits.
- More time is spent on exhibits which line the path along the shortest route between the entrance and exit of an exhibit.
- Just as (western) people read from top-left to bottom right, they will also scan exhibits in this pattern.
- People tend to be drawn to brighter and larger objects.
- People have an average attention span of about 30 minutes in an exhibit.

If you went out and conducted the study suggested in Box 5.10, you may have found it rather difficult to test Dean's model. Perhaps this is because museum planners are often reflexive about human movements and viewing patterns. Museum experts have a message to get across and a space to fill. They will often have used knowledge of the kind we divulge here in order to plan the exhibit and distribute people around and through it. Dean suggests various strategies that museum planners can use to shape exhibits and head off habitual patterns of action. These include:

BOX 5.10   MUSEUM BEHAVIOUR EXERCISE

Are Dean's findings valid? Visit your local museum and make predictions about which exhibits in a particular room will be more popular according to his criteria. Now record people's movements in the selected exhibit. You can do this either by tracking people around the complex, or by sitting in a room and making notes. Do people seem to have other behavioural patterns that the list above does not cover? Think about ways of quantifying your data. For example, record the comparative amount of time spent at exhibits you have previously coded as 'dull' and 'bright'.

- using barriers to force people to turn left on entry
- promoting movement in 'unnatural' directions through the use of light, colour and other gimmicks
- getting people to look at displays of 'dull' and 'boring' but scientifically important things that they feel the public should know about (e.g. shards of old pottery, bones) by using dramatic lighting effects
- generating curiosity or a sense of mystery that will encourage people to circulate or explore out-of-the-way spaces. This can be done through light, design, and sound.

In the previous chapter we looked at the ways that a museum display might encode a process or 'story' like human evolution through the arrangement of artefacts in a case. Such a process can operate at a macro level too. An important factor in determining the lay-out and design of a museum exhibit is the total 'narrative' message of the display (Dean, 1994: 55). Unstructured approaches are common where there is no specific story being told. This might be found in an art gallery. A given room might display paintings by 'impressionists', treating them as a school with common properties. In such a location floor plans tend to be open, and human movement discretionary. 'Directed' approaches to human movement are found in displays with a stronger story line. These might document the chronology of a phenomenon, like the evolution of stone tools or the development of Monet's style during his career. Here we can expect to find a floor plan which pushes the reader from earlier

---

BOX 5.11   COMPARATIVE MUSEUM EXERCISE

Return to the museum you studied in the last assignment. How many of the devices listed above can you note in the exhibit? What evidence can you collect to claim that they work? Again, think about a tally or using a stopwatch to record the amount of time spent at a given exhibit.

It is reasonable to expect that not all museums will use the same devices. We can predict that large, well-funded museums (like malls and supermarkets) are better able to afford 'gimmicks' and traffic direction technology. They are also more likely to have professionally trained staff who are aware of the sorts of technologies and concerns we have revealed in this chapter. Try to contrast two museums, one a local, low-budget affair (e.g. a local history society or library or amateur collection) and the other a 'professional' state or national museum. Contrast the use of exhibition technologies and human traffic movements in these museums. What does this tell you about the degree of reflexivity and professionalism in each?

to later stages. An alternative might be a display on something technical, where earlier exhibits introduce fundamentals and later exhibits introduce finer detail that cannot be understood without a grasp of the fundamentals. An exhibit on Monet's techniques and materials or on atomic power might follow such a pattern. The two diagrams in Figure 5.2 illustrate the kinds of human traffic flow one might expect to find in each setting.

Movement in the shopping mall

Whilst virtual shopping and catalogue shopping are viable options, for most people shopping has a kinaesthetic dimension, it is 'about moving in the city, malls and shops, that is, in a space that makes purchasing possible and where the openness and plurality of possibilities are fundamental' (Lehtonen and Maenpaa, 1997: 143). As discussed previously, the shopping mall is not just a place where functional needs for survival are met. It is also a place where people have fun and fulfil social needs. Lehotonen and Maenpaa (ibid.: 144) distinguish two ideal types of shopper. One kind sees shopping as a 'necessary maintenance activity'. For these people it is a means to an end, where time is viewed as scarce, where shopping is an everyday routine and where planning and discipline are involved. The other kind of shopping is pleasure oriented. Here shopping is an end in itself, it is a fun activity for spending time and is seen as being an escape from everyday life. In this latter kind of activity one need not actually make any purchases to have a good shopping trip! The pleasure of shopping comes in part from looking at goods, trying them on, walking around the mall and experiencing its atmosphere, seeing and being seen (yes, it's that *flâneur* again!!). It can also provide social opportunities for meeting friends and spending time with them.

A similar distinction is made by Colin Campbell (1997), who argues on the basis of a focus group study that these distinctive shopping styles are gendered. According to Campbell the analysis of his transcripts suggests that the 'male view of shopping is, in essence, one in which a "need" is identified, an appropriate retail outlet is visited, and a suitable item purchased, after which the shopper returns home' (ibid.: 169). Males, then, tend to be time-conscious and to see shopping as a work-type activity which needs to be completed efficiently and quickly. By contrast women are interested in browsing and refer to 'the pleasure to be had in "just looking around"' and to 'refer to shopping in terms which suggest that a fundamentally aesthetic and expressive gratification is involved' (ibid.: 170). Women see shopping as a form of leisure and are also more likely to take advantage of the parallel opportunities provided to enjoy coffee, movies and social experiences offered by the mall.

Issues of shopping experience and shopping style are, of course, related to subjective experiences and personal meanings. Interview studies and ethnography may be required to flesh these out. Nevertheless, some are

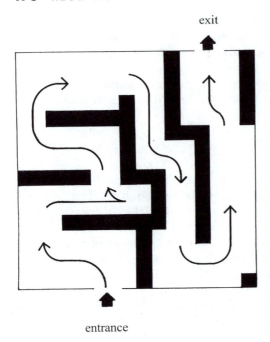

exit

Exhibit floor plan
allowing only directed
movement

entrance

entrance or exit

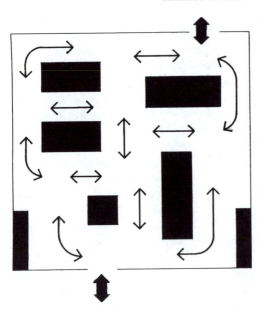

Exhibit floor plan
allowing unstructured
movement

entrance or exit

FIGURE 5.2   *Unstructured and directed human traffic flows in a museum.*
Adapted from Dean (1994: 54)

BOX 5.12   MUSEUM TRAFFIC FLOW EXERCISE

Visit a museum, select one or more exhibits that seem to have a strong narrative theme. What is the narrative being told by the exhibit? How is this embodied in the floor plan? Sketch the floor plan and indicate with arrows how the various components of the narrative are arranged spatially within the exhibit. How effective is the floor plan in carrying out its mission? This last part of the assignment is quite hard. Are there blind alleys and corners with important information that people never get to see? Are there bottlenecks, where the practical task of moving people through the exhibit clashes with the didactic needs of the exhibit? If people seem to skip some sections, why is this?

amenable to exploration from the viewpoint of visual research to the extent that they can be seen. Contrasting orientations towards shopping should be reflected in human movements around the mall, or in contrasting uses of mall facilities. These kinds of behavioural data can be directly observed and provide a complement to the attitudinal data that is collected through shopping ethnography. The exercise in Box 5.13 suggests some ways to explore this issue.

Another approach to shopping centre movements is to explore questions of architectural design and flow, much as we looked at questions of flow in the museum. Shopping centre managements like to build multistorey malls as this maximizes the amount of retail space they can place on a given area of land. A problem, however, can be to get customers to circulate to the upper levels of the mall. Various devices can be established to attempt to do this. These include the use of glass and light to draw people upwards, locating up-escalators in more visible places than down-escalators, and (the more risky strategy) of locating anchor attractions on these floors, such as food courts. Basement areas can also be a problem.

Postmodernism and disorientation

One of the most substantial claims about postmodern spaces is that they exert a disorienting effect on people. Fredric Jameson's influential thesis is that such places embody the spatial and cultural logic of late capitalism. They engender confusion that prevents the contemporary subject from understanding the totality of the situation in which they find themselves. Whilst people might be able to navigate the grid-like streets of a modernist city like New York, they find themselves perplexed when dealing with a multi-level, postmodern space with curves and blind alleys, etc. Jameson's own evidence for this finding was his personal experience of

BOX 5.13   GENDER AND SHOPPING STYLES EXERCISE

Here we suggest three ways of exploring gendered shopping styles and seeing if the orthodoxy holds up.

- Trail men and women around the mall from the moment they enter the door. Using a prepared map of the mall, mark their route and keep a record of where they are every five minutes by placing a mark on the map. Analyse the maps. If the theory is correct we should expect that men's routes will be more direct than women's and involve less back-tracking. They should also spend less total time in the mall.
- Position yourself by an entrance and make a note of the number of men and women entering the mall. Work out the proportion of each sex. Now visit areas of the mall that offer non-shopping experiences such as coffee shops, food halls and movie theatres. Count the number of men and women in each location. If the theory is correct, it will be found that women are over-represented in these places.
- Position yourself in a location with a good view of a stretch of mall corridor (e.g. on a balcony looking down). Using a watch, time how long it takes men and women to cover the stretch between two identifiable points (e.g. shop fronts, rubbish bins, plant pots). If the theory is correct, men will cover the distance more rapidly thanks to their purposeful, time-efficient shopping style and desire to leave the mall as soon as possible.

Notes: (1) You might want to obtain permission from mall management to conduct these studies. The first one in particular might attract the attention of store security or may spook the customer into thinking you are a stalker. The second two are more unobtrusive and should be easier to carry out. (2) You may locate interesting differences according to the day of the week. Weekends, for example, are socially defined as leisure time. You might find a trend towards the leisure shopping pattern at this time. (3) Aside from gender, age and race offer other demographics along which you can structure your study.

being lost in the Los Angeles Bonaventure Hotel. Although from a methodological perspective one might find this evidence inadequate, his claim has often been repeated as a fact by leading sociological scholars. Rob Shields (1994: 206), for example, writes that contemporary shopping malls 'enfold and engulf us in their interior spatial logic' and that they have the power to 'guide but also deny human will . . . on terms prescribed by the designers, display artists and operators of the shopping centre'. According to Shields, the architecture of labyrinthine passages and stairways and escalators moving in directions opposite to those we wish make it difficult for people to engage in rational, planned movement through the mall. Consequently we are forced to become a *flâneur*, moving with the flow of people whether we like it or not.

Such ideas have recently come under scrutiny. Peter Jackson and Nigel Thrift (1995: 210), for example, assert that the 'residual influence of Marxian political economy' in the study of malls has led to a rather one-sided picture of the mall as 'an essentially threatening presence, able to bend consumers to its will'. They suggest that more research should focus on the active role of consumers in negotiating meanings and lines of action in the mall. We return to this issue of action in public spaces in a later chapter. For the meantime, let's focus on disorientation claims. Shopping malls provide an excellent location for a more thorough test of generic claims about postmodern spaces and their ability to overwhelm the human subject. The project in Box 5.14 taps into this opportunity.

BOX 5.14   DISORIENTATION IN THE MALL PROJECT

In a thesis we supervised (Woodward, 1996), shoppers were surveyed in three malls, ranging in style from the mildly postmodern to the highly postmodern. The less postmodern malls were essentially older, linear malls which had had some postmodern features bolted on to them. Shoppers were asked questions about feelings of confusion and the need to consult store maps. The results showed remarkably little difference between the malls, with people quickly learning layouts and plans so that after a few repeat visits, they were no longer disoriented in the postmodern malls. Such a methodology, of course, has little to do with visual research. Yet, it should be possible to replicate this study with little difficulty using purely observational methods. Sit near to the mall maps and note how often they were consulted at the various malls. If the postmodernists are correct there should be marked differences between consultation patterns in the two kinds of malls. Obviously you will have to think about visiting each mall at various days of the week etc. so as to capture the full range of mall users. The advantage of this method over Woodward's is that you are using a non-reactive observational measure. As we have argued earlier in this book, these present advantages for visual sociology over traditional reactive social research. Your findings, therefore, should not be influenced by normative responding or by faulty recall or by variations in the ways that respondents interpret survey questions and scales.

Spaces and uses

The previous studies in this section have looked at movement. Another way to approach people in places is with a synchronic or snapshot approach, mapping who is where doing what at particular points in time. Once again, a purely visual or observational sociology can turn up interesting findings. Because the next chapter deals with people interacting with each other, we are unable to follow these issues at length here. Our focus is restricted to how people interact with the space. The following examples are taken from Carr et al. (1992).

- In New York City's minute Greenacre Park, most users sit facing the waterfall. Elderly people, by contrast, sit near the entrance looking out towards the street. This is so they can look out for acquaintances passing by. For these people the park is essentially a meeting place.
- Sports and games could be found throughout parks in Los Angeles, but in Paris they tended to be restricted to certain areas of parks (Lyle, 1970).
- Play areas attract mostly children and their parents. Skateparks attract teenagers, etc.
- People tend to sit facing the flow of pedestrian traffic, not with their backs to it.
- Women prefer to sit near other people, especially women, and in places with escape routes. They tend not to sit on their own or in isolated positions.
- People will avoid sunny locations on hot days and sit in the shade, and vice versa for cold days.
- Shopping malls attract people for many reasons other than shopping. The food and drink areas, for example, provide locations for people to hang out. Shields (1994) reports that Somali refugees used a food court area of a Canadian mall as an area to sit and chat over long, drawn out cups of coffee. The area became a sort of social space for solidaristic interaction. For pensioners, the unemployed and others on fixed incomes, public spaces provide a way to get out of the home and cope with potential isolation. Such groups will typically colonize particular areas of a public space, but spend little money. Young people are another poor and marginalized group who use public spaces to hang out (White, 1990). Conflicts with police often arise if they are perceived to be loitering or causing a public nuisance, or with mall management if they are seen to be not engaged in shopping activity.

Visibility, invisibility and the gaze

In previous chapters we have touched on issues of vision, visibility and invisibility. In the chapter on objects, for example, we spoke about the

BOX 5.15   SPACES AND USES PROJECT

Select a small public space such as part of a mall, park or plaza. Using observation at hourly intervals, record:

- the spatial distribution of people in this area on a sketch map at various times of the day
- their activities (active/passive, alone or in groups)
- age and gender.

What kinds of patterns do you detect in terms of the links between types of person and the uses of space? How do routines associated with the time of day alter this (e.g. morning joggers, lunch hour brown baggers)?

Note: The suggested project above is very open ended. It is a grounded project in that there is no specific originating hypothesis. If you require a theory or issue to test, the gendered distribution of people is one which is theoretically interesting and easy to explore in purely visual terms (unlike, say ethnicity, which may not be visible). Do women and men have different patterns of using public space? To what extent can safety issues explain these? You may want to use a camera to illustrate the kinds of interaction you find at various times.

contrast between hidden objects and those which are displayed in public. In this section we return to the issue. We are particularly interested in the organization of spaces in terms of visibility and invisibility and links to power, control and civility. An adjunct theme concerns the kinds of gaze that are promoted in various places, their ties to the social meanings and to profit.

Panopticon spaces

At various points in this book we have alluded to Foucault's (1979) work on spaces and disciplinary practices. Central to this work were ideas of surveillance and the ways that this surveillance caused people to regulate their behaviour within repressive institutions. Foucault drew attention to a Victorian-era architectural device known as the panopticon. This consisted of a central tower with an invisible guard, around which various cells were arrayed. People in the cells could never be certain if they were being watched or not. As a result they would have to constantly monitor and check their behaviour, conform to institutional rules and so on. Foucault argues that the principles of the panopticon have become widespread in our society as a technique of social control. Evidence for this can be seen in the proliferation of security cameras in shopping malls, high streets and even universities like ours!! In other words, vision and visibility are central to the maintenance of social order. Earlier in this chapter we discussed a study by Lindsay Prior in which built form was used as a means of decoding knowledge and belief systems in relation to children's hospital wards. We return to that study here.

In addition to looking at the hospital, Lindsay Prior (1988) also studied the asylum. He shows that early asylums embodied the kind of disciplinary architecture Foucault discusses. Inmates are enclosed and cut off from the outside world, and were separated from each other in cells located in wings, whilst functionaries work in the 'hub' of the panopticon design. There is more to the design than simply panopticism. Prior suggests that the stress placed on the individual cell reflects 'a desire to emphasize the individuality of the occupant, and a desire to control the occupant' (ibid.: 102). In other words, there was a tendency in the prevailing discourses to treat the inmate as an individual, rather than as a member of a class of people with a common problem. Other features of designs also catch Prior's attention. On the plans he sees 'bathrooms, day rooms, airing grounds, wash-houses, bed-rooms' which 'spell out in some detail the elements of a culture in which the body and its functions are closely regulated' (ibid.: 105). In addition, one can decode an obsession with hierarchy from the plans, with supervisors given more room than keepers and so on. Looking at more recent designs, Prior comments that as madness came to be seen as more like an illness, asylum designs have come to resemble hospital designs more than prisons. Moreover, contemporary designs incorporate spaces for social workers and occupational therapists. This again reflects changing discourses about madness and how it intersects with the interests of various professions.

Some contemporary critics argue that we are living in a 'surveillance society'. Is this true, and if so, to what extent? How can we tell if surveillance is effective? Many scholars argue that Foucault fails to take account of 'resistance' and the innovative abilities of people to locate secret spaces. Certainly Goffman's (1961) study of *Asylums* suggests this may be the case. Using ethnographic methods Goffman found that inmates of the asylum had secret places which were relatively immune from staff supervision. Here they would engage in illicit activities like smoking, drinking and gambling. Goffman's findings may be applicable more widely to high-surveillance locations.

Mutual surveillance in institutional settings

Behaviours in public places are strongly regulated not only by norms, but also by issues of visibility and invisibility. The panopticon need not be operated by people in authority, but can also arise from self-policing of populations thanks to mutual visibility. To illustrate this theme, let us return to

BOX 5.16   THE PANOPTICON SHOPPING MALL PROJECT

Visit your local shopping mall. What forms of surveillance can you detect (e.g. security cameras, guards)? When you have worked out what forms of surveillance are in operation classify areas of the shopping mall according to whether they are high, medium, or low surveillance. The next thing to do is to collect data on deviance. Itemize visual evidence of deviance (e.g. graffiti, litter, drug needles, used condoms) for each of these areas. To supplement this project, you might also want to conduct visual observation of some of these areas. Look for 'deviant' activities like skateboarding, or groups of young people hanging out. You can write up the study in either a quantitative or qualitative way. If taking the quantitative path, think about scoring the evidence and constructing a scale for the amount of deviance (e.g. item of litter = 1, graffiti = 3, drug needle = 5). Do your findings tend to support Foucault's views about the power of surveillance, or Goffman's about the ability of people to find creative ways to avoid it?

one of our favourite sites for visual research – the museum. Writing about the nineteenth century, Tony Bennett argues that 'the museum explicitly targeted the popular body as an object for reform, doing so through a variety of routines and technologies requiring a shift in the norms of bodily comportment' (1995: 100). The intention was that the working classes (and other less refined groups) might become more cultivated not only by studying the exhibits, but also through genteel promenading in a civilizing environment. The implicit contrast was with the street, the pub and the fair, where licentious and boisterous behaviour was predominant. The problem for museum managers was to enforce new norms of behaviour without having to employ armies of guards. The solution lay in internal architectures in which the public's view of itself came to be as significant as the public's view of the exhibits. New museum designs had open galleries and halls, replacing and eliminating small rooms and dark corners. Because it was constantly visible in galleries to itself, the public came to self-regulate, 'thus placing an architectural restraint on any incipient tendency to rowdiness' (1995: 101). Bennett sees this technique as being consistent with Foucault's work on surveillance, with the gaze being used as a normalizing device to discipline the unruly body.

Kinds of gaze

Environments are not simply places where we see things in a passive way. They are also locations where we must look in active ways. In an earlier

BOX 5.17   VISIBILITY AND BEHAVIOUR EXERCISE

Visit your local museum, yet again. Note down areas where levels of mutual public visibility are high and areas where they are low. Areas of high visibility might include galleries and walkways. Areas of low visibility might include dead-end rooms, less visited locations on the top floors, and places that are kept dark for dramatic effect or to protect the displays. Using observational techniques, code examples of less formal modes of behaviour like laughter, touching, joking, kissing, running, slouching, etc. You will probably need to keep a tally of the number of people passing through each location so that you can express your 'unruly' behaviours as rates. In this way you can control for the potential effects of the less-visible locations being the less visited. Do you notice significant differences in comportment in these areas? Do your findings support Bennett's ideas about public-to-public visibility leading to civil conduct?

Note: One reason you might experience problems in conducting the project above is that, as we have discussed, today museums are trying to jazz up their image and encourage signs of life in their visitors. You easily can modify the project by making the central plank of your research an evaluation of whether these strategies work. Discussions with museum management might help to clarify the intention of various exhibits and the kinds of public behaviours that are to be expected or tolerated in each location. You can then look to see if reality conforms to expectation.

chapter we looked at the ways that adverts and other texts encourage particular kinds of gaze. Sexist adverts, for example, usually encourage a 'male gaze' of an objectified female body. Environments can be coded in much the same way to encourage particular kinds of looking. Using post-structural language, we can argue that places work to anchor different kinds of 'scopic regimes'. Pasi Falk (1997) suggests some of the ways that this can take place. Both the chapel and the shop work to halt the moving body and pull it away from the flow of the street. Yet there are differences. The chapel, he argues, 'promotes a kind of inward meditative look as an aspect of a peace-seeking mind, while the shop invites a more extroverted and active look' (ibid.: 179). The art gallery is like the shop in that it is organized to stimulate the active gaze. However, in the case of the art gallery the gaze is directed in such a way as to maintain distance, whilst in the shop it may 'lead to close encounters and the use of contact senses. Thus the shopping gaze is reminiscent of the approaching gaze of the hunter. . .' (ibid.: 182).

Fiske et al. (1987) provide some further indications of the kinds of fundamental ways in which the gaze structures shops and shopping. They assert that shopping is structured around the 'pleasure of looking'. It is a spectacle in which one is both performer and spectator. Fiske et al. point to the extensive use of 'glass, light and reflective surfaces' which make window shopping into a 'stroll through a hall of mirrors' (ibid.: 98). They also point to the omnipresence of places for looking, like balconies, where shoppers can gaze at the passing parade. In combination these stimulate consumption by making people more aware of their bodies, identity and image. Narcissism, voyeurism and identity formation come together in complex ways in the shopping experience.

Naturally people don't always gaze in the normative way. Shields (1994: 221), for example, argues along similar lines to Fiske et al. that malls work to direct the gaze towards objects, oneself and others and to stimulate consumption. Yet he also points out that such gazes may take deviant forms as people make use of the opportunities the mall presents. Men, for example, may use the plethora of glass and escalators for voyeuristic looking, whilst children might count bald heads from a balcony or take an interest in rubbish on the floor.

Visibility, invisibility and symbolic classification

Work looking at the gaze typically explores issues of visibility and invisibility in terms of power, control and the body. Another approach to these issues is to think about the social meanings of objects and the ways in which they are encoded. In the previous chapter we showed that some objects in the house are displayed and others are hidden because of taboo, shame, or embarrassment. Earlier in this chapter we also approached this question when discussing public and private spaces in the home. Similar cultural logics can be detected in other places too.

BOX 5.18   PLACES AND GAZES EXERCISE

This is a small exercise to get you thinking about the gaze and the ways it is encouraged and shaped. Select two contrasting locations where looking is a major activity. Tourist spots, sports grounds, strip clubs, casinos and hair salons, for example, are all organized spatially and in terms of mood to encourage particular kinds of looking. What kind of gaze is encouraged at your locations? Is it active or passive? Public or hidden? How does the architecture and design of the location encourage a particular gaze? Conduct some observational studies. To what extent do people engage in the gaze that is being encouraged?

In the shopping mall and shops, for example, visibility is strongly linked to the desire to sell commodities. Hence goods that are for sale and shop floors are likely to attract attention. Other objects may be hidden from view or may be seen but not noticed. Rooms associated with animal bodily functions, toilets and baby changing rooms, are likely to be hidden away in the mall. Perhaps this is because of a symbolic association with pollution. As Mary Douglas (1969) has asserted, distinctions between the pure and the polluted structure a substantial proportion of our cultural life. That which is deemed dirty, infected, dangerous or disordering must be excluded from that which is orderly, tidy and pure. A similar point has been made by Norbert Elias (1978) in a historical argument about the rise of the modern norms of civility. Elias asserts that over the past several centuries the dirty, violent and 'animal' sides of human activities (defecation, sex, etc.) have been hidden away and excluded from public view. Whilst these were once performed in public settings, today we see them as threatening to our sense of self-worth and dignity. Such normative shifts can be seen in the design of buildings, with the modern toilet and bedroom, for example, arising in step with this historical shift. Other, less visceral cultural codings may also structure the display and location of mall objects. Equipment necessary for the efficient or safe functioning of the mall might also be hidden (e.g. air conditioning plant) or else displayed so that we don't really notice it, even though it does not carry negative connotations of pollution. As Rob Shields (1994: 215) notes, in the mall things which are useful in everyday life 'suffer a loss of legitimacy' relative to things which are for sale. Examples in the latter class might include fire-fighting equipment, rubbish bins, phones, seats and so on. Such objects should be in working order, and we should be able to find them if we actively look for them, but they should not intrude on the experience of commodities. These form the privileged objects within the mall. Consequently the mall can be read as a kind of 'frame' which serves to highlight certain objects (the goods for sale) and hide supporting objects (infrastructure).

BOX 5.19   VISIBILITY, INVISIBILITY AND OBJECT CLASSIFICATION EXERCISE

Select a public space other than a mall. You may wish to look at a church, a school, a nightclub, a museum, or an office. Which objects and spaces are privileged in this location? Why are they privileged? Which objects and spaces are devalued? How does the spatial arrangement of the building and the objects, or patterns of display frame these relative statuses?

Conclusion

In this chapter we have explored various dimensions through which places can provide a resource for the visual researcher. We have looked at how they can be decoded, at ways in which they are used and looked at, and at ways in which people move around them. Towards the end of the chapter, vision, gaze, civility and behaviour in public places came to the fore as essential themes for understanding relationships between people and environments. The next chapter builds on these issues but in a new direction. In this chapter our concern was with the ways that built forms influence human action and human movements. In Chapter 6 our attention shifts to consider how interaction with other humans, and their visual availability to us, influences how we behave. This area of interpersonal interaction is, in many ways, far more complex and methodologically challenging.

Note

1   This finding has a history extending back to the Chicago school studies of the 'urban transition' zone. Its most recent incarnation is as the 'broken windows' hypothesis which supports 'zero tolerance' policing. We looked at this at the end of the last chapter.

6

Living Forms of Visual Data: Bodies, Identities and Interaction

In our final chapter we extend our investigation of visual data to embrace what is arguably its most ubiquitous but least self-evident manifestation: the activities of people in everyday interaction. Our primary concern is to identify the ways in which these activities and the relationships they embody can be captured using the visual method of observation. In previous chapters we have explored the issue of people interacting with spaces and objects, and the ways that questions of sociological relevance can be addressed by exploring movements and behaviours. Things become more complex when we explore how people react in relationship to each other. This is because people, as we all know, are not objects. Consequently we all modify our behaviours when we know they will be interpreted by other people. The study of interaction can therefore become a study of people as bearers of signs which mark identity, status and social competence. Because the production and reception of many of these signals is in the visual register (exceptions are things like perfume, and, of course, language) social interaction is inherently a visual activity organized in large part around observable symbolism. For this reason, the study of persons in interaction is very much amenable to visual inquiry. Every day each person gives off hundreds of signals which are intended to be read. As visual researchers, all that is required is that we attend to these signals in theoretically and methodologically disciplined ways.

In this chapter we will:

- introduce theoretical perspectives through which visual research can look at people and bodies in mutual interaction
- explore questions of gaze, territoriality, gesture and presentation of self
- consider how the transformations of modernity have impacted upon the visual organization of interpersonal relations in contemporary urban life.

In this chapter we are primarily interested in behaviour which is publicly observable by virtue of its occurrence in streets, parks, shops and department stores, restaurants and waiting rooms and so on. Among the issues we consider are the ways in which much of this everyday public behaviour has a spatial or territorial component to it. The study of the ways humans utilize or orient to space in their everyday interaction is a specialized area of investigation and is referred to as proxemics; closely related is the field of kinesics or communication through gesture and body language. Whilst these are both highly technical fields, we briefly consider each of them in this chapter and present examples of the ways that a low-tech observational study can ask and answer interesting questions.

To some extent many of the issues we canvass in this chapter are well known: indeed they have become part of sociological wisdom, particularly for those who work within the symbolic interactionist tradition. Erving Goffman's voluminous writings (e.g. Goffman, 1963, 1971) on interactional conduct in public settings are probably the best examples of sociological work which takes the minutiae of everyday conduct seriously. Our aim, however, is not to present yet another reworking of Goffman's ideas but to extend and apply these in specific ways. It is an oft-repeated remark that, although Goffman presents fascinating insights, there is a surprising lack of methodological rigour to his writings. That is, Goffman is seldom – if ever – concerned with testing the validity of his observations in systematic empirical ways. The examples for project work we suggest in this chapter can be seen as a small contribution to putting Goffman – and the visual sociology he so clearly outlines – on a more secure empirical footing. There is also the related question of the historical relevance of his vision of everyday conduct. Goffman's concepts were forged in a period of high modernity: the late 1950s and 1960s. As sociological theorists continually remind us, we now live in postmodern times. The question naturally arises: to what extent are the cultural changes associated with postmodernity reflected in the social organization of day-to-day public conduct? Goffman presents his observations of interactional behaviour as if this was somehow eternal and universal. In fact the dynamics of public conduct which seem so taken-for-granted to us today are historically specific and came into being at a particular time. Before going any further it is useful to consider this historical specificity in more detail.

The transformation of the public domain

There is a powerful expectation in modern society – we use this term as a convenient shorthand for the developed western industrial countries – that, in public, people have a right to enjoy privacy or silence. Although it is not illegal to initiate a conversation with a fellow passenger on a bus or train, or with a stranger whilst strolling in a park or browsing through a department store, there are strong moral or social pressures against doing so. We tend to regard people who do this as a little odd or strange – perhaps even threatening. And yet this attitude to what is permissible in public interaction has by no means always existed. Simmel was, perhaps, the first sociologist to comment on the changing expectation concerning public intercourse. In his essay on 'The Sociology of the Senses', Simmel (1921[1908]) drew attention to one of the key features of modern life, that interaction is based on sight rather than sound. Noting the calm and peaceful disposition which the blind – those who hear but do not see – generally display towards their surroundings, Simmel observed that the converse – when interaction is based on seeing but without hearing – was at the root of the emotional problems of life in the modern metropolis:

> Social life in the large city as compared with the towns shows a great preponderance of occasions to *see* rather than *hear* people. . . . Before the appearances of omnibuses, railroads, and street cars in the nineteenth century, men were not in a situation where for periods of minutes or hours they could or must look at each other without talking to one another. Modern social life increases in ever growing degree the role of visual impression . . . and must place social attitudes and feelings upon an entirely changed basis. The greater perplexity which characterizes the person who only sees . . . brings us to the problems of the emotions of modern life: the lack of orientation in the collective life, the sense of utter lonesomeness, and the feeling that the individual is surrounded on all sides by closed doors. (Simmel, 1921[1908]: 360–1, emphasis in original)

The thesis concerning the transformation of public life has been given its most extended treatment by Richard Sennett. In *The Fall of Public Man* (1977) Sennett develops an argument concerning the imbalance which has developed between the public and private domains. Whereas there was once a thriving public culture in which individuals actively sought rewarding contact with strangers, the contemporary citizen manifests an entirely different approach to public behaviour. The 'stranger' is now perceived as a threatening figure, and individuals have withdrawn into the private domain of the family. As a consequence, Sennett believes that private life and sexuality have become distorted as we engage in increasingly narcissistic forms of self-absorption. Sennett's thesis is complex, and we do not have the space to fully document all that he has to say about these changes. Moreover, we are less interested in his target – the indictment of the psychological malaise of modern culture – than in what we have apparently lost and the conditions which underpinned the 'original' vibrant character of public interaction. Sennett sees the apotheosis of 'public man' in the expanding urban centres of London and Paris during the eighteenth century and dates its decline with the passing of the *Ancien Régime* under the twin influences of industrialization and secularization. According to Sennett,

> the citizens of the 18th Century capitals attempted to define both what public life was and what it was not. The line drawn between public and private was

essentially one on which the claims of civility – epitomized by cosmopolitan, public behaviour – were balanced against the claims of nature – epitomized by the family. They saw these claims in conflict, and the complexity of their vision lay in that they refused to prefer the one over the other, but held the two in a state of equilibrium. Behaving with strangers in an emotionally satisfying way and yet remaining aloof from them was seen by the mid-18th Century as the means by which the human animal was transformed into a social being. (Sennett, 1977: 18)

A central plank for Sennett's thesis is provided by Goffman's dramaturgical model. *The Fall of Public Man* weaves together a fascinating series of examples from architecture, politics, fashion, manners, and – importantly – the theatre to demonstrate its argument that in the public life of the eighteenth century, men[1] behaved almost literally as actors. In the public domain conventions of speech, clothing and appearance immediately established a person's place in society. As a consequence people from all social strata could mingle freely, secure in the knowledge that they could readily identify their fellow citizens. Sennett argues that the principle of dressing the body as a mannequin, constituting it as a marker of established conventions, actually drew the upper and lower classes closer together. Amongst the upper orders the body became even more objectified through elaborate ornamentation of wigs, hats, masks and facial colouring:

Marking the face with little patches of paint was the final step in obliterating the face. The practice was begun in the 17th Century but by the 1750s it had become widespread. In London patches were placed on the right or left side of the face, depending on whether one were Whig or Tory. During the reign of Louis XV, patches were placed to indicate the character of the Parisian: at the corner of the eye stood for passion; centre of the cheek, gay; nose, saucy. A murderess was supposed to wear patches on her breasts. (Sennett, 1977: 70)

The demise of this 'visually stratified' public domain, in Sennett's view, took place gradually during the nineteenth century. One strand in this process came from the developments in merchandizing associated with capitalist industrialization. Clothing increasingly became mass produced and available through the new department stores which encouraged passive consumption rather than the active haggling in the street markets of earlier times. The sartorial heterogeneity through which occupational groups had once been differentiated was thus eliminated. Coupled with this, however, was an equally important secular change regarding human nature and the manner in which this was ascertainable. The eighteenth-century notion which saw the human animal as having a fixed repertoire of behavioural traits became eroded in favour of a view which saw individuals as developing – through their unique experiences – their own individual personalities. If human nature was no longer a transcendental category but instead immanent in observable actions then the appearance of emotion and the inner nature of the person expressing this became one and the same. Whereas in the eighteenth century, clothing, forms of speech and gestures were masks, in the nineteenth century these things were now seen as signs of personality. Consequently, Sennett argues, people became increasingly self-conscious about their appearances in public:

> In this society on its way to becoming intimate – wherein character was expressed beyond the control of the will, the private was superimposed on the public, the defence against being read by others was to stop feeling – one's public behaviour was altered in its fundamental terms. Silence in public became the only way one could experience public life, especially street life, without feeling overwhelmed. In the mid 19th century . . . there grew up the notion that strangers had no right to speak to each other, that each man possessed as a public right an invisible shield, a right to be left alone. Public behaviour was a matter of observation, of passive participation, of a certain kind of voyeurism. The 'gastronomy of the eye', Balzac called it. (Sennett, 1977: 27)[2]

Sennett's thesis about the decline of public life and the claustrophobic or narcissistic character of our personal lives has not gone unchallenged. Giddens (1991), in particular, has argued that the course of modernity has in fact been one of the expansion of the public realm and of the possibilities which individuals have for participating within this. Nevertheless Sennett's writings provide a fascinating source of ideas all of which offer possibilities for the study of visual aspects of modern urban life. Erving Goffman and Lyn Lofland are two writers who have addressed these issues empirically.

Goffman and 'civil inattention'

One of the consequences of the transformation of the public domain is the development of new norms or behavioural codes which govern our interaction with others in such settings. One of Goffman's earliest and most fertile concepts was forged with the explicit aim of documenting this behavioural sensibility. When persons are mutually present in a public place but not otherwise interactionally engaged Goffman suggests that there are particular norms operating which regulate the kind of eye contact deemed permissible between individuals. Specifically we accord other parties 'civil inattention', a process which involves giving the other

> enough visual notice to demonstrate that one appreciates that the other is present (and that one admits openly to having seen him), while at the next moment withdrawing one's attention from him so as to express that he does not constitute a target of special curiosity or design. In performing this courtesy the eyes of the looker may pass over the eyes of the other, but no 'recognition' is typically allowed. Where the courtesy is performed between two persons passing on the street, civil inattention may take the special form of eyeing the other up to approximately eight feet, during which times sides of the street are

apportioned by gesture, and then casting the eyes down as the other passes – a kind of dimming of lights. In any case, we have here what is perhaps the slightest of interpersonal rituals, yet one that constantly regulates the social intercourse of persons in our society. (Goffman, 1963: 84)

Gardner has observed that the simple act of walking past another person may involve activities 'that are not breaches of civil inattention but constitute mere markers of the act' (Gardner, 1980: 329). Women are particularly liable to receive such paralinguistic signs of their presence. These communicative markers can range from such things as mechanical noises – a truck driver noisily applying air breaks as his vehicle keeps pace with a female pedestrian, or youths who jingle bicycle bells as a rhythmic accompaniment to a walker – to physiological signals such as belches or nose blowing as well as more elaborate activities which appear more contrived or intentional. Gardner offers the following description:

A young white father wheeling his child in a stroller looks up and down at the young woman crossing Fifth Avenue opposite him. Eight feet away from her he gives stroller and child an extra push and lets go – no hands: and with one of his free hands he begins patting his thigh and, at the same time, begins to whistle continuing both activities until he and the woman have passed. Other men rhythmically tap some object at hand – a walking cane, a magazine, a gallery program. . . . These types of markers of passage thus salute civil inattention by obeying its boundaries and simultaneously undermine it by incorporating attention-getters such as gaze and noise into those boundaries. (Gardner, 1980: 331)

Gardner's example draws attention not only to the presence of tokenistic markers, but also to Goffman's relative insensitivity to issues of gender in the public domain. Leaving this issue aside for the time being, we note that more overt linguistic breaches of civil inattention are also to be found. For example where there is some obvious similarity between two passersby – persons with children of the same age or dogs the same breed – then there is a licence both to give and receive remarks. Gardner also mentions situations when, for whatever reason, we exit the role of a properly comported citizen we become an 'open person' (Goffman, 1963: 126) and liable to comments from passers-by. On these occasions we may be anxious ourselves to proffer reasons or extenuating circumstances for the discrepant appearance. People en route to a fancy dress party by foot or transporting unusual objects, such as large items of furniture from one location to another, are examples of this.

Goffman appears to assume that civil inattention operates as a universal norm governing all forms of public contact between individuals, at least in contemporary western societies. But this is not the case. On the contrary there are situations in which contact between passers-by appears to be governed by what we might term a norm of *civil attention* – the inverse of Goffman's category – when *not* to speak or openly engage with the other party constitutes a breach of pedestrian etiquette. We have in mind here as an example the sort of contact that takes place between citizens who pass each other on the walking or jogging tracks which have become a conspicuous feature of many suburbs of large cities. At least in the Australian context with which we are familiar, walkers appear duty bound to explicitly acknowledge fellow exercisers. The encounter assumes the following form. As two walkers (or walking parties) approach each other on a track, something like the typical norm of civil inattention appears to operate until a space of about 3 metres separates them. That is, the walkers momentarily monitor each other, adjusting their positions in readiness for passing. As the gap between them narrows, eye contact is deliberately engaged and greetings, typically verbal but occasionally gestural, are exchanged as the parties pass. In Brisbane, where we reside, it is common for up to 20 such greetings to be given during an early morning stroll. We speculate that such greetings might be a way of mutually acknowledging the 'worthiness' of each other. That is, the person is recognized as someone 'who has made an effort' or 'got out of bed early' and is now actively disciplining the self and the body in Foucault's sense of these terms. Walking tracks are frequently busy as early as 5.00 am in Brisbane: in the summer months it is light by then and people take advantage of this – and the relative coolness at this time of day – to exercise before heading off to work.

A study conducted some years ago by Melbin has some potential bearing on this phenomenon. Melbin (1978) postulated that in contemporary times the night time had become a new frontier. More specifically he argued that just as the process of land settlement displayed spatial colonization, so the tendency for humans to spend an increasing number of hours during the night awake and active represented the colonization of time. But even more intriguingly he hypothesized that if this was the case then perhaps the behavioural norms which operated in the land frontier might also be found operating at night. In order to investigate this he devised a number of small-scale experiments to see whether the norms of helpfulness and friendliness which had historically been identified with frontier life could also be found in the night time. For example, were there any differences in how people responded to requests for directions or when approached to answer surveys at different times of the day? Was there any evidence that shoppers and clerks at supermarket checkout counters engaged in more sociable forms of contact during the night time opening hours? Melbin's research is doubly interesting in that his hypothesized behavioural norms run counter to our typical understandings of night time conduct. That is, we generally regard the hours of darkness as a more threatening time when people would be reluctant to engage with strangers. In fact Melbin's research demonstrated that this was not the case: his experiments supported his prediction 'that night-time is a period of more helpfulness and friendliness than other portions of the day' (Melbin, 1978: 17).

BOX 6.1   TEMPORAL DIFFERENCES IN CIVIL ATTENTION PROJECT

Building on Melbin's research it would be interesting to explore whether the incidence of civil attention we have earlier associated with walkers who meet in the early mornings occurs at other times of the day. Although a direct replication of Melbin's research design is not possible – recreational walkers appear to be only active during the daylight hours[3] – there are still a sufficient number of hours of daylight to explore variations in the kind of behaviour we have identified. If, as we have suggested, the mandatory greetings which appear to be exchanged between early morning walkers is a function of the perceived worthiness of the activity at that time of the day, then do walkers who meet later in the day, when the activity carries less sense of disciplining of the self, feel compelled to acknowledge each others' presence? Or is it the case that a situation more like civil inattention and the aversion of the gaze comes into play?

To explore these rival hypotheses you would need to systematically assume the role of a recreational walker over the entire span of daylight hours. For example, walks could be undertaken at 2 hour intervals from earliest light until dusk and the degree or kind of contact exchanged recorded. It would be possible to quantify this in an elementary way: a verbal greeting representing the full civil attention end of the spectrum could be scored 2, a gestural greeting 1, and the aversion of eye contact at the moment of passing representing civil inattention 0. As in all such experiments the design of the research would be enhanced by incorporating other variables such as gender, age and locale. Is there more evidence of same-sex greeting behaviour – that is civil attention – between walkers regardless of the time of the day that they meet? Other factors could be introduced into the research design: for example you could try roller-blading instead of walking and see whether this has any impact on previously established patterns of contact; or you might take along a pet dog with you.

Whilst we are on the subject of pets, the role that they can play in facilitating interaction between strangers has been explored in a paper by Robins, Sanders and Cahill (1991). As we observed above, Gardner suggests that people in public places who are accompanied by a child or an animal are more likely to be cast as 'open persons' in Goffman's sense of this term, that is persons who are deemed more available to face engagements, to be addressed or have other breaches of civil inattention performed upon their persons. This is because the pet operates as a visual marker which tells us something about the moral qualities of its owner. Robins et al. sought to investigate the actual processes through which persons with pets become aquainted and whether there were any limitations to the kind of sociability that ensued. The setting for their research was a public park in which a group of loosely acquainted dog owners gathered most mornings to exercise their pets. Simply by entering the same area of the park with his own dog Robins was able to ascertain 'the typical fate of unfamiliar dog owners who happen upon that group' (ibid.: 5). Their research suggested that a number of steps were involved. In the first place there was a period of 'unfocused interaction' in which the existing pet owners and the outsider engaged in mutual observation. If the outsider moved on quickly to another area of the park then the second stage of focused interaction involving verbal communication did not occur. Robins et al. found that it was the regulars who initiated verbal contact and this was typically done by addressing the dog rather than the owner: e.g. remarks such as 'you're so cute', 'you're friendly aren't you?'. Initiating contact with a stranger carries the potential for loss of 'face' if such contact is not reciprocated in the expected manner, and by addressing the dog first this minimizes any potential embarrassment. The dog thus serves as a 'bridging device' (Goffman, 1963: 126) or a conduit between the two humans. Cain (1983) has coined the term 'triangling' to refer to this process of pet owners directing remarks to each other through the medium of their animals. A period of small talk between the owners then followed, this being limited to dog-related matters. Subsequently the new owner would be invited to unleash her or his dog so that it could join the other dogs already at play. If the dog 'passed' this initiation test, that is if it demonstrated that it was not aggressive with the other animals, then the new owner embarked upon a period of 'probationary membership' (Robbins et al., 1991: 13) with the group. In this phase, although conversations with the other dog owners became more extensive, they were still largely restricted to dog-related matters. Finally the newcomer becomes identified as a regular, and conversational topics become more varied and intimate. In Robins' case this occurred after a period of about five weeks had elapsed. An indicator of this final status is revealed when the newcomer him or herself – rather than the pet – is greeted by the other members of the group on arrival at the park and their return anticipated in the closing salutations exchanged after each exercise period.

In the project described in Box 6.2 we suggested looking for differences between cities and small towns. This has long been a theme in urban research. One of the conventional wisdoms in sociological thinking concerns the differences in sociability between life in cities as opposed to small towns or rural areas. Cities are held to be more impersonal or unfriendly places where people remain anonymous – although this latter point has also been cited as an advantage of city living. Some commentators (e.g. Milgram, 1970) have advanced the thesis of 'communication overload' as a way of accounting for the withdrawal of city people from interpersonal contacts. Simply put, life in metropolitan areas is so crowded or congested

BOX 6.2   PET-FACILITATED INTERACTION EXERCISE

As is so often the case with qualitative research, questions have to be raised about the generalizability of the findings of Robins et al. (1991). Their study was undertaken in a park in Los Angeles, a large 'postmodern' city known, in part, for being dangerous. It is possible that a very different interaction pattern might be observed in other locations, such as a small town (see discussion below) where we could expect higher levels of trust to be found. Moreover, questions should always be asked about generalizing from one national or ethnic context to the globe more widely. Accompanied by a pet (borrowed if necessary) hang out in your local park. Does the interaction pattern detected by Robins prevail? How long does it take before people speak directly to you? Robins found a strong boundary to exist between dog owners and non-owners. Do non-owners speak to you as well? How can you account for the similarities/differences with Robins' findings?

Note: You might be able to modify this project in various ways. Try using a weird pet like a snake or rat. Do people still want to talk to you? What does this suggest about the role of animal symbolism in mediating breaches of civil inattention?

that it is impossible to have contact with every person we encounter, and so we refrain from any attempt to do so. In contrast, life in small towns is supposed to be more gregarious, with inhabitants readily exchanging greetings not only with each other but with strangers or visitors. These contrasts have become enshrined in popular cultural representations of the city and the country as well as the introductory sociology textbooks. However, the limited empirical evidence which has been collected in regard to this issue is not always in agreement. Two studies which employed visual techniques as part of their research design are relevant here. In one, Newman and McCauley (1977) undertook an investigation of the rates of eye contact between strangers. Male and female experimenters were positioned outside the front door of a centrally located building such as a post office or a store in three different locales – a city, a suburban area and a small town – and were instructed to attempt to make eye contact with everyone entering the door. The results showed that eye contact with strangers in the central city was relatively rare (an overall success rate of 15 per cent), more common in the suburb (45 per cent), and most frequent of all in the small town (75 per cent). Moreover the rate of eye contact did not appear to vary with the sex of the experimenter or with the interaction between the sex of the experimenter and the subject.

In contrast Wright (1989) reports the results of a 'friendly student exercise' which came to opposing conclusions with regard to the sociability of rural settings. Wright describes his exercise as an attempt to 'debunk the folk wisdom that the bucolic world is predominantly personal and intimate' (Wright, 1989: 485). In his research he requested students, enrolled in an introductory sociology class at the rural based university where he teaches, to approach strangers and to attempt to initiate interaction with them using an innocuous greeting or a casual remark about the weather. Students were advised to work in pairs: one undertook the attempted interaction and noted the verbal component of the stranger's response whilst the second student observed the interaction from a distance and took note of any non-verbal component such as body language and facial expression. To minimize any suggestions of sexual interest, students only approached same-gender strangers. The strangers' responses generally fell into one of four types. Most common was what Wright categorizes as 'mistaken identity'. Here the stranger's response indicated that the student had mistaken them for someone he or she knew, and the stranger then rapidly withdrew from the encounter. A second type of response was 'Your face is familiar, but I can't place your name'. Here the stranger indicated that they were at fault in not being able to reciprocate the initial greeting. A third response was classified as 'insults and irritation'; in content these were somewhat similar to the responses which Garfinkel observed in his ethnomethodological breaching experiments (Garfinkel,

---

BOX 6.3   COMMENTS AND SUGGESTIONS FOR FURTHER RESEARCH

Which of the experiments – by Newman and McCauley (1977) or by Wright (1989) – do you think has yielded the most convincing results? Is it possible that they are both reporting accurate outcomes? Can you identify any aspects of their research designs which might account for the discrepancy in the results? For example Wright's research was carried out only in the one locale – the rural area – an obvious limitation, as he himself acknowledges. If the 'friendly student exercise' were replicated in the other two locales investigated by Newman and McCauley, what do you think the outcome might be? Do you think that the time of day would have an impact on the results as indicated by Melbin's research? Can you identify an important difference between Wright's and Melbin's research as regards the operationalization of their core concepts?

Either of these studies would be relatively easy to replicate for a student group project. Are there any ethical issues which you think need to be addressed in research such as this?

1967). Finally, but least likely of all, were 'friendly' responses by the stranger involving the acceptance of the greeting and the development of the encounter through further conversation.

Lofland and anonymous interaction in the city

Although she rarely cites Simmel, in *A World of Strangers* Lyn Lofland (1973) takes a rather Simmelian line in suggesting that the modern city, in contrast to the village, provides an environment characterized largely by the constant interactions of strangers. As Lofland points out: 'To live in a city is, among many other things, to live surrounded by large numbers of persons whom one does not know. To experience the city is, among many other things, to experience anonymity. To cope with the city is, among many other things, to cope with strangers' (1973: ix–x). According to Lofland: 'A stranger is anyone personally unknown to the actor of reference, but visually available to him' (ibid.: 18).

Lofland identifies a number of adaptations which allow people to deal with the complexities of living in a world of strangers through 'urban public behavior'. Citizens will typically learn to read the city using 'appearential and locational and behavioral clues to make identifications' (ibid.: 97). They learn to code the appearance of individuals as clues to their identity and personality, and to read urban locations. They also learn to colonize certain settings, such as bars or street corners, where they can be surrounded by friends or like-minded people. Often, however, the urbanite is alone in a public space which they are unable to transform through group activity. Here they need to employ strategies to create privacy around themselves – to remain inconspicuous whilst signalling that they are not willing to participate in interaction.

Lofland analyses two common situations in which the urbanite might find themselves – movement from one public space to another and waiting behaviour. The 'entrance sequence' refers to movement from an outdoor to an indoor environment – say from the street to an office or hotel reception area. The entrance sequence runs as follows. Typically the citizen will check their appearance and arrange their clothing and hair just outside the door. Physical needs may also be attended to at this time, like belching, scratching and coughing. Upon entering the setting the citizen has to read a barrage of visual signals about interior layout, people and so on. Pausing can provide an opportunity to do this, but at the same time it can make one the object of scrutiny by others. The entry is usually a place of high visibility where people do not like to linger. According to Lofland the most common strategy is to keep moving straight ahead, but also to scan rapidly with the eyes so as to take information on board. Another is to justify a pause with some delaying tactic, like removing sunglasses or a hat. Alternately the individual may avoid taking a complete reading by focusing single-mindedly on one aspect of the environment, such as a news-stand in a railway station, and heading towards that goal. The full environment can be surveyed after reaching the stand or purchasing a magazine. Some people just follow others so as to get away from the entrance area quickly or look only at the floor and feet and navigate in that way. The aim of all people entering a setting, however, is to find an inconspicuous position where they can stop or attain a goal (e.g. a ticket queue) where their place in the setting is justi-fied.

Waiting provides a similar problem in that 'the trick is to sustain one's inconspicuousness and to continue to make very clear that one is not open for interaction' (ibid.: 146–7). In a Goffmanesque way, Lofland identifies three major 'styles' through which this is accomplished. The *sweet young thing* is assumed primarily by young women. This involves having a very correct posture, sitting still and 'reading' a book or magazine. These combine to signal that one is a respectable person. The reading material, however, is rarely read. Instead it is scanned, with much attention being spent on reading the environment for danger. This is attained without risking eye contact. When she moves away from her place of rest, she will move purposefully rather than strolling. The *nester* tends to have large numbers of items of personal property which they spend time arranging and caring for. They arrange these around themselves and spend a lot of time in body movement as they fiddle with them. They will be constantly delving into bags, reading and folding newspapers, counting change, moving their bags around and so on. Involvement with these props gives the nester an excuse to avoid eye contact and signals that they are too busy to be approached for possible interaction. According to Lofland, young men and middle-aged women are most likely to be nesters. The *investigator* spends a lot of time exploring the inanimate objects of the setting. They might look at the contents of vending machines, read signs, time-tables and brochures, and study the architecture. Investigators are pri-marily men from the age of 30 upwards.

Territoriality, space and interaction

Some aspects of Lofland's book, like the idea of the 'nester' or the dis-cussion of the colonization of particular spaces by groups of friends, touch on the issue of 'territoriality'. This concept centres on ideas of ownership of spatial environments and provides a further fruitful avenue for visual social science. This is because territories are nearly always marked out by visual signs of occupation. These are designed so that others can see them and know not to interfere. Research into territoriality has been genuinely interdisciplinary, with important contributions from anthropologists, social psychologists, architects and designers as well as sociologists. Closely related to the study of territory is the study of the ways humans utilize space. This latter field has been termed 'proxemics' by its founder Edward Hall (see e.g. Hall, 1963, 1966, 1974). Hall emphasizes that spatial

BOX 6.4   ENTERING AND WAITING BEHAVIOUR PROJECT

Symbolic interactionism has often been accused of being relatively insensitive to gender issues. Feminist critics have argued that what for men is 'civil inattention' is for women a more defensive action designed to ward off sexual harassment and danger. Although Lofland discusses gender differences in behaviour, it is not always with great sensitivity. For example the concept of the 'sweet young thing' seems rather patronising, whilst the evidentiary basis for some claims about gender differences in behaviour is unclear. Gender-based criticisms of symbolic interactionism have also pointed to the fact that it seems to generalize wildly from casual observations of white males in 1950s America. Whilst Lofland's book was published in the 1970s, it seems to share this patina and, like some of Goffman's work, aroused scathing comment from several of our female students. Yet it is important to separate out the formal content of an argument from its illustration and from the substantive empirical claims that are being made. Issues such as the presentation of self in public, gaze and eye contact avoidance are features of social life which should be studied. We would suggest that one way to put such studies on a firming empirical footing is via efforts at quantification which allow stronger inferences to be made about the population distribution of various interactional strategies. The following two projects suggest ways that this can be done:

1.   Select a suitable public space like a waiting room, bus depot, or railway station. Observe the entrance sequences of men and women. Using a code sheet, code activities like preparatory grooming and pausing as well as observable social characteristics of the people, like gender and age. Do you detect any significant differences?

2.   Conduct a similar project coding waiting room strategies. Do the demographic differences claimed by Lofland still exist? One possible hypothesis is that younger women who have been socialized in a post-feminist era will be more assertive in the use of public space than older women. They might be behaving as 'detectives' rather than 'sweet young things'. One might also compare strategies in different settings or times of day. In more dangerous areas and later at night, one might find 'sweet young thing' strategies becoming more common for both sexes. This suggests that the strategies people adopt are context dependent rather than being inherently gendered.

awareness is very much a cultural phenomenon, and a good deal of his most influential book on proxemics, *The Hidden Dimension*, is devoted to cross-cultural differences in spatial sensitivity. Although much of this is valuable, Hall has a tendency to resort to rather questionable national and gendered stereotypes which are now little more than historical anachronisms. Women, for example, are presumed to be concerned with the space of the kitchen, Arabs with body odours. Proxemic research has explored such issues as the different types of space or territorial contexts that humans appear to recognize, the kinds of behaviours that are associated with each of these, and how persons deal with questions of defence or invasion of these various spaces. A number of typologies of space, spatial distances and types of territory have been advanced; we shall look at the most influential of these before turning to suggest how research based upon the visual aspects of proxemics might be undertaken by students.

Common to a number of accounts of proxemics is the idea that human behaviour can be understood as located within a number of zones of spatial influence. For example Hall (1966, chs 9, 10) distinguishes between three major types of space: 'fixed-feature space', 'semifixed feature space' and 'informal space'.[4] Fixed feature space is that which we associate with the built environment. This includes the spatial layout of towns and cities as well as the interior features of the buildings comprising these settlements. With regard to building interiors Hall notes that contemporary notions of privacy which westerners take for granted are of relatively recent origins. Until about the eighteenth century, rooms were not differentiated by functions and people ate, slept and otherwise spent their time in the same locale. One concomitant of these arrangements is that the concept of childhood with its requisite specialized forms of domesticity was unrecognized (Aries, 1962). The spatial arrangements of buildings can be seen as shaping social life at a more macro-level. Winston Churchill, for example, argued that the characteristic two-party system in British politics was largely due to the shape of the House of Commons, where political opponents sat facing each other. After the war Churchill opposed the idea of redeveloping the Commons to resemble the 'horse-shoe shaped' chamber of many of the European parliaments, fearing that this would lead to a profusion of minor parties once the spatial opportunity for this had been offered. The European systems, Churchill thought, made it too easy for people to locate their own shade of grey. Minor parties could emerge simply by parliamentary representatives shuffling along the benches to a new political home. In the House of Commons, by contrast, 'crossing the floor' to vote against the government required a more momentous and determined decision. In earlier chapters of this book we have looked at homes, museums, shopping malls, etc. Readers may wish to revisit these chapters and think of them as explorations of the characteristics of fixed-feature spaces.

'Semifixed-feature space' embraces spatial arrangements which are more flexible and which can be altered if desired. Hall refers to a distinction between two diametrically different forms of semifixed-feature space termed 'sociofugal' and 'sociopetal'. Sociofugal space typical of most hospital, airport, or railway waiting areas serves to keep people apart. Sociopetal arrangements, of which the best illustration is provided by European sidewalk cafes, tend to bring people together. Hall recounts an experimental intervention undertaken by a physician Humphrey Osmond and psychologist Robert Sommer into the spatial organization of a large female geriatric ward. Although the ward was new, brightly painted and apparently cheerful there was almost no interaction between the patients. The problem was that the ward had too many sociofugal spaces and as a consequence the patients were coming to resemble the furniture: 'permanently and silently glued to the walls at regular intervals between the beds' (Hall, 1966: 102). Osmond and Sommer had earlier noted that in the hospital cafeteria the maximum number of conversations occurred when patients were seated diagonally across the corner of tables in the a–f configuration (see Figure 6.1) .

Conversations here were twice as frequent as those when patients were in the c–b positions (side to side), and this in turn yielded three times as many conversations as the c–e or b–f arrangement. By redesigning the ward along sociopetal lines – essentially this meant introducing a number of smaller tables to maximize the number of across-the-corner (a–f) opportunities for interaction – they were able to double the number of conversational encounters between the patients.

In later research Sommer (1969) reported a relationship between seating arrangements and the kind of task that was to be undertaken. Students were asked to imagine sitting at a rectangular table with a same-sex friend and performing a number of different tasks: *conversation*, in this context

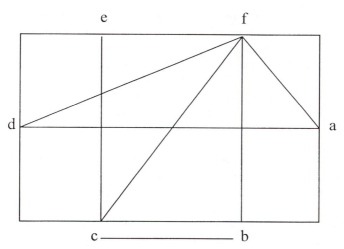

FIGURE 6.1   *Possible combinations of seating arrangements at a rectangular table. Source: Hall (1966: 102)*

meaning talking prior to a class; *cooperation*, or studying together for the same test; *coaction* or studying for different tests and finally *competition* when the aim was to be the first to solve some puzzles. For conversation seating positions a–f and b–f were most frequently nominated; for cooperating the preference was for the c–b positions; coacting elicited preferences for the diagonal c–f and to a lesser extent the across-table b–f positions; whilst for competing, students were most likely to nominate b–f, the diagonal c–f or the end-to-end a–d positions.

Finally Hall refers to informal space or the distances which we maintain in encounters with others. This is the category which has become associated with the concept of personal space and which has received the most significant amount of attention from social psychologists and ethnologists as well as those who work more directly within the field of proxemics. Hall's account is largely devoted to a specification of the zones (intimate, personal, social and public) which appear to constitute informal space

BOX 6.5 GENDER DIFFERENCES IN SEATING PROJECT

According to social psychologists, pop psychologists and a good deal of feminist literature, women are supposed to be caring, supportive and cooperative, whilst men are said to be more individualistic, selfish and confrontational. If this is the case, we might expect such orientations to be manifested in seating preferences. In other words, seating preferences can serve as an observable indicator of gendered norms and personality traits. In a casual visit to a coffee shop on the University of Queensland campus, we noted that men in conversation tended to sit facing each other, whilst women tended to sit side by side. However, our observations were unsystematic. In order to explore this more thoroughly, select a suitable location such as a canteen or a coffee shop which has a number of tables. After selecting your location, draw a plan of the table layout and code seating patterns by placing an 'M' for a male or 'F' for female. Once you have recorded a sufficient number of observations prepare a quantitative summary of your findings. What are you able to conclude about gendered differences?

Note: The project can be extended by comparing different locations where one might expect the clientele to have taken on board particular value patterns. For example, one might expect to find confrontational patterns in a coffee shop occupied by city centre commodities traders (capitalism is institutionalized competition) but supportive patterns in places frequented by participants in the arts or a women's support group where norms of empathy prevail.

together with a brief specification of the kinds of behaviour with which each is associated. As we note later in this chapter a great deal of research work here tends to be experimental and/or laboratory based and of less relevance to those whose research interests are visual or observational inquiry. However, Goffman's contribution to this field stands as a particularly relevant lead for visual researchers, so accordingly we shall look at his account of these issues.

Goffman and public interaction

Goffman (1971: 28–60) deals most clearly with the questions of space and interaction in chapter 2 of *Relations in Public*. He identifies eight 'territories of the self'. We shall consider the ones which are of most relevance to visually oriented research. First, and of most importance, is personal space. By this he understands the 'space surrounding an individual, anywhere within which an entering other causes the individual to feel encroached upon, leading him to show displeasure and sometimes to withdraw' (1971: 29–30). Legitimate claims on personal space are situationally contingent, with what is to count as an 'infringement' liable to moment-by-moment re-evaluation. The social organization of co-waiting provides some useful illustrations of these themes. Goffman notes that to sit or stand next to a

---

BOX 6.6   PERSONAL SPACE AND DEPARTURE ETIQUETTE EXERCISE

Building upon Goffman's observations it would be interesting to discover if there are any differences in how people react to newly created places from one type of location to another. For example a comparison could be made of the strategies that people use in doctors' waiting rooms, which tend to be rectangular with seating arranged around the periphery of the room, compared with that of a bus or a train where passengers typically are seated in pairs. How do people in each setting manoeuvre to new locations? Which is more difficult – in the sense of its potential to give offence – to accomplish: relocation in a waiting room or relocation in a bus? Are there any additional features in the two settings which can be utilized for this purpose? For example relocations in doctors' waiting rooms may be ratified by a conspicuous display of interest in a health poster or leaflet pinned on the wall near the newly vacated seat, but this is an option which is unlikely to be available for bus or train patrons. Consequently it may be the case, as Goffman notes, that as a bus or train empties 'there will be a period when two individuals signal by proximity a relationship that does not in fact exist' (1971: 32).

stranger in a waiting area or lift would be regarded as more intrusive if the area were relatively unpopulated than if this were the only place available. Typically, then, waiting rooms fill on the basis of a series of continual readjustments as people move closer to others to accommodate later arrivals. But departures create a more complex problem. For example an individual who moves seat immediately to take up one recently vacated may be seen as unduly offending his former neighbour. However when the two persons are of the opposite sex then *not* to move to a more distant seat may indicate a sign of inappropriate interest in the other. Accordingly waiting rooms and elevators empty on a different basis from that which regulates how they fill with occupants waiting for a tactful moment before moving to more open space (see Box 6.6).

Goffman, secondly, refers to 'the stall', or 'space to which individuals can lay temporary claim, possession being on an all-or-none basis' (1971: 32). In contrast to personal space, which has more fluid boundaries, stalls have easily visible and defendable boundaries. Examples would be such things as a particular favourite chair, or a telephone booth, but Goffman suggests they can also refer to the use of a towel on the beach as a means of indicating residence or occupancy.[5] Another difference is that a stall can be temporarily vacated whilst maintaining a continuing claim upon it, but personal space cannot. The issue then arises as to how possession of a stall can be indicated through the use of various markers. A useful illustration of this can be found in Nash's (1982) discussion of the way in which campers signal their occupancy of campsites. Nash is referring primarily to campers in the North American context who use recreational vehicles or other forms of 'self-contained' mobile camping units. The problem at issue here is for campers to mark the occupancy of their campsite when the family decide to drive to a nearby lake or to the local town for provisions and literally take their (temporary) home with them. Nash's research suggested that the objects which campers have devised to mark their continued occupancy of a site carry different symbolic meanings, and the more demand there is for a particular favoured site then the more likely it is that campers will use objects which carry greater personal value. So a campsite which is marked by items of clothing such as a special sweat shirt is seen as more likely to be successfully defended than one which has been marked by a cheap item of camping equipment such as a saucepan from a discount store. In New Zealand, which also has a large market in camper van holidays, we noted that the problem of occupancy has been solved in a more institutionalized way. Every van comes with a bucket. If you wish to leave your site you just fill the bucket with water and leave it in the spot. The advantage here is that the institutionalized meaning is less ambiguous. The cheap saucepan or sweatshirt may be assumed by newcomers to have been lost or thrown away rather than purposively left to mark a territory. The disadvantage of the New Zealand system is that varying levels of willingness to 'fight' for the prime spot cannot be signalled with a standardized symbol.

There are a number of places or settings which feature stalls and their defence which could be researched by visual methods. Park benches and picnic tables are obvious examples. A rather comic illustration of this took place during the performance of Wagner's Ring Cycle in Adelaide in 1998. There are four operas in the operatic cycle, which take place on different evenings. Long intervals between acts allowed patrons time to picnic and to therefore avoid expensive food prices. During the four operas, practices of territoriality among the penny-pinching arts elite became progressively more marked. Pressure for picnic tables mounted as more and more people cottoned on to the idea of bringing a picnic, bottle of wine, etc. During the first opera a few patrons wandered casually out to the tables during the interval. By the third opera there was an undignified mass stampede for the tables, only to find they had been sneakily reserved during the first act by means of a table cloth. By the fourth opera people had arrived an hour early and, taking no chances, were setting up the tables with glasses, ice buckets, tableware and candles as a sign of determined occupancy!

Picnic tables, library tables and seats present additional problems for single people. These are typically of a size that will accommodate more than one individual and yet they are often understood as 'taken' (i.e. they

---

BOX 6.7   STALL DEFENCE AND TERRITORIALITY IN THE GYM EXERCISE

An alternative example of 'body contamination' being used as a means of territorial defence can be found in the use of gymnasiums. Items of equipment in weight-training establishments or gymnasiums have the characteristics of stalls in that they can have temporary territorial claims laid upon them. Research has shown (see Ogilvie, 1994) that there are important differences in the ways in which these are used by men and women, including the use of territorial claims on equipment items. Equipment is typically used serially with patrons exercising different muscle groups on different machines. Ogilvie's research suggested that it was a relatively common practice for a patron to reserve an item of equipment by draping a (sweaty) towel over it whilst they exercised on another machine. Her research suggested that this was an exclusively male practice and, even though it was met with disapproval by patrons of both sexes, it invariably worked as a means of stall defence. Ogilvie's research demonstrated that there were a range of other practices which men engaged in which served to prioritize their use of the gym over that of women. If you are a regular visitor to gymnasiums (male or female) can you identify what some of these might be?

become 'stalls') under conditions of single occupancy. When crowding increases then pressure is put upon such occupants to give up their exclusive claims to possession. Goffman suggests that those already ensconced can use a variety of tactics to prevent this from eventuating. For example in relation to bus and train seating which is typically designed to accommodate two persons first occupants can use possessions, avoidance of eye contact and even a 'contaminating part of himself, such as his feet' (1971: 34) as means to reserve the territory for themselves (see Box 6.7).

'Use space', Goffman's third territorial form refers to the area immediately around or in front of an individual to which he can lay some temporary instrumental claim. An example is provided by the expectation that visitors to art galleries will be able to view a picture without another person entering into their viewing frame. Similarly we generally try to avoid stepping in between a photographer and the object of their attentions. When two persons are momentarily engaged in conversation on opposite sides of a passage or corridor then a third party who wishes to pass through will typically engage in some minimization of the offence: lowering their head or quickening their gait.

Goffman fourthly considers 'the turn', essentially the mechanisms which regulate queues and the socially organized practices constituting queuing behaviour. Above all else, queues must operate with some sort of ordering rule – 'first come first served' – and also some sort of claiming device which can serve to validate the first principle. For example queues at delicatessen counters in supermarkets operate with a ticketing system. Indeed in these situations, because the order of the queue is not visible since customers will typically position themselves along the counter in front of the object they intend to purchase, the ticketing system is the only evidence that there is a queue in operation. But we more typically associate queues with visible forms of organization ranging from bus stops to large-scale sports events.[6] Given this concern with organized visibility it is not surprising that queues and turn-taking in public spaces more generally have attracted some interest from ethnomethodological researchers (e.g. Ball and Smith, 1986). Ball and Smith argue that queues have visible self-organizing features such that we can readily distinguish between queue members and non-queue members: in short, queues have in-built mechanisms which work to maintain their orderliness. Members of queues, they suggest, are continually engaged in interpretive work that centres upon the reflexive monitoring of visual information relating to the direction the queue is heading and the appropriate distances which queue members are required to keep between each other, and so on. They refer to this feature as the '"visual availability" of queueing's local organization' (Ball and Smith, 1986: 28). As with other ethnomethodologically based accounts (e.g. see Chapter 3) their focus is on the practical ways in which queues are commenced and maintained.

BOX 6.8 QUEUING EXERCISE

As forms of spontaneous spatial organization which rely on visual information, queues are a great setting for visual inquiry – and sabotage! Recruit four or five accomplices and head for an ATM machine in a busy location and a busy time of day – a Saturday morning near a supermarket would be ideal. One member of the team should occupy him or herself with operating the ATM machine whilst the other team members organize themselves into a particular 'deviant' queuing arrangement but without giving any indication that they all know each other. For example try queuing with a distance of about 4 or 5 metres between yourselves rather than the normal 1–2 metres which operates in such queues. Take note of how the queue develops as more people arrive: for example do they seem uncertain that there is in fact a queue in existence? Do they maintain the 4–5 metre distance that you have instigated?

After a while you could reform the queue so that instead of a large gap between its members you now apparently violate each other's personal space by standing so close that you are almost touching. There should be no problems in this configuration with new queue members working out that this is a queue, but do they maintain the same distance? Finally you might like to try taking the queue in an unorthodox direction (e.g. circling round a nearby traffic sign) simply by organizing yourselves in a particular way. When you have finished, spend time observing the ATM from a discreet distance. How long does your pattern last? Under what circumstances does it disappear? Which kinds of pattern seem to be more robust than others. What does this tell us about the norms related to queuing?

Note: Given that queue members typically do not turn round to look at others in the queue (the norm of civil inattention) you may need to have an additional team member positioned some distance from the ATM machine who can record these details.

Body, clothing and display

As we have seen earlier in this chapter, scholars like Lofland, Simmel and Goffman point to the importance of display in everyday social life. They suggest that people work to give off meanings and impressions. These facilitate everyday social interaction by providing visual clues to others as to who one is and what one is doing. Aside from the gaze, the body provides one of the major tools that people have for accomplishing this complex task. Broadly speaking we can identify three ways in which this is accomplished. Firstly the body can be directly modified (e.g. tattoos), secondly the body can be adorned (e.g. clothes) and thirdly the body can be moved (e.g. gestures). In this section we briefly explore these forms of visual data.

The body

The body itself is an increasingly central theme in visual research. By modifying the body people are able to express their identities to others. These modifications might allow them to signal individual personality, political or religious beliefs, conformity, or group membership. Whilst some modifications of the body (e.g. genital piercing) are not readily available for a casual visual inquiry, many others can be observed. There is an extensive literature on body hair and the ways that hair (or its absence) can signify things as diverse as sexuality (the supermodel), rebellion (the rastafarian, the skinhead), conformity (the army crew cut) and so on (for a review see Synnott, 1993). Beards, tattoos, scars and piercings are also significant identity symbols which can be used in analogous ways. It is arguably the case that such uses of the body are becoming more prevalent. They might be thought of as rebellions against the anonymous and bland conformist identities of modernity of the kind that Simmel and Goffman wrote about. Anthropologist Daniel Rosenblatt (1997), for example, discusses this trend as a kind of 'modern primitivism' in which members of affluent western societies seek to mobilize exotic motifs as a form of resistance to dominant social and cultural structures. More specifically, by mobilizing what they think of as the 'primitive', they are resisting rationalism, the concept of progress, secularization and the alienation of the self.

Makeup also has an important role to play in modifying the body. In western societies the use of makeup tends to be gender specific and to be tied to idealized notions of femininity. One indirect result of this is that the makeup user tends to be seen as a dupe of consumer trends and powerful ideologies. As Jennifer Craik (1994: 153–4) points out, whilst body decoration is often seen 'as active and purposeful behaviour, the use of makeup and cosmetics is interpreted as passive and trivial behaviour'. Both can be more accurately – and neutrally – thought of as techniques for expressing or presenting the self through the body to others. Whilst sociologically and economically of great importance, makeup can be rather difficult to study. When skillfully applied, makeup is difficult to detect. As a result, interview studies might be of more use than direct observation in public settings. Advertisements, of course, offer another form of visual data that can be explored here. They offer particular opportunities for tracing changing norms and fashions in the use of makeup.

As the issue of makeup emphasizes, one problem with conducting visual research on the body is that the data that is derived from pure observation can be rather hermeneutical, 'thin' and purely descriptive. For those interested in society and culture, rather than kinesics, etc., it is hard to get much theoretical leverage from this kind of material. For this reason most studies in this area (when they don't make use of rich advertisement data) tend to make use of interviews, ethnography, or texts alongside visual materials. James Myers' (1992) study of genital piercing and other non-mainstream body modification illustrates this trend. Although Myers provides pictures of pierced genitalia, the main data source for his paper is an ethnographic account of workshops which allows him to explore motivations and subcultural values. Daniel Rosenblatt's (1997) discussion of tattooing, body piercing and scarification goes even further, avoiding visual materials entirely and using textual materials to recreate the meanings of these practices.

Clothes

Studies of clothing and fashion cover a vast area, including the economics of the industry, historical changes in styles and their ties to changing social structure, links to gender ideologies, the decoding of advertisements, and so on. As we noted in Chapter 3, fashion is an intriguing area for quantitative study because of the longevity of the historical record that is available for investigation. Here we wish to explore the practical semiotics of clothing: the ways people use clothes to give off visual information. Our particular concern, in line with the theme of this chapter, is to focus on issues of presentation of self.

As is so often the case with cultural phenomena, Simmel (1957[1904]) got there first! Simmel argues that fashion can only exist in a society with social mobility. In a society without mobility, dress differences between classes are permanent and clothes act like a uniform which signals status (there are clear parallels with Sennett on 'public man' here). According to Simmel the rise of fashion corresponded to the rise of the urban middle class. This group aped the clothing of the aristocracy. The aristocracy wished to differentiate themselves from the middle classes, and so tried to improvise new styles. These in turn were copied. The result is a kind of race in which new styles have to be created rapidly and then discarded before they are adopted by groups further down the social ladder. Aside from indicating social status, Simmel asserted that fashion had other uses. It enabled people to assert their self-identify and/or their simultaneous membership of a group. It also enabled people to be reflexive and instrumental in that they could work with clothing to present a desired image or identity in various settings. Simmel's work, then, suggests that clothing can be used in remarkably complex ways to assert personal and group identity and social status.

Another influential study of fashion by a leading social theorist was Roland Barthes' (1983) *The Fashion System*. This difficult book suggests we can decode clothing as a network of structured signs. Contrasts between, say bright and dark, top and bottom can be used to formally analyse clothing combinations and fashion changes. It is probably fair to say that the book has had little influence on the analysis of fashion in cultural studies. Whilst the generic point that clothing can be decoded has been accepted, most studies of clothing tend to rely on common-sense judgements to work out the meaning of particular fashions. They tend to be decoded as 'conservative', 'retro', 'vulnerable', 'fetishistic', etc. on the basis of allegedly 'self-evident' features rather than complex semiotic structures. In the project described in Box 6.9 you will also be required to use your common-sense knowledge of this kind to interpret clothing.

Subsequent research on clothing has tended to take up the sorts of themes developed by Simmel and Barthes. Some studies are more involved with looking at the social uses of clothing (à la Simmel) and others with decoding garments (à la Barthes). Ruth Rubinstein's (1995) *Dress Codes* integrates these two paths in providing a comprehensive examination of the symbolic uses of clothes in western society. One theme is to dramatize power. Royal regalia and dictators' uniforms exemplify this use. Clothing can be used to demonstrate wealth, through the use of expensive materials and accessories. Experiments by Hoult (1954) confirmed the importance of dress in evaluating the perceived social status of strangers. Models, some 'dressed up' and others 'dressed down', were presented to subjects who were asked to allocate a rank to them on various social dimensions. Results showed that being dressed up was likely to increase perceived status.

Uniforms are of great sociological interest (e.g. Davies, 1989). They work to show a number of things. They demonstrate one is properly qualified, that one is a member of a group, and that one supports the group's norms. Ethnographic studies have indicated the significance of uniforms in regulating interaction in various settings. In medical examinations, for example, the white coat of the doctor can be used to establish a professional personality which can head off embarrassment in the patient. Whilst we tend to think of uniforms in the context of people like the police, medical staff and military, it is clear that other kinds of para-uniform exist. In the modern business world the dull suit and conservative tie operate as a kind of uniform to show one is a competent professional. Deviation from this norm of self-restraint can result in a loss of business. Similarly, fashion trends among the young often amount to de facto uniforms. Adolescents are often anxious about being the 'odd one out' and so will copy one another in an effort to maintain a group identity. Trends can shift rapidly from year to year in high schools as Adidas and Nike sneakers, Malcolm X baseball hats, and whatever Madonna, the Spice Girls or the next functional equivalent are wearing, move onto and off the fashion stage. In universities one will also find various looks available. At the time of writing (as these things change quite quickly) students may wish to appear as a studious 'preppy' or 'swot' or take on a more counter-cultural look influenced by surf culture, grunge, metal, rap, etc. The default setting for those who wish to be anonymous seems to be jeans, sneakers and T-shirt or sweat shirt. Such variety in clothing trends is useful because it enables people to remain members of groups, whilst at the same time allowing them to express a personal identity. The process perfectly exemplifies Simmel's claim that fashion allows people to satisfy competing demands of being an individual and claiming a collective affiliation.

Another use of clothing is to establish a gender identity. Feminists have pointed to the arbitrary nature of gender conventions, showing that ideals about female beauty and attire change from age to age and setting to setting. Modesty in dress, for example, might be prescribed in some eras, at others a glamorous and seductive look might be preferred, whilst in yet others a vulnerable look could be the ideal. Debate rages among feminists as to whether women's fashions are the product of a male gaze or are a woman-centred practice (see e.g. Kunzle, 1977). Discussion about the pop star Madonna in the late 1980s and early 1990s exemplified this dilemma. Some authors claimed her revealing costumes and steamy videos were pornographic and pandered to male fantasy, whilst others asserted they were a creative and empowered female sexuality. Research on gay sub-cultures and straight masculinity has shown how these, too, have dress codes which signal in gendered ways. More recent theoretical work has explored issues of cross-dressing and the ways in which it challenges or refutes the mainstream gender order.

Whilst clothing can be analysed *in situ* on the body, it seems to be the case that the majority of work makes use of 2D data – at least in western societies. In other words there is a far more extensive literature decoding advertisements and photographs of clothing than ethnographic studies of clothing in action. We suggest several possible reasons for this. Firstly, questions about changing historical norms can best be explored with con-sistent longitudinal data – such as pictures in the same magazine over a period. Second, magazine data allows for systematic sampling methods and the acquisition of a large sample. We saw both of these advantages in Richardson and Kroeber's research discussed earlier in the book. Thirdly, photographs and advertisements seem to lend themselves to the kind of elaborate cultural studies decodings that we discussed in Chapter 3. This is particularly the case where the cultural connotations of items of cloth-ing need to be uncovered. As with body modification discussed above, it is difficult to write theoretically involving work based on purely obser-vational material from everyday life. Magazine material provides a way of obtaining richer material with which to work because the clothing is explicitly embedded in a thick texture of signifiers.

An example of cultural studies research which uses magazine material to good effect to explore clothing is Kaite's (1989) study of the uses of the high-heeled shoe in soft and hard core pornography. Using complex psychoanalytic cultural theories to explore relationships between the body, shoe and viewer, Kaite interprets the shoe in these photographs as a kind of surrogate penis. It would be difficult to undertake such an analy-sis using direct observational data, even if the meanings being investi-gated were non-sexual. To understand the semiotic universe of the loafer or deck shoe, for example, one might do better to look at advertisements and catalogues. These would no doubt feature sail boats and ivy league colleges, suggesting connotations of privilege and high cultural capital. A study of people wearing them in the street or library, by contrast, would probably be rather semantically thin.

Having confessed that representations of clothing are often a better resource for cultural studies than their uses, it can be worthwhile to explore clothing on real bodies. For example, the questions about the city and modernity we have asked throughout this chapter have direct relevance for uses of clothing. The view of the city developed by Lofland, Goffman and others suggests that most people wear clothing in conformity with social norms. They wish to demonstrate that they are normal and dependable and, in the context of the city, invisible. Improvisation which expresses personality exists, but is usually within limits. It might extend to the choice of tie or handbag (conservative, retro, etc.) or to the colour of a shirt or blouse. Is this really the case? It has been argued that the postmodern city is a place of plural lifestyles and tastes, inhabited by 'neo-tribes' rather than by drably homogeneous citizens. If this is so, one might expect it to be characterized by diversities in style, many of them indicating dissent from mainstream norms and affiliation to those of a deviant or minority subculture. Examples here include the Hare Krishna saffron robes and shaven heads, punks with their confrontational use of leather, tartan, torn clothes and bondage paraphernalia, and bikers with their leather and gang emblems. One might also think of groups like Rastafarians, ferals, and hippies. However, it is important to remember that dissent can also be conservative in orientation. Examples here are the Hasidic Jews of New York, who wear traditional long coats and hats and sport beards, and also fundamentalist Muslims. Such groups may disagree with mainstream social values but in a conservative way, arguing for the need to return to Holy Scripture, to revive the family and with it traditional gender roles. With such peoples, clothing can be used as an indicator of religious conformity. Those who wear the full kit can be supposed to be 'more religious' than those who wear just one or two items. In his ethnographic study of Hasidic Jews Solomon Poll (1962) makes just this point, suggesting that garments ranged from the 'extremely Hasidic' through to those which were worn with modern clothes but could serve as a minimal token of belonging. In this context clothing is perhaps better thought of as an indicator of tradition/modernity rather than deviance/conformity. In Chapter 1 we also looked at Enninger's study of the Amish, which discussed the clothing codes as an indicator of social status within that community. In some third-world countries one can look at the tension between traditional and western clothing in this way. In Himalayan Nepal, for example, women tend to wear traditional dress, whilst men often wear baseball caps, T-shirts and jeans. This suggests that women's roles remain traditional and that they have been to some extent excluded from a 'westernization process' (Smith, 1986). The exercises in Boxes 6.9 and 6.10 draw upon these sorts of uses of clothing as an indicator.

BOX 6.9   BODY AND CLOTHING AND CONFORMITY EXERCISE

This project makes use of the idea that the body and clothing can be used as an indicator of deviance and conformity with respect to mainstream norms. Whilst it is tempting to think of clothing and the body as dramatizing conformity and deviance to mainstream norms in a binary way, the distinction is more likely to be in degree. There is a continuum between wearing formal business clothing and being a punk. In between these extremes we will find things like wearing a shirt with no tie, aggressive rap and heavy metal T-shirts, the Malcolm X baseball cap, baggy trousers and skate pants. Research has to take account of this diversity. Select a public space in your city such as a mall or plaza. Along with a friend, code people's clothing on a scale of 1–5 according to what you perceive to be levels of deviance from mainstream norms (e.g. man in suit and tie = 1, feral = 5). Also record their apparent age, gender and ethnicity. After some pilot work compare your sheet with your co-researcher. You may wish to develop formal criteria for your coding sheet to increase the rigour of the project. Analyse your data looking for patterns linking socio-demographic characteristics with deviant identities. What conclusions are you able to draw? Which demographics seem to be conformist, which partly conformist and which deviant? What kinds of social forces might lead these patterns to arise? Do we live in a city of 'neo-tribes' or is conformity still the dominant pattern?

BOX 6.10   CLOTHING AND EXPERTISE EXERCISE

In her study of the gym Emma Ogilvie (1994) noticed that clothing styles correlated strongly with claims to expertise. The 'baggy T-shirts' were novices who were ashamed of their bodies and didn't know how to use the equipment. Advanced users of the gym tended to wear more revealing lycra and to have specialist accessories like leather weight belts (back supports) and gloves. Select a suitable location for investigating this sort of issue. The finishing line of a triathlon or marathon can be a good spot, as can a sports club or a popular river for fishing. How is clothing used to signal status? Draw annotated sketches to illustrate your findings with 'ideal types' of the novice, journeyman and expert.

Whilst much attention has been given to clothing, accessories are also a potential resource for visual research. In his long distance hike around remote parts of Wales in the nineteenth century, the writer George Borrow noticed that carrying an umbrella improved his social relationships.

... who doubts that you are a respectable character provided you have an umbrella...? And what respectable man when you overtake him on the way and speak to him will refuse to hold a conversation with you, provided you have an umbrella? No one. The respectable man sees you have an umbrella and concludes that you do not intend to rob him, and with justice, for robbers never carry umbrellas. (1934[1862]: 397)

Borrow noted, then, that umbrella was read as a sign that he was a trustworthy human being. In today's society many artefacts (like children and dogs as we have discussed above) have this kind of signifying property too. Glasses, jewellery, walking sticks, back packs and watches are not just 'functional'. They can all be used to signal information and to assert individual or group identity. Cigarettes and smoking equipment also provide identity clues. Such objects do not only have a sign value in themselves, but also can be manipulated in various ways to send out extra messages. In Hollywood *film noire* for example, the cigarette could be smoked in various ways. Peter Lorre's style suggested nervousness. He was always stubbing out his cigarettes and taking short drags. Bogart and Bacall, by contrast, tended to signal coolness and eroticism with long plumes of smoke and shared matches.

Gesture and posture

The use of the body in interaction is also a potent source of visual data. Humans use 'body language' consciously or unconsciously to convey information to others about things as diverse as emotion, social status, openness to interaction and sexual arousal. There is a vast and diverse literature in this field but, although human gesture and expression is very much visual data, much of this research can be only of limited use in the context of this book. There are several reasons for this.

BOX 6.11   USE OF ACCESSORIES EXERCISE

This exercise does not have an originating hypothesis, but will test your skill as an observer and your decoding ability as a competent member of society. As usual, situate yourself in a public space. We prefer coffee shops. Observe the use of accessories by people around you. How many expressive uses are you able to detect (e.g. the item is used to convey information by the actor)? How many of these uses are unconventional in that they require an item to be used in a way that was not intended? How are accessories used by waiting people rather than those in conversations? What kinds of opportunities arise for people to display their accessories to others?

1. It is often difficult to hook up observations on the use of the body to mainstream social theory. Much research is rooted in psychological and biological rather than social and cultural theory. The point of a study might be to draw analogies with the behaviours of animals or to hunt for psychological universals in the expression of emotion or to ask which kinds of gestures will help influence and persuade people. Such research is essentially in a different paradigm from the qualitative social science and cultural studies orientation of this book. A popular and entertaining example of such work is zoologist Desmond Morris' (1977) *Manwatching*, which interprets human behaviours (e.g. grooming, expressions) via analogies with our primate cousins.

2. Cutting edge research on body language often involves the use of expensive equipment (e.g. video, brain electroencephalograms, etc.) and technical languages for transcribing movement and, possibly, its links to mental and physiological states. Birdwhistell's studies on kinesics (movement) exemplifies work in this tradition which is closest in orientation to mainstream social science. Other research uses conversation analytic techniques to look at the association between gesture and speech, noting how gestures assist people in mutual orientation and communication (e.g. Goodwin, 1986). Conducting research in these sorts of areas requires specific training that is beyond the scope of this text.

3. Many studies and books on gesture often add up to little more than endless lists of types of gesture or their social function: e.g. as 'reinforcing', 'encouraging', 'illustrating', 'isolating', etc. An alternative approach, such as that of Norton (1983) is to identify styles of body movement and gesture. Norton locates 'dramatic', 'dominant', 'animated', 'relaxed', 'attentive', 'open', 'friendly', 'contentious' and 'impression leaving styles', each of which has its own kind of body language. Still other studies look to identify and document standardized sequences of movement in episodes like greeting and courtship. A related trend in the literature is to note cultural variations in gesture meanings or gesturing styles. David Efron (1972), for example, noted that East European Yiddish-speaking Jews gestured in ways which reflected the logical structure of a conversation. Southern Italians, by contrast, tended to perform concrete illustrative gestures which were 'pantomimic' of the action being talked about. Such work seems to be content to document differences rather than explain them. It draws attention to the importance of gesture in everyday interaction, its forms and variations, but tends to be descriptive in orientation. By contrast our concern in this book (and we hope that of our readers) is to connect analysis of the body and gesture to mainstream social and cultural theory.

4. As the work of Simmel, Goffman, etc. attests, much of the most interesting theory is on the role of gaze and eye contact in contemporary

social life. Such work is difficult to conduct, because of the unobservability of the gaze. Using expensive equipment and/or laboratory research one can explore some issues related to the gaze, but often not under naturalistic conditions. For example, walking round with a video camera strapped to your head to record gazes will not encourage people to gaze at you in a normal way!! So for a routine visual inquiry, we often have to restrict ourselves to the more observable motions of the body.

Having expressed these reservations there is still a vast store of information that could be used for visual research. Here we are restricted to a few examples of the kinds of themes that can be used to inform research by taking the gestures and movements of the body as indicators of social process. Many of these impinge on issues of territoriality discussed earlier. Some of the most interesting studies have looked at status differences in the uses of the body (LaFrance and Mayo, 1978). Findings from these include the following.

- Higher-status people are freer to touch than lower-status people.
- When a subordinate initiates a conversation they tend to be further away from the other party than when a superior initiates a conversation.
- Higher-status people also tend to sprawl when they sit and to adopt asymmetrical positions. Subordinates, by contrast, will tend to occupy less space and sit upright, in a symmetrical posture. (This is shown in the photograph (Figure 6.2) of a student consulting a professor.)
- High-status people gaze at the other when they are talking, but tend to look away when they are being talked to.

Whilst conducted in another academic tradition, such results provide remarkably strong support for Bourdieu's assertions about the importance of embodied *habitus* as a mode of domination. According to Bourdieu, posture and a sense of being at ease are characteristic of the dominant classes. These embodied attributes are ones of which we are largely unaware and which subordinate classes can rarely learn, unlike, say, textbook forms of cultural capital. Studies of posture, such as the one described in Box 6.12, provide one way of exploring Bourdieu's theory.

Gender differences in posture have also been frequently noted. Zdenek Klein's (1984) study of sitting postures in males and females provides a representative example of a project with a well-thought-out sociological method, but a typically disappointing biological spin to the analysis. Klein recorded sitting postures in public transportation in Prague outside of rush hour. In each case postures were coded 30 seconds after the bus or tram left the station. In such public settings the sitters were unlikely to know each other or engage in conversation. Postures were recorded in 600 men and 600 women, with a second coder being used to establish the

FIGURE 6.2   *University professor and undergraduate student in typical sitting positions. Observe how the professor looks relaxed and is adopting an asymmetrical posture. By extending his arms and raising one knee he consumes the maximal amount of space. In contrast the student sits bolt upright with her arms by her sides. Notice also how the professor's desk furniture creates a barrier which serves to mark out his personal space and thereby dramatize status differences. Reflecting back on the themes of Chapters 4 and 5 we can detect other semiotic processes at work in the photo. The desk top cluttered with academic papers, books and journals signifies that the room belongs to a specialist in complex knowledges and the lap-top computer denotes leading edge technological skills.*

reliability of the coding. For males the preferred posture was one with knees and ankles kept apart. For females, postures with close contact of the knees were more prevalent (see Figure 6.3). Klein is able to discount the explanation that this was due to modesty, by showing that there was no association between the type of clothing worn by the woman (skirt or trousers) and posture adopted. Older woman were more likely than younger women to adopt a 'masculine' posture. Men's positions were not influenced by mode of transport, but women were more likely to adopt a 'masculine' posture when in a tram than a train. Klein believes this reflects seating patterns. Train seats faced one another, giving rise to situations of mutual visibility. Tram seats, like bus seats, all faced the same direction, making visual contact difficult.

Whilst this methodology for exploring gender, posture and seating is exemplary, like so much of this type of literature Klein's interpretation of the data is sociobiological and hence less satisfactory from the viewpoint

BOX 6.12   STATUS AND POSTURE PROJECT

Ask several members of staff in your department if you can sit in their office during consultation hours with students, but don't tell them why you wish to be there. In this interactional setting academics are high status and students low status. Devise a coding sheet which captures aspects of 'space-eating' and 'slouching' behaviours (e.g. 'feet on desk', 'poor posture', 'arms behind head') as well as 'space-minimizing' behaviours (e.g. arms folded, 'sitting upright'). Sit in a quiet corner where it is difficult for the parties to observe you, and code behaviours of academics and students. Do your results confirm the theory? By comparing results within your sample, what kinds of status attributes seem to have the largest impact on postures of both academics and students (gender, age, academic rank/numbers of years as a student, dress, accent)? What can you conclude from your visual data about the major sources of interpersonal status in academic settings?

Note: In theory you could also conduct this study in other places like doctors' surgeries, police stations, offices. In practice gaining access may be difficult, but if you have an entrée it might provide a rewarding research site.

(a)

FIGURE 6.3   *Types of leg posture in females and males. These photographs were taken at various locations at the University of Queensland and Brisbane city*

(b)

(c)

centre. Photos (a) and (b) show examples of what Klein considers to be typical female and male leg postures respectively. Photo (c) depicts four people seated on a bench. They are all exhibiting conventional postures. Can you identify the gender of each person? Photos (d) and (e) suggest that we may be observing changes from the patterns Klein identified . In (d), which contains only females, the posture of the person on the right might be thought of as more 'masculine'. In contrast to (e) which shows two males at a bus stop, the figure on the left has adopted a strongly feminine posture with both knees and ankles touching.

(d)

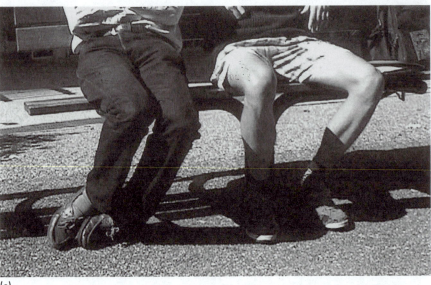

(e)

of mainstream sociology and cultural studies. Drawing on data derived from primates he suggests that the male seating posture is one that allows for immediate motion (for defence or flight) and tends to 'increase the contour of masculine stature' (Klein, 1984: 128). Women's posture is a kind of 'female courtship behavior' which 'presents the individual's more attractive somatic characteristics' (i.e. legs?) to the opposite sex. Klein sees support for this argument in the fact that older women and women in the non-eye contact trams were less likely to adopt a 'female' posture. From a sociological perspective one might be able to offer alternative explanations

BOX 6.13   GENDERED PUBLIC POSTURES PROJECT

Klein's study was conducted in the early 1980s. Gender norms have changed considerably since that time. If they are the determining factor, it is possible that there will be less difference between the sexes than Klein detected. If biology is a key factor, then one might expect to find results very similar to Klein's. Try to replicate Klein's study on public transport in your own town. Do your results match his? How, if at all, do they differ? Do you detect differences between participants in terms of variables like age and race? What, if anything, are you able to conclude about the power of gender norms versus biology as an explanation?

that focus on men's tendency to dominate space and their socialization into culturally specific postural norms. A woman sitting with her legs apart, whatever she is wearing, is likely to be perceived as loose and may be subject to sexual harassment. Looked at from this viewpoint, posture is an indicator of gendered norms, habitus and power structures rather than biological imperatives.

Touch is another kind of gesture that is observable in public settings and is used to signal information between people. Heslin (1974), providing yet another of those innumerable typologies that characterize the field, suggests there are many types of touch ranging from the professional touch of the doctor, through the polite touch (e.g. kiss, handshake), the friendship touch (e.g. hugs at airport meetings), and on to intimate and sexual touching. To this list we should add forms of touch that dramatize power such as physical or sexual abuse or the arresting hand of the police officer (Synnott, 1993). In all societies touching is subject to norms. In some cultures touching is seen as an invasion of the self. There are also taboos due to the anxiety caused by the potentially sexual interpretation of human touching (see Richmond, McCroskey and Payne, 1991: 241ff). For this reason many people feel embarrassed when touched by a stranger, or have to apologize if they accidentally touch someone. Norms are also often place specific. Sexual touching, for example, is more acceptable in a private setting than in a public one.

As Simmel and others have noted, the modern city has brought people into proximity. This has caused a problem not only for the use of vision and the gaze (qua civil inattention as discussed earlier) but also, on occasion, for touch. Subway trains present a particular problem in that they require people to be pushed up close against one another, violating the customary norms against contact with strangers. Edward Hall remarks that subway riders have 'defensive devices' which take the intimacy out of contact in such public spaces. He writes:

BOX 6.14 GENDER AND TOUCHING NORMS PROJECT

Studies have documented cross-cultural and gender variation in touching. It has been widely held that women are more 'touch oriented' than men. Is this still the case? Arguably we are living in an era when traditional gender roles are breaking down. All those sensitive new-age guys should have fewer inhibitions than their fathers. Moreover, questions have to be asked as to whether the 'postmodern city' is as replete with repressive norms as its modernist counterpart. This question forms the basis of the project.

Select a public location such as a coffee shop (again?!) or mall (ditto!). Code instances of touching that you observe according to the parties involved, using a simple coding sheet (e.g. woman touches child, man touches woman). You may also be able to include additional variables like age and race, but our main focus here is on gender. Remember to make an estimate of the relative populations of men and women so that your estimates take account of the gender balance at your locale. Do men touch less than women? Are young men more likely to touch than older men? What other patterns can you identify? What do your results suggest about the touching norms in our society?

Note: This project can be made even more interesting if converted into a comparative study by identifying functionally-equivalent locations with different populations. For example, we might expect a trendy inner city coffee shop frequented by executives to differ from a roadside 'greasy spoon' frequented by truckers and bikies. A gay bar might differ from a straight bar. A mall in an 'ethnic' area might differ from a mall in a 'white' area. This sort of comparative dimension might allow you to make inferences about the strength of orthodox touching norms in various communities.

The basic tactic is to be as immobile as possible and, when, part of the trunk or extremities touches another person, withdraw if possible. If this is not possible, the muscles in the affected areas are kept tense. (1966: 112)

Greetings and farewells

These are the last bodily activity that we will explore in this chapter. Goffman (1971) argued that such activities are a central kind of supportive interchange in everyday social interaction. Consequently a great deal of effort goes into ensuring they are done correctly. Kendon and Ferber

(1973) filmed interactions in order to understand the sequence of greet-ings. They claim that greetings follow a sequence involving sighting each other, demonstrating recognition through a wave, nod or head toss, approaching, grooming oneself followed by a handshake, kiss, or embrace. It can be instructive to watch this process at work by hanging out at a popular meeting place and observing. As with greetings, farewells seem to vary in routine according to the levels of intimacy of the parties. Another important variable might be the duration of the anticipated parting. Bakken (1977) compared farewells at a student union and an airport. At the union, partings might be assumed to be casual and rela-tively unimportant. Bakken observed them to be accomplished by mutual and simultaneous rotation until the parties were facing in different direc-tions. Sequences of head tossing and a small wave could often come before a verbal goodbye. In the airport there was (1) far more frequent touching, (2) verbal goodbyes preceded the last physical contact, and (3) the remain-ing party stayed stationary whilst the passenger moved away (see Box 6.15).

In the above section we have suggested some of the ways that bodies in interaction can be studied using direct observation. It is worth remem-bering, however, that photographs also provide a way of studying these sorts of issues, even if one does not use the kinds of formal techniques advocated by Birdwhistell. Whilst they are not naturalistic, magazine photographs at least provide an insight into idealizations and cultural conventions regarding the body, posture, gesture and dress. At the risk of intruding on the territory of Chapter 2, we suggest here some brief exam-ples of studies that have used this data source. Goffman's *Gender Adver-tisements* (1979), as discussed previously, used the body as an indicator of gender ideologies. Morgan's (1989) exploration of dominatrix pornogra-phy deftly combines the analysis of facial expression, clothing and body posture in arguing that the genre subverts traditional gender characteriz-ations of the kind Goffman describes. According to Morgan (1989: 116) the 'rhetoric of dominatrix pornography is a revolutionary one, for it seeks to persuade its audience to experiment with sexual difference, to re-play the game of sexual power otherwise'. Morgan notes that in such pictures the clothing and hair of the dominatrix mark her out as feminine. Yet posture and expression have masculine connotations. In a typical photograph the woman stands over the man and dominates him, inverting the kind of rep-resentation we usually find in pornography or, indeed, *Gender Advertise-ments*. Moreover her facial expression is aggressive. She will often have a scowl, and a concentrated Medusa-like stare. This denotes that she despises and hates men rather than looking up to them supportively.

Dean MacCannell's (1989) study of facial semiotics in pornography takes the study of facial expression in a more systematic direction. MacCannell demonstrates that photographs of the face during intercourse are conven-tionalized – we are able to read the face for emotions and feelings. A knotted brow and screwed-up face indicates pain. Ecstasy is denoted by eyes closed

---

BOX 6.15 FAREWELLS PROJECT

Bakken's study of farewell behaviour in airports raises as many questions as it answers. Does the farewell ritual here reflect an orientation towards a predicted long time apart? Does it reflect the fact that the people who have taken the passenger to the airport are likely to be family members or a close friend (unlike the student union interactants)? Does it reflect a perception of the danger of flying? Or perhaps it reflects the spatial organization of airports or the simple fact that one person is being dropped off and the other is remaining (unlike the student union, where both people are likely to be going about their business)? Some of these questions can be addressed with a comparative visual project. Using a coding sheet which records the three typical airport behaviours noted above, and perhaps a video, note the number of times 'airport-style' farewells take place.

1. Compare farewells at the international terminal with the domestic terminal. This should enable you to explore whether a predicted long time apart is a critical variable. It is a reasonable presumption that on average the persons travelling overseas will be away longer. In large countries you may be able to conduct the whole study in the domestic terminal. In domestic airports it is usually possible to go to the gates yourself, so you know how far people are travelling and can infer how long they will be apart. Make observations at short-haul (e.g. New York–Washington) and longer (e.g. New York–Alaska) flights. Are there any differences?
2. Compare farewells at a railway station or bus terminal and at the domestic airport. This should allow you to see if there is anything unique to flying, or the style of farewell is the product of a generic passenger/non-passenger sequence in 'terminal' style settings.
3. The family/friend issue is a tricky one. You may have to ask people what their relationship is to the passenger.
4. Aside from these questions, also code to see to what extent the 'student union' style farewell has invaded the airport setting. What does this tell you about the routinization of flight as an aspect of everyday life? Were Bakken's findings the product of an era when flying was more expensive, unusual and dangerous?

---

and mouth open. Feats of self-control are demonstrated by upper-face, lower-face antagonism, such as closed eyes but clenched teeth. MacCannell suggests that many expressions in pornography are rarely found in everyday, asexual emotion. Whilst in everyday life expressions of intense emotion often involve upper and lower face and bilateral symmetries, 'the

BOX 6.16   FACES, BODIES, CLOTHES AND PHOTOGRAPHS EXERCISE

Thanks in part to feminist scholarship and social concern, much academic attention has been given to the body in pornography and advertising. Scholars have also devoted considerable attention to non-reflexive bodily and facial expression in everyday life. Rather less study has been made of photographic data on everyday life which involves staged or idealized social relationships. Weddings represent an important social event in most people's lives where there are strong conventions and performative norms that have to be upheld. Many of these relate to the expression of socially appropriate emotions and the dramatization of appropriate social roles.

Locate a wedding album belonging to yourself, a friend, or a relative. Carefully analyse the photographs. How do faces, bodies (including gestures) and clothes symbolize the following things: gender roles, social solidarity, love, fun and excitement? Which photographs seem 'fake' to you in terms of expression and which seem spontaneous or more 'genuine'? How can you tell?

Note: There is potential to make this project considerably more extensive by means of time series data (old wedding albums), cross-cultural data (wedding albums belonging to people with a different ethnic background) or other comparative data (e.g. class). Comparing the album to a videotape of the wedding may allow you to explore issues of selectivity in the construction of an idealized version of the wedding.

pornographic frame is often the site of spectacular whole-face muscular antagonisms that are not found in other areas of life' (1989: 159). Hard-core pornography works, then, not by mimicking everyday asexual expression, but rather via claims to difference.

This last item (Box 6.16) has brought us full circle back to the study of the two-dimensional photographic image. In this book we have not sought to replace such images in visual research, but rather to suggest that they should be augmented by other methodologies and supplemented by theoretically informed research questions. Visual research is not just about *the* photograph or conducted *through* the photograph. It is the study of the visible domains of social life and the visual languages and sign systems through which we communicate with each other. It includes objects, buildings and people as well as images. We have argued that direct observation, interpretative skills and a powerful theoretical imagination are the core resources for doing good visual research, not the camera nor the photograph. Thinking in this way allows us not only to revitalize visual research as a concept, but also to understand its ongoing but unrecognized centrality throughout the social sciences and cultural studies fields.

Notes

1 Sennett is mostly concerned with men. Questions need to be asked about the position of 'public woman', both in the past and today. We cannot address historical issues here, but much of our project work in this chapter is designed to foreground contemporary gender-based differences in public displays of the self.

2 One non-visual way to explore this shift from public sociability to public withdrawal is through the novel. In Dickens' early work, such as *The Pickwick Papers*, which was written in the 1830s, conversations and relationships with strangers seem to be casually struck up during stage coach journeys and at inns. These venues offered, we suggest, a device for introducing new characters and plot twists that would be not only familiar to his audience, but also plausible. By the end of the nineteenth century, however, public transportation in the novel serves merely to move people from one geographical location to another. In E.M. Forster's writing, for example, there are innumerable train journeys which are alluded to, but which have no direct impact on the story that is being told. Accidents, freak events and considerable dramatic artifice are required in order for fateful relationships between strangers to be initiated. These textual characteristics reflect more contemporary norms in which breaches of civil inattention between strangers require an elaborate explanatory framework.

3 Goffman alludes to an additional factor which may be operative when people meet during the night time which can affect the occurrence of contact between them. He refers to 'the tack occasionally taken by a man passing a strange woman at night on a narrow isolated walk: instead of conspicuously according the female civil inattention, the man may proffer a fleeting word to show that, unlike a would-be assailant, he is willing to be identified' (Goffman, 1963: 128).

4 In a somewhat similar vein Lyman and Scott (1967) refer to four different types of territories through which we progressively reach the domain of embodied activity: 'public', 'home', 'interactional' and 'body' territories.

5 In Chapter 4 we suggested that many of the stones on the breakwater at Nambucca Heads can be seen as a type of stall. Once a stone has been identified as the 'preserve' of a family unit by an inscription then the stone is unlikely to be used for additional graffiti messages.

6 Mann (1969) offers a useful discussion of the cultural aspects of queueing, based on material collected from queues for tickets for Australian Rules football finals outside the Melbourne Cricket Ground (MCG). He mars an otherwise helpful discussion by referring to the MCG as 'the Melbourne Football Stadium'.

References

Adorno, T. and Horkheimer, M. (1979) [1947] *Dialectic of Enlightenment*. London: Verso.
Alba, V. (1966) 'The Mexican revolution and the cartoon', *Comparative Studies in Society and History*, 9: 121–36.
Alexander, V.D. (1994) 'The image of children in magazine advertisements from 1905 to 1990', *Communication Research*, 21(6): 742–65.
Aries, P. (1962) *Centuries of Childhood*. New York: Alfred Knopf.
Atkinson, J.M. (1982) 'Understanding formality: notes on the production and categorization of "formal" interaction', *British Journal of Sociology*, 33: 86–117.
Bakken, D. (1977) 'Saying goodbye: an observational study of parting rituals', *Man–Environment Systems*, 7: 95–100.
Ball, M.S. and Smith, G.W. (1986) 'The visual availability of queueing's local organisation', *Communication and Culture*, 19(1): 27–58.
Ball, M.S. and Smith, G.W. (1992) *Analyzing Visual Data*, Qualitative Research Methods Series No 34. London: Sage.
Banks, M. and Morphy, H. (eds) (1997) *Rethinking Visual Anthropology*. New Haven: Yale University Press.
Barnes, J. (1974) *Scientific Knowledge and Sociological Theory*. London: Routledge.
Barthes, R. (1973) *Mythologies*. St Albans: Paladin.
Barthes, R. (1977a) 'The photographic message', in R. Barthes, *Image, Music Text*. London: Fontana.
Barthes, R. (1977b) 'Rhetoric of the Image', in R. Barthes, *Image, Music Text*. London: Fontana.
Barthes, R. (1981) *Camera Lucida: Reflections on Photography*. New York: Hill and Wang.
Barthes, R. (1983) *The Fashion System*. New York: Hill and Wang.
Bates, J. and Martin, M. (1980) 'The thematic content of graffiti as a nonreactive indicator of male and female attitudes', *The Journal of Sex Research*, 16(4): 300–15.
Bateson, G. and Mead, M. (1942) *Balinese Character: a Photographic Analysis*. New York: New York Academy of Sciences.
Baudrillard, J. (1988) *Selected Writings*, edited by M. Poster. Cambridge: Polity.
Baudrillard. J. (1990) *Revenge of the Crystal: Selected Writings on the Modern Object and its Destiny, 1968–1983*, edited and translated by P. Foss and J. Pefanis. Leichardt, NSW: Pluto.
Becker, H.S. (1974) 'Photography and sociology', *Studies in the Anthropology of Visual Communication*, No 1: 3–26.
Becker, H.S. (1979) 'Preface', in J. Wagner (ed.), *Images of Information: Still Photography in the Social Sciences*. Beverly Hills: Sage.
Becker, H.S. (1981) *Exploring Society Photographically*. Chicago: University of Chicago Press.
Becker, H.S. (1986) *Doing Things Together*. Evanston, IL: Northwestern University Press.
Belknap P. and Leonard II, W.M. (1991) 'A conceptual replication and extension of Erving Goffman's study of gender advertisements', *Sex Roles*, 25(3/4): 103–8.
Benjamin W. (1973) 'The work of art in the age of mechanical reproduction', in his *Illuminations*, edited and introduced by H. Arendt. London: Fontana.

Benjamin, W. (1985)[1931] 'A small history of photography', in W. Benjamin, *'One Way Street' and Other Writings*. London: Verso.

Bennett, T. (1995) *The Birth of the Museum*. London: Routledge.

Bennett, T., Emmison, M. and Frow, J. (1999) *Accounting for Tastes: Australian Everyday Cultures*. Melbourne: Cambridge University Press.

Birdwhistell, R.L. (1971) *Kinesics and Context: Essays on Body Motion Communication*. Harmondsworth: Penguin.

Bloor, D. (1976) *Knowledge and Social Imagery*. London: Routledge.

Borrow, G. (1934) [1862]. *Wild Wales*. London: Oxford University Press.

Bourdieu, P. (1984) *Distinction: a Social Critique of the Judgement of Taste*. Cambridge, Mass.: Harvard University Press.

Bourdieu, P. (1990) 'The Kabyle house or the world reversed', in P. Bourdieu, *The Logic of Practice*. Cambridge: Polity. pp. 271–319.

Bourdieu, P., Boltanski, L., Castel, R. and Chamboredon, J.-D. (1990) *Photography: a Middlebrow Art*. Stanford: Stanford University Press.

Cain, A. (1983) 'A study of pets in the family system', in A. Katcher and A. Beck (eds), *New Perspectives on our Lives with Companion Animals*. Philadelphia: University of Pennsylvania Press. pp. 71–81.

Campbell, C. (1997) 'Shopping, pleasure and the sex war', in P. Falk and C. Campbell (eds), *The Shopping Experience*. London: Sage. pp. 166–76.

Carr, S., Francis, M., Rivlin, L. and Stone, A. (1992) *Public Space*. Cambridge: Cambridge University Press.

Chaplin, E. (1994) *Sociology and Visual Representation*. London: Routledge.

Chavez, D. (1985) 'Perpetuation of gender inequality: a content analysis of comic strips', *Sex Roles*, 13(1/2): 93–102.

Chevalier, S. (1998) 'From woollen carpet to grass carpet: bridging house and garden in an English suburb', in D. Miller (ed.), *Material Cultures*. Chicago: University of Chicago Press. pp. 47–72.

Cintron, R. (1997) *Angels' Town*. Boston: Beacon.

Clancy, S. and Dollinger, S.J. (1993) 'Photographic depictions of the self: gender and age differences in social connectedness', *Sex Roles*, 29(7/8): 477–508.

Clifford, J. (1995) 'Paradise', *Visual Anthropology Review*, 11(1): 92–117.

Collier, J. Jr and Collier, M. (1986) *Visual Anthropology: Photography as a Research Method*. Albuquerque: University of New Mexico Press.

Couch, C. (1987) *Researching Social Processes in the Laboratory*. Greenwich: JAI Press.

Coupe, W. (1966) 'The German cartoon and the revolution of 1848', *Comparative Studies in Society and History*, 9: 137–67.

Craik, J. (1994) *The Face of Fashion*. New York: Routledge.

Dean, D. (1994) *Museum Exhibition: Theory and Practice*. London: Routledge.

Debord, G. (1958) 'Theorie de la derivé', *Internationale Situationiste*, 2: 19–23.

Dingwall, R., Tanaka, H. and Minamikata, S. (1991) 'Images of parenthood in the United States and Japan', *Sociology*, 25(3): 423–46.

Donald, J. (1995) 'The city, the cinema: modern spaces', in C. Jenks (ed.), *Visual Culture*. London: Routledge. pp. 77–95.

Douglas, M. (1969) *Purity and Danger*. London: Routledge.

Dowdall, G. and Golden, J. (1989) 'Photographs as data: an analysis of images from a mental hospital', *Qualitative Sociology*, 12(2): 183–213.

Duncan, M.C. (1990) 'Sports photographs and sexual difference: images of women and men in the 1984 and 1988 Olympic Games', *Sociology of Sport Journal*, 7: 22–43.

Edelman, B. and Roskis, E. (1998) 'Beyond the frame', *The Guardian Weekly*, 25 October: 15.

Efron, D. (1972)[1941] *Gesture, Race and Culture*. The Hague: Mouton.

Elias, N. (1978) *The Civilizing Process*. Oxford: Blackwell.

Emmison, M. (1983) ' "The Economy": its emergence in media discourse', in H. Davis and P. Walton (eds), *Language, Image, Media*. Oxford: Blackwell. pp. 139–55.

Emmison, M. (1986) 'Visualising the economy: fetishism and the legitimation of economic life', *Theory, Culture & Society*, 3(2): 81–97.

Emmison, M. and McHoul, A. (1987) 'Drawing on the economy: cartoon discourse and the production of a category', *Cultural Studies*, 1(1): 93–112.

Enninger, W. (1984) 'Inferencing social structure and social processes from nonverbal behaviour', *American Journal of Semiotics* 3(2): 77–96.

Evans-Pritchard, E.E. (1940) *The Nuer*. Oxford: Oxford University Press.

Falk, J.H. and Dierking, L. (1992) *The Museum Experience*. Washington, DC: Whalesback Books.

Falk, P. (1997) 'The scopic regime of shopping', in P. Falk and C. Campbell (eds), *The Shopping Experience*. London: Sage.

Ferrell, J. (1993) *Crimes of Style: Urban Graffiti and the Politics of Criminality*. New York: Garland.

Fiske, J., Hodge, B. and Turner, G. (1987) *Myths of Oz*. Sydney: Allen and Unwin.

Foucault, M. (1973) *The Birth of the Clinic*. London: Tavistock.

Foucault, M. (1979) *Discipline and Punish*. London: Penguin.

Frow, J. (1998) 'Gift and commodity', in J. Frow, *Time and Commodity Culture*. Oxford: Oxford University Press. pp. 102–217.

Fyfe, G. and Law, J. (eds) (1988) *Picturing Power: Visual Depiction and Social Relations*, Sociological Review Monograph No. 35. London: Routledge.

Gardner, C.B. (1980) 'Passing by: street remarks, address rights, and the urban female', *Sociological Inquiry* 50 (3/4): 328–56.

Garfinkel, H. (1967) *Studies in Ethnomethodology*. Englewood Cliffs, NJ: Prentice Hall.

Garfinkel, H., Lynch, M. and Livingstone, E. (1981) 'The work of a discovering science construed with material from the optically discovered pulsar', *Philosophy of Social Sciences*, 11: 131–58.

Giddens, A. (1991) *Modernity and Self-Identity: Self and Society in the Late Modern Age*. Stanford: Stanford University Press.

Glasgow University Media Group (1976) *Bad News*. London: Routledge.

Glasgow University Media Group (1980) *More Bad News*. London: Routledge.

Goffman, E. (1961) *Asylums: Essays on the Social Situation of Mental Patients and Other Inmates*. New York: Doubleday & Co.

Goffman, E. (1963) *Behaviour in Public Places: Notes on the Social Organization of Gatherings*. New York: Free Press.

Goffman, E. (1971) *Relations in Public: Micro Studies of the Public Order*. London: Allen Lane The Penguin Press.

Goffman, E. (1974) *Frame Analysis: an Essay on the Organization of Experience*. Harmondsworth: Penguin.

Goffman, E. (1979) *Gender Advertisements*. London and Basingstoke: Macmillan.

Gombrich, E. (1996) 'The visual image: its place in communication', in R. Woodfield (ed.), *The Essential Gombrich: Selected Writings on Art and Culture*. London: Phaidon.

Goodwin, C. (1986) 'Gestures as a resource for the organization of mutual orientation', *Semiotica*, 62(1–2): 29–49.

Gottdiener, M. (1995) *Postmodern Semiotics: Material Culture and the Forms of Postmodern Life*. Oxford: Blackwell.

Graham, H. (1977) 'Images of pregnancy in antenatal literature', in R. Digwall, C. Heath, M. Reid and M. Stacey (eds), *Health Care and Health Knowledge*. London: Croom Helm.

Hall, E.T. (1963) 'A system for the notation of proxemic behaviour', *American Anthropologist*, 65(5): 1003–26.

Hall, E.T. (1966) *The Hidden Dimension*. New York: Doubleday.

Hall, E.T. (1974) 'Handbook for proxemic research', *Studies in the Anthropology of Visual Communication*, No 3: 2–124.

Hall, S. (1973) 'The determinations of news photographs', in S. Cohen and J. Young (eds), *The Manufacture of News: Deviance, Social Problems and the Mass Media*. London: Constable.

Hall, S. (1991) 'Reconstruction work: images of post-war black settlement', in J. Spence and P. Holland (eds), *The Meanings of Domestic Photography*. London: Virago.

Halle, D. (1993) *Inside Culture: Art and Class in the American Home*. Chicago: University of Chicago Press.

Hamilton, P. (1997) 'Representing the social: France and Frenchness in post-war humanist photography' in S. Hall (ed.) *Representation: Cultural Representation and Signifying Practice*. London: Sage.

Hansen, A., Cottle, S., Negrine, R. and Newbold, C. (1998) *Mass Communication Research Methods*. London: Macmillan.

Harper, D. (1987) 'Life on the road', in J. Wagner (ed.), *Images of Information: Still Photography in the Social Sciences*. Beverly Hills: Sage. pp. 25–42.

Harper, D. (1988) 'Visual sociology: expanding sociological vision', *The American Sociologist*, Spring: 54–70.

Harper, D. (1994) 'On the authority of the image: visual methods at the crossroads', in N. Denzin and Y. Lincoln (eds), *Handbook of Qualitative Research*. London: Sage.

Harper, D. (1997) 'Visualizing structure: reading surfaces of social life', *Qualitative Sociology*, 20(1): 57–77.

Harris, A. (1977) 'Sex and theories of deviance: towards a functional theory of deviant type-scripts' *American Sociological Review*, 42(Feb): 3–16.

Harvey, D. (1989) *The Condition of Postmodernity*. Oxford: Blackwell.

ten Have, P. (1998) *Doing Conversation Analysis: a Practical Guide*. London: Sage.

Heath, C. (1997) 'The analysis of activities in face to face interaction using video', in D. Silverman (ed.), *Qualitative Research: Theory, Method and Practice*. London: Sage. pp. 183–200.

Heath, C. and Luff, P. (1997) 'Convergent activities: collaborative work and multimedia technology in London underground line control rooms', in D. Middleton and Y. Engestrom (eds), *Cognition and Comunication at Work: Distributed Cognition in the Workplace*. Cambridge: Cambridge University Press.

Henry, L. (1986) 'A short history of visual sociology', *Current Sociology*, 34(3): 1–4.

Heritage, J.C. (1984) *Garfinkel and Ethnomethodology*. Cambridge: Polity.

Heritage, J.C. (1989) 'Current developments in conversation analysis', in D. Roger and P. Bull (eds), *Conversation: an Interdisciplinary Approach*. Avon, Hampshire: Multilingual Matters. pp. 21–47.

Hermer, J. and Hunt, A. (1996) 'Official graffiti of the everyday', *Law & Society Review*, 30(3): 455–80.

Heslin, R. (1974) *Steps towards a taxonomy of touching*. Conference paper cited in V. Richmond, J. McCroskey and S. Payne (1991) *Nonverbal Behaviour in Interpersonal Relations*. Englewood Cliffs, NJ: Prentice Hall. p. 140.

Hoult, T.F. (1954) 'Experimental measurement of clothing as a factor in some social ratings of selected American men', *American Sociological Review*, 19: 324–8.

Hull, J. (1990) *Touching the Rock*. Melbourne: David Lovell.

Jackson, P. and Thrift, N. (1995) 'Geographies of consumption', in D. Miller (ed.) *Acknowledging Consumption*. London: Routledge. pp. 204–37.

Jameson, F. (1991) *Postmodernism, or the Cultural Logic of Late Capitalism*. Durham, NC: Duke University Press.

Jenefsky, C. and Miller, D. H., (1998) 'Phallic intrusion: girl–girl sex in Penthouse', *Women's Studies International Forum*, 21(4): 375–85.

Kaite, B. (1989) 'Reading the body textual: the shoe and fetish relations in soft and hard core', *American Journal of Semiotics* 6(4): 79–93.

Katz, J. (1988) *Seductions of Crime*. New York: Basic Books.

Kazdin, A.E. (1979) 'Direct observations as unobtrusive measures in treatment evaluation', in L. Sechrest (ed.), *Unobtrusive Measurement Today*. San Francisco: Jossey-Bass. pp. 19–31.

Kellehear, A. (1993) *The Unobtrusive Researcher: a Guide to Methods*. St Leonards: Allen & Unwin.

Kelling, G. and Coles, C. (1996) *Fixing Broken Windows*. New York: Martin Kessler Books.

Kendon, A. and Ferber, A. (1973) 'A description of some human greetings', in R.P. Micaheal and J.H. Crook (eds), *Comparative Ecology and Behaviour of Primates*. New York: Academic Press.

Kinsey, S., Pomeroy, W.B., Martin, C.E. and Gebhard, P.H. (1953) *Sexual Behavior in the Human Female*. Philadelphia: Saunders.

Klein, Z. (1984) 'Sitting posture in males and females', *Semiotica*, 48(1–2): 119–31.

Kloftas, J. and Cutshall, C. (1985) 'Unobtrusive research methods in criminal justice: using graffiti in the reconstruction of institutional cultures', *Journal of Research in Crime and Delinquency*, 22(4): 355–73.

Kress, G. and van Leeuwen, T. (1996) *Reading Images: the Grammar of Visual Design*. London: Routledge.

Kuhn, T. (1970) *The Structure of Scientific Revolutions*. Chicago: University of Chicago Press.

Kunzle, D. (1977) 'Dress reform as anti-feminism', *Signs*, 2(3): 570–9.

LaFrance, M. and Mayo, C. (1978) *Moving Bodies: Nonverbal Communication in Social Relationships*. Monterey: Brooks/Cole.

Lakoff, R. (1975) *Language and Women's Place*. New York: Harper & Row.

Lash, S. (1988) 'Discourse or figure? Postmodernism as a "regime of signification"' *Theory, Culture & Society*, 5: 311–36.

Law, J. and Whittaker, J. (1988) 'On the art of representation: notes on the politics of visualisation', in G. Fyfe and J. Law (eds), *Picturing Power: Visual Depiction and Social Relations*, Sociological Review Monograph 35. London: Routledge.

Leal, O. (1990) 'Popular taste and erudite repertoire: the place and space of TV in Brazil', *Cultural Studies* 4(1): 19–29.

Lehtonen, T.-K. and Maenpaa, P. (1997) 'Shopping in the East Centre Mall', in P. Falk and C. Campbell (eds), *The Shopping Experience*. London: Sage. pp. 136–65.

Leiss, W., Kline, S. and Jhally, S. (1990) *Social Communication in Advertising: Persons, Products and Images of Well-being* (2nd edn). London: Routledge.

Lidchi, H. (1997) 'The poetics and politics of exhibiting other cultures', in S. Hall (ed.), *Representation: Cultural Representations and Signifying Practices*. London: Sage. pp. 151–222.

Lodge, D. (1989) *Nice Work*. Harmondsworth: Penguin.

Loewenstein, H., Ponticos, G. and Paludi, M. (1982) 'Sex differences in graffiti as a communication style', *Journal of Social Psychology*, 117: 307–8.

Lofland, L. (1973) *A World of Strangers*. New York: Basic Books.

Lyle, J.T. (1970) 'People watching in parks', *Landscape Architecture*, 60: 51–2.

Lyman, S.M. and Scott, M.B. (1967) 'Territoriality: a neglected sociological dimension', *Social Problems*, 15: 236–49.

Lynch, K. (1960) *The Image of the City*. Cambridge, MA: Technology Press.

Lynch, M. and Edgerton, S. Jr (1988) 'Aesthetics and digital image processing: representational craft in contemporary astronomy', in G. Fyfe and J. Law (eds), *Picturing Power: Visual Depiction and Social Relations*, Sociological Review Monograph 35. London: Routledge.

Lynch, M. and Woolgar, S. (eds) (1990) *Representation in Scientific Practice*. Cambridge, MA: MIT Press.

Lyotard, J.-F. (1984) *The Postmodern Condition: a Report on Knowledge*. Translated by G. Bennington and B. Massumi. Minneapolis: University of Minnesota Press.

MacCannell, D. (1989) 'Faking it: comment on face-work in pornography', *American Journal of Semiotics*, 6(4): 153–74.

Mann, L. (1969) 'Queue culture: the waiting line as a social system', *American Journal of Sociology*, 75: 340–54.

Marcuse, H. (1968) *One Dimensional Man*. London: Sphere.

Marcuse, P. (1988) 'Neutralising homelessness', *Socialist Review*, 18(1): 69–96.

Matacin, M.L. and Burger, J.M. (1987) 'A content analysis of sexual themes in *Playboy* cartoons', *Sex Roles*, 17(3/4): 179–86.

McGregor, G. (1995) '*Gender Advertisements* then and now: Goffman, symbolic interactionism and the problem of history', *Studies in Symbolic Interactionism*, 17: 3–42.

McHoul, A. (1982) *Telling How Texts Talk: Essays on Reading and Ethnomethodology*. London: Routledge.

McHoul, A. (1991) 'Taking the children: some reflections at a distance on the camera and Dr Barnado', *Continuum*, 5(1): 33–50.

Melbin, M. (1978) 'Night as frontier', *American Sociological Review*, 43(Feb): 3–22.

Milgram, S. (1970) 'The experience of living in cities', *Science*, No. 167: 1461–8.

Miller, D. (1988) 'Appropriating the state on the council estate', *Man*, 23: 353–72.

Miller, T. and McHoul, A. (1998) *Popular Culture and Everyday Life*. London: Sage.

Millns, C. (1998) 'Arty tarts and geekgirls: young women, art and new technologies', BA Honours thesis, Dept of Anthropology & Sociology, University of Queensland.

Millum, T. (1975) *Images of Women: Advertising in Women's Magazines*. London: Chatto & Windus.

Morgan, T.E. (1989) 'A whip of one's own: dominatrix pornography and the construction of a post-modern (female) subjectivity', *American Journal of Semiotics*, 6(4): 109–36.

Morley, D. (1995) 'Television: not so much a visual medium, more a visible object', in C. Jenks (ed.), *Visual Culture*. London: Routledge. pp. 170–89.

Morris, D. (1977) *Manwatching*. New York: Harry Abrams.

Morris, R. (1992) 'Cartoons and the political system: Canada, Quebec, Wales and England', *Canadian Journal of Communication*, 17: 253–8.

Myers, J. (1992) 'Nonmainstream body modification: genital piercing, branding, burning and cutting', *Journal of Contemporary Ethnography*, 21(3): 267–306.

Nash, J.E. (1982) 'The family camps out: a study in nonverbal communication', *Semiotica*, 39(3–4): 331–41.

Neuman, W.L. (1994) *Social Research Methods: Qualitative and Quantitative Approaches*. Boston, MA: Allyn & Bacon.

Newman, J. and McCauley, C. (1977) 'Eye contact with strangers in city, suburb and small town', *Environment and Behaviour*, 9(4): 547–8.

Nir, Y. (1977) 'US involvement in the Middle East conflict in Soviet caricatures', *Journalism Quarterly*, 54: 697–726.

Norton, R. (1983) *Communicator Style: Theory, Applications and Measures*. Beverly Hills: Sage.

Ogilvie, E. (1994) 'An ethnography of corporeality and sexual difference within the gym', BA Honours thesis, Dept of Anthropology & Sociology, University of Queensland.

Penner, M. and Penner, S. (1994) 'Publicizing, politicizing, and neutralizing homelessness: comic strips', *Communications Research*, 21(6): 766–81.

Petersen, A. (1998) 'Sexing the body: representations of sex differences in Gray's *Anatomy*, 1858 to the present', *Body & Society*, 4(1): 1–16.

Poll, S. (1962) *The Hasidic Community of Williamsburg*. New York: Free Press.

Prior, L. (1988) 'The architecture of the hospital: a study of spatial organization and medical knowledge', *British Journal of Sociology*, 39(1): 86–113.

Psathas, G. (1979) 'Organizational features of direction maps', in G. Psathas (ed.), *Everyday Language: Studies in Ethnomethodology*. New York: Irvington. pp. 203–25.

Quimby, M. (ed.) (1978) *Material Culture and the Study of American Life*. New York: Norton.

Rathje, W.L. (1979) 'Trace measures', in L. Sechrest (ed.), *Unobtrusive Measurement Today*. San Franciso: Jossey-Bass.

Richardson, J. and Kroeber, A.L. (1940) 'Three centuries of women's dress fashions: a quantitative analysis', *Anthropological Records*, 5(2): 111–53.

Richmond, V., McCroskey, J. and Payne, S. (1991) *Nonverbal Behavior in Interpersonal Relations*. Englewood Cliffs: Prentice Hall.

Riggins, S.H. (1994) 'Fieldwork in the living room', in S.H. Riggins (ed.), *The Socialness of Things*. New York: Mouton de Gruyter. pp. 101–48.

Robins, D.M., Sanders, C.R. and Cahill, S.E. (1991) 'Dogs and their people: pet facilitated interaction in a public setting', *Journal of Contemporary Ethnography*, 20(1): 3–25.

Robinson, D. (1976) 'Fashions in shaving and trimming of the beard: the men of the *Illustrated London News*, 1842–1972', *American Journal of Sociology*, 81(5): 1133–41.

Rosenblatt, D. (1997) 'The antisocial skin: structure, resistance and "Modern Primitive" adornment in the United States', *Cultural Anthropology*, 12(3): 287–334.

Rubinstein, R. (1995) *Dress Codes*. Boulder, CO: Westview Press.

Sacks, H. (1972) 'On the analyzability of stories by children', in J. Gumperz and D. Hymes (eds), *Directions in Sociolinguistics*. New York: Holt, Rinehart and Winston. pp. 325–45.

Schegloff, E.A. (1988) 'Goffman and the analysis of conversation', in P. Drew and T. Wootton (eds), *Erving Goffman: Exploring the Interaction Order*. Cambridge: Polity. pp. 89–135.

Schlereth, T. (1985) *Material Culture: a Research Guide*. Lawrence: University of Kansas Press.

Schwartz, D. (1989) 'Visual ethnography: using photography in qualitative research', *Qualitative Sociology*, 12(2): 119–54.

Schwartz, H. and Jacobs, J. (1979) *Qualitative Sociology: a Method to the Madness*. New York: Free Press.

Scott, J. (1991) *A Matter of Record: Documentary Sources in Social Research*. Cambridge: Polity.

Sechrest, L. and Flores, L. (1969) 'Homosexuality in the Philippines and the United States: the handwriting on the wall', *The Journal of Social Psychology*, 79: 3–12.

Sechrest, L. and Phillips, M. (1979) 'Unobtrusive measures: an overview', in L. Sechrest (ed.), *Unobtrusive Measurement Today*. San Francisco: Jossey-Bass. pp. 1–17.

Sennett, R. (1977) *The Fall of Public Man*. Cambridge: Cambridge University Press.

Shanas, E. (1945) 'The AJS through Fifty Years', *American Journal of Sociology*, 50: 522–33.

Sharrock, W.W. and Anderson, D.C. (1979) 'Directional hospital signs as sociological data', *Information Design Journal* 1(2): 81–94.

Shields, R. (1994) 'The logic of the mall', in S. Riggins (ed.), *The Socialness of Things*. New York: Mouton de Gruyter. pp. 203–29.

Silverman, D. (1987) *Communication and Medical Practice: Social Relations in the Clinic*. London: Sage.

Simmel, G. (1921)[1908] 'Sociology of the senses: visual interaction', in R. Park and E. Burgess (eds), *Introduction to the Science of Sociology*. Chicago: University of Chicago Press. pp 356–61.

Simmel, G. (1957)[1904] 'Fashion', *American Journal of Sociology*, 62: 541–58.

Small, A. (1905) 'A decade of sociology', *American Journal of Sociology*, 9: 1–10.

Smith, P. (1986) 'Trekking Tourism in Nepal', MA thesis, University of Edinburgh.

Smith, P. (1999) 'The elementary forms of place and their transformations: a Durkheimian model', *Qualitative Sociology*, 22(1): 13–36.

Soja, E.W. (1996) *Thirdspace: Journeys to Los Angeles and Other Real-and-Imagined Places*. Cambridge, MA: Blackwell.

Sommer, R. (1969) *Personal Space: the Behavioural Basis of Design*. Englewood Cliffs: Prentice Hall.

Sontag, S. (1977) *On Photography*. Toronto: McGraw-Hill.

Stasz, C. (1979) 'The early history of visual sociology', in J. Wagner (ed.), *Images of Information: Still Photography in the Social Sciences*, Beverly Hills: Sage. pp. 119–36.

Stimson, G.V. (1986) 'Place and space in sociological fieldwork', *Sociological Review*, 34: 641–56.

Stoppard, M. (1985) *Pregnancy and Birth Book*. London: Dorling Kindersley.

Streicher, L. (1966) 'On a theory of political caricature', *Comparative Studies in Society and History*, 9: 427–45.

Synnott, A. (1985) 'Symbolic replica: a sociology of cemeteries', *International Journal of Visual Sociology*, 3(2): 46–56.

Synnott, A. (1993) *The Body Social*. London: Routledge.

Tagg, J. (1988) *The Burden of Representation: Essays on Photographies and Histories*. London: Macmillan.

Trachtenberg, A. (ed.) (1980) *Classic Essays on Photography*. New Haven, CT: Leete's Island Books.

Turner, B.S. (1984) *The Body and Society*. Oxford: Blackwell.

Veblen, T. (1912) *The Theory of the Leisure Class*. New York: Macmillan.

Wagner, J. (ed.) (1979) *Images of Information: Still Photography in the Social Sciences*. Beverly Hills: Sage.

Wagner-Pacifici, R. and Schwartz, B. (1991) 'The Vietnam Veterans' Memorial', *American Journal of Sociology*, 97: 376–420.

Walker, M. (1978) *Daily Sketches: a Cartoon History of British Political Cartoons*. London: Granada.

Webb, E.J., Campell, D.T., Schwartz, R.D. and Sechrest, L. (1966) *Unobtrusive Measures: Nonreactive Research in the Social Sciences*. Chicago: Rand McNally.

White, R. (1990) *No Space of their Own: Young People and Social Control in Australia*. Cambridge: Cambridge University Press.

Williamson, J. (1978) *Decoding Advertisements: Ideology and Meaning in Advertising*. London: Marion Boyars.

Willis, P. (1978) *Profane Culture*. London: Routledge.

Wilson, J.Q. and Kelling, G. (1982) 'Broken windows', *The Atlantic Monthly*, 249(3): 29–38.

Woodward, I. (1996) 'A sociological account of the shopping mall as a postmodern space', BA Honours thesis, Dept of Anthropology & Sociology, University of Queensland.

Woodward, I. (1998) 'The shopping mall, postmodern space and architectural practice: theorising the postmodern spatial turn through the planning discourse of mall architects' *Architectural Theory Review*, 3(2): 45–56.

Woodward, I., Emmison, M. and Smith, P. (2000) 'Postmodern space and human disorientation: a modest test of an immodest theory', *British Journal of Sociology*, 51: June (forthcoming).

Worth, S. and Adair, J. (1972) *Through Navajo Eyes: an Exploration in Film Communication and Anthropology*. Bloomington: Indiana University Press.

Wowk, M. (1984) 'Blame allocation, sex and gender in a murder interrogation', *Women's Studies International Forum*, 7(1): 75–82.

Wright, E.O. (1997) *Class Counts: Comparative Studies in Class Analysis*. New York: Cambridge University Press.

Wright, R.A. (1989) 'The "friendly student" exercise', *Teaching Sociology*, 17: 484–8.

Ziller, R.C. (1990) *Photographing the Self: Methods for Observing Personal Orientations*. Newbury Park: Sage.

Ziller, R.C. and Rorer, B.A. (1985) 'Shyness–environment interaction: a view from the shy side through auto-photography', *Journal of Personality*, 53: 626–39.

Index